100 CLASSIC HIKES in™

WASHINGTON

North Cascades • Olympics • Mount Rainier & South Cascades • Alpine Lakes • Glacier Peak

Ira Spring & Harvey Manning

THE
MOUNTAINEERS

Published by
The Mountaineers
1001 SW Klickitat Way, Suite 201
Seattle, WA 98134

First printing 1998, second printing 1999, third printing 2000, fourth printing 2001, fifth printing 2002, sixth printing 2004, seventh printing 2005

Published simultaneously in Great Britain by Cordee, 3a DeMontfort Street, Leicester, England, LE1 7HD

Manufactured in China

Maps by Gray Mouse Graphics
All photographs by Ira Spring
Cover and book design by Jennifer Shontz
Layout by Gray Mouse Graphics

Cover photograph: *Image Lake and Glacier Peak, Hike 31*
Frontispiece: *Chickamin Glacier on Dome Peak, Glacier Peak Wilderness*

Library of Congress Cataloging-in-Publication Data

Spring, Ira.
    100 classic hikes in Washington: North Cascades, Olympics, Mount
  Rainer & South Cascades, Alpine Lakes, Glacier Peak / Ira Spring &
  Harvey Manning.—1st ed.
       p.   cm.
  Includes index.
  ISBN 0-89886-586-7
    1. Hiking—Washington (State)—Guidebooks. 2. Mountaineering—
Washington (State)—Guidebooks. 3. Washington (State)—Guidebooks.
I. Manning, Harvey. II. Title.
GV199.42.W22S67 1998
917.9704'43—dc21   98-13632
                                                       CIP

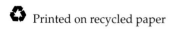

100

CLASSIC
HIKES in ™

WASHINGTON

CONTENTS

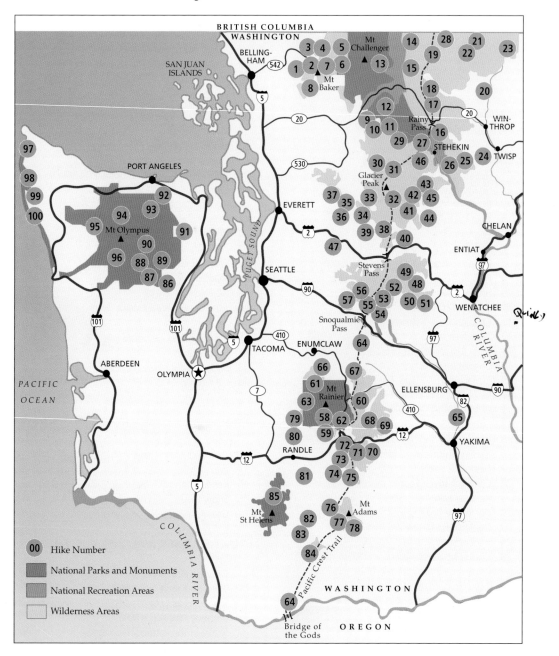

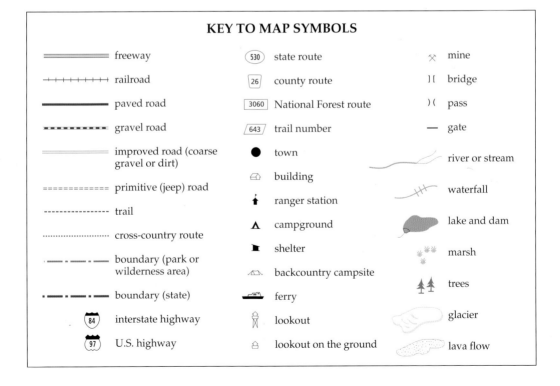

KEY TO MAP SYMBOLS

══════ freeway	(530) state route	⤬ mine
┼┼┼┼┼┼┼┼ railroad	[26] county route	)(bridge
━━━━━ paved road	[3060] National Forest route	)(pass
▪▪▪▪▪▪ gravel road	/643/ trail number	— gate
═════ improved road (coarse gravel or dirt)	● town	∿ river or stream
═════ primitive (jeep) road	⌂ building	⤞ waterfall
------------ trail	⭭ ranger station	⬬ lake and dam
·················· cross-country route	▲ campground	※ marsh
·—·—·—· boundary (park or wilderness area)	▪ shelter	♣ trees
·—··—··— boundary (state)	⌂ backcountry campsite	glacier
(84) interstate highway	⛴ ferry	
(97) U.S. highway	⛫ lookout	lava flow
	⌂ lookout on the ground	

Glacier Peak from Miners Ridge trail, Hike 31

My father, Ira Spring, passed away on June 5, 2003, at the age of eighty-four. Ira inspired three generations of outdoor enthusiasts with his breathtaking photographic images and his work as a trail lobbyist. Ira was cofounder of the Washington Trails Association and received the Theodore Roosevelt Conservation Award for his volunteer efforts toward trail funding and preservation. In 2004 Ira will be remembered at the dedication of the newly built Ira Spring Trail on Bandera Mountain off the I-90 corridor.

Ira's unswerving activism was recently recognized again when the drafters of the NOVA (Nonhighway and Off-Road Vehicle Activities Program) bill named the nonmotorized portion of the new law the Ira Spring Fund.

Ira also campaigned for the Wild Sky Wilderness Area, which is close to becoming a reality. One of Ira's last book projects was *55 Hikes Around Stevens Pass: Wild Sky Country*, written with Rick McGuire, showcasing the best hikes in the Wild Sky area of Washington.

The legacy of Ira Spring (and his wife and hiking partner, Pat Spring) on Washington hiking trails will be felt for years to come. My sister, Vicky, and I are following our own missions in life, but we are committed to ensuring the continuation of our father's work. In December 2000, Ira founded a nonprofit organization called the Spring Family Trail Fund, to which all proceeds from his royalties are donated. By combining individual donations with Ira's royalties, even small donations can become part of powerful programs. The Spring Family Trail Fund is a natural extension of Ira's tireless efforts to preserve hiking opportunities in Washington State. Please visit *www.springtrailtrust.org* to see the types of projects we fund.

As Ira regularly reminded us, there is a lot of power in sending a letter to your legislator or land manager. I sit on many committees for trails and I can tell you how often a few letters change the way our society manages itself. Please join the Ira Spring Family in continuing to make sure hikers are heard. A little goes a long way in letters, financial donations, and volunteering for trail maintenance. You can be a part of the legislative power of voters taking care of our heritage: Simply by purchasing this book you have helped preserve trails for the future. Please don't hesitate to contact me for more ideas about how you can help.

— John E. Spring
Manager
Spring Family Trail Fund
www.springtrailtrust.org
johnespring@seanet.com

GREEN BONDING FOR A GREEN FUTURE: THE MOUSE THAT IS LEARNING TO ROAR

What is "green-bonding"?

"Bonding" is the term for the development of ties of any offspring to its parent—a newborn baby to its mother, a newborn fawn to its doe. "Green-bonding" describes the emotional ties a person develops while hiking wildland trails, enjoying the flowers, trees, wildlife, and views. Green-bonding generated a green constituency that prompted thousands of people to write their Congressmen urging passage of the 1984 Washington Wilderness Act. Their pleas were heard because of our ten Congressional delegates, six were, while growing up, green-bonded by hiking in the Cascades and Olympics. Again, during Forest Management Planning by the U.S. Forest Service, 10,000 people wrote the Mount Baker–Snoqualmie National Forest stressing the importance of trails.

However, there is other bonding than green—to decent homes, to good schools, to adequate streets and highways, to convenient shopping malls, to pleasure domes for athletic

Buttercups

contests. As the nation continues a population growth that entails more wooden houses, more factories, more vacation retreats accompanied by the desire for helicopters pads in parks and wilderness areas, the result is a massive de-greening by money-bonded entrepreneurs who efficiently organize and heavily fund a nigh-religious crusade to despoil the public green for private profit. The 1996 session of Congress entertained serious proposals to decommission "surplus" park and wilderness land and hand it over to the "private sector." Fortunately, in 1996 there were enough green-bonded people in the nation to halt the giveaway. But further raids must be expected. Will there be enough green-bonded people in the year 2005 or 2010 to protect public lands?

Prior to World War II the White Chuck River country had many trails but few hikers—too few to prevent a postwar logging road up the valley nearly to Kennedy Hot Springs (Hike 32), converting a long backpack of many days to an afternoon stroll. We had the Golden Horn (Hike 17) all to ourselves, but because there was no trail, few had been there and no constituency existed large enough to obtain it for the North Cascades National Park. The Ragged Ridge, Eagle Rock, and Jackman Creek roadless areas had no trails, so again they had insufficient constituency for 1984 designation as wilderness—and since these areas still have no trails they

may lack enough green-bonded support for the next go-around.

The money-bonding of commercial-industrial entrepreneurs is the heart of the matter, is the essence of our economy. It cannot be kept in check simply by our taking a hike. However, with lots of green-bonded support it can be redirected. By our feet. That's what this book is for—to mobilize feet.

In the 1950s the trail to Snow Lake was hiked by 800 people a year. The number now is 20,000 a year! When I worked at Mount Rainier in 1937, on a fine summer Sunday perhaps as many as 300 walkers would be met on the flower trails of Paradise. Now the count is sometimes 3,000. In the 1960s we were amazed when 300 climbers a year reached the summit. Now it's often 300 in a day. Granted, the backcountry was uncrowded back then; that was the good news. Unfortunately, the bad news outweighs the good—there wasn't enough public support (green-bonding) to prevent logging roads from gobbling up thousands of miles of trails.

Hikers are by nature individuals who mostly hike with one or two friends and have no reason to join other hikers. Our independence has cost us dearly. Of the thousands of green-bonded people in this state, few join hiking-oriented organizations that publish newsletters discussing day-to-day trail situations. Only when a major threat reaches the mass media do they react. On one such occasion 5,000 letters were sent to the

Wenatchee National Forest opposing motorcycles on trails and over 10,000 letters to the Mount Baker–Snoqualmie. Untold thousands were sent to our Congressional delegates in support of the 1984 Wilderness Act.

That's what we need. More letters. (Write them!) More well-informed hikers. (Join a group!) More greenpower. (Flex your muscles!)

Is it too late for feet to save our heritage? No. Not if each of you takes up paper and pen and postage stamps and joins the letter-writing militia. Go walking. Fill your feet with the feel of the land. Then, returned home, let your fingers do the walking on pages and mail them to your supervisors of national forests (see page 11 for the addresses), Congresspersons and Senators, and newspaper editors. All these need to know what your feet have learned. This wildland is your land, and it is your obligation to be its steward and its advocate.

Well-informed letters about the wildland are crucial. Your feet, taking one step at a time at a studiously slow pace, know the land better than the heads of any elected officials. Insert into those heads what your feet know. Your feet bones are connected to your leg bones, leg bones to the hip bones, hip bones to the backbones, backbones to the head bones, head bones to the letter-writing finger bones.

Your feet have *information*, direct boot-on-trail knowledge of the earth. Really-truly information, not the showtime sound-bites of this Age of Misinformation. Your fingers—by typewriter, ballpoint pen, pencil, goose quill—produce *personal* letters, the postage stamp on the envelope promising authenticity; which indeed lies within, guaranteed by the words that conjure up the pain of blisters and the reek of sweaty socks. A few years ago timber companies used to print up postcards by the bushel and stuff them in pay envelopes for loggers and mill-workers to sign. Now the slicks mass-produce form letters by machinery and punch buttons to vomit them into the etheric roar of e-mail and Fax. Our friends in government tell us that the torrent of robot communications is conscientiously tabulated by robot—but that *human letters are read*. Forest Service personnel tell anecdotes of hot debates in staff meetings when one or two really-truly human letters were passed around and turned the tide in our favor. You think one letter doesn't make a difference? Your one letter to the Wenatchee National Forest, added to 4,999 others, convinced a federal judge to return the North Fork Entiat to non-motorized use.

Warning: Informants also tell us of occasions when their office wires were clogged by electronic yap, but no human letters having been received, the decision-makers concluded that hikers didn't care.

So write. Join a trail oriented-organization in your area.

And get *cracking!*

—Ira Spring

WHERE TO FIND INFORMATION

Addresses of Trail-oriented Organizations

Sierra Club, Cascade Chapter
8511 15th Avenue Northeast, #201
Seattle, Washington 98115

The Mountaineers
300 Third Avenue West
Seattle, Washington 98119

Washington Trails Association
(publishers of *Signpost* Magazine)
1305 Fourth Avenue
Room 512
Seattle, Washington 98101

Other Organizations with Trail Interests

ALPS (Alpine Lakes Protection Society)
Washington Wilderness Coalition
North Cascades Conservation Council
Wilderness Society
Methow Valley Council
Mount Rainier Park Associates
Olympic Park Associates
Mid-fork
IATC (Issaquah Alps Trail Club)

OUR GREENBOOKS AND HOW THEY GREW

As the familiar epigram has it, those who are ignorant of history are doomed never to have any. A third of a century having passed since Ira and I (and The Mountaineers, willy nilly) got into the guidebook business, a few more people than presently do ought, in my opinion, to know the how and the why.

The how, appropriately, was *Mountaineering: The Freedom of the Hills,* which dawned quietly the summer and fall of 1953, at my typewriter, where I was melding the lecturers' outlines from the previous five years of The Mountaineers' Climbing Course into a master outline file. When I dropped the completed work in the lap of Climbing Chairman Jack Hazle, he pronounced this "1953 Lecture Book," as it came to be called, none other than the starting point for the new textbook we'd been thinking about, a replacement for the excellent but now obsolescent *Climbers' Notebook* of 1940. It fell to me to commence planning, and this continued until 1955, when the Climbing Committee said, "Time's a-wastin'. Get crackin'." The committee I assembled did so with knee-jerk alacrity, and the crackin' awoke the Board of Trustees, where a fit of dunder und blitzen was the squall-line forerunner to years of sturm und drang. However, in 1960 the sun broke through, birds sang, and a chorale hailed the new textbook.

We printed 5,000 copies, estimated to last 5–7 years; before the year was up I'd ordered a second 5,000, and so it went, and so it still does.

Much of that early dunder and continuing sturm had been engendered by an understandable distrust of climbers, in this case aggravated by our committee's internal use of various provocative working titles, such as "Hillwalking: The Lowdown on How to Get High." There was, of course, the normal difficulty any old, large organization has in undertaking any new, large project. However, the obstacle too formidable to overcome by a good rhetorical physicking was poverty. We climbers could not believe the club had no money and suspected a flim-flam (especially since petitions demanding the book be publicly aborted were being circulated at club gatherings and ski lodges) until one of our own volunteered for the onerous job of club treasurer and after lengthy scrutiny of quill-pen scratchings in the accounts concluded, "It's true. The club is living—and not too well—from hand to mouth." Paul Wiseman, one of a series of club presidents who squared up to the problem, appointed an ad hoc committee of club elders to review "our" treasurer's report. I was invited to attend as an observer at the meeting where they faced the quandary. As they sat dumb I reviewed in my mind the options our group had discussed; among them was taking the book, and probably the Climbing Course, and leaving the club. Leo Gallagher broke the silence: "It must be done." He got out his checkbook, which was joined in the next several weeks by a hundred other checkbooks. The loans were secured by the book; any loaner who lost patience could demand repayment in copies to hawk in the street.

That never was necessary. Embarrassment came from the other direction—sudden, unexpected riches. Sales of the first 5,000 books repaid the loans and netted enough to pay for the second 5,000, and sales of these, and the next 5,000s, began amassing what was, to a bare-bones club, a fortune. In various heads there began dancing visions of sugarplums, such as new ski lodges. Meanwhile, receipts from book sales were being put in the club's General Fund from which they might be plucked at any meeting of the Board of Trustees, for any requested purpose, by an ordinary majority vote, no referendum, no appeal.

Didn't seem right to me. The *Freedom* riches were not a shower of gold from Heaven rewarding the club for the inherent virtue of its manifold activities in the woods and snows, on the dance floor and stage, they were the market value, the cashing-in of seven years of unpaid volunteer labor by me and a hundred fellow members in the writing and editing, and of the philanthropy of Leo and the hundred others who put up the money for the publication—and of a tradition dating from the 1934–35 founding of the Climbing Course and, even farther back, from the first ascent of Mount Olympus in 1907 by the club's first Summer Outing. Leo and several other club elders, including President Jesse Epstein, saw it the same way I did. The trustees voted to separate book receipts from the General Fund in a Literary Fund.

Thus the how. Now, the why.

The cards of history were so dealt that 1960 was the year not only of our *Freedom* but the Sierra Club's *This is the American Earth*, inaugural volume in the revolutionary Exhibit Format series created by Dave Brower. Thanks to the book (and Dave) the Sierra Club grew explosively and enormously in size and influence, nationally and internationally. The book—the series—and Brower—may be said to have ushered in the Age of Environmentalism. The founding of The Mountaineers in 1906 had been an expression of Muirism; it seemed fitting to the Literary Fund Committee to embrace, in 1960, Browerism. In 1964 we published Tom Miller's *The North Cascades*, an economy-size "format," which combined with Dave's 1965 full-size Format *The Wild Cascades: Forgotten Parkland* to make a thundering salvo in the battle for a North Cascades National Park, won in 1968.

Our Literary Fund of the 1960s was insufficiently robust to stage Dave Brower-scale operas (though in 1972 Tom and I, as envoi to our years as unpaid leaders of Mountaineer Books, produced the only Brower-scale, Brower-style Exhibit Format the club has ever published, *The Alpine Lakes*). The question in the mid-1960s was, what Brower-like things might we do on, say, a chamber-music scale? Brower stirred the minds, the hearts, the spirits of America and the world. Might we serve in our home hills, on a more pedestrian level, by stirring the feet? Stirring—and steering—to wildlands that needed sensitive feet to repel tyrannical wheels?

Guidebooks were rarities hereabouts in the 1960s. In 1965 there fell into our hands a most extraordinary manuscript, *Routes and Rocks: Hiker's Guide to the North Cascades from Glacier Peak to Lake Chelan*, by Dwight Crowder and Rowland Tabor. So dazzled was our Literary Fund Committee by the book's geographic and geologic and literary merits, and the sale of more than 2,000 copies in a matter of weeks, that we were scheming a series of the same—until a bit of calculation showed that for such a series we would need either a few hundred Crowders and Tabors or a few hundred years or both.

We couldn't wait. For two reasons. For one, though membership in The Mountaineers was not keeping pace with the area's population growth (there exists in the soul of many wilderness walkers a hard core of non-joiner philosophical anarchism), wilderness walking was *more* than keeping pace. Tom Miller complained that with the first sunshine of spring there came from all over Boeing a parade flocking and knocking at his office door, asking directions to the Mount Si trail.

For the other, the Conservation Division's plate of threatened wildlands was full-to-overflowing. *Routes and Rocks*, in selling 2,000 copies overnight, had in very short order put a minimum of 4,000 boots in the North Cascades heartland we were seeking as the core of a North Cascades National Park. Boots. Feet bones connected to the leg bones, leg bones connected to the hip bones, hip bones to the backbones, backbones to the head bones, head bones to the letter-writing and voting-machine-lever-pulling finger bones and the testifying-and-howling mouth bones and the jumping-up-and-down feet bones.

Tom Miller brought to a meeting of the Literary Fund Committee an English edition of a German guidebook he'd run across, *Salute the Mountains: 100 Walks in the Alps* (translated in 1962 from the 1959 *Berg Heil: Die hundert schönsten Bergwanderungen in der Alpen*, by Walter Pause). That was our ticket, the model for Tom's maestroship of *100 Hikes in Western Washington* in 1966, the first and so far only hiking guide to top the local bestseller chart. There being many more than 100 matters on the Conservation Division's plate, there had to be a second *100*, and another *100*, and *100* more, etc.

* * *

If guidebooks were rare hereabouts in the 1960s, the same cannot be said of the 1990s. Ira and I take the precaution of not reading any of

Mount Shuksan from tarn on Kulshan Ridge, Hike 7

the row upon row of newcomers to bookstore shelves in order to avoid the ever-present dangers of unconscious plagiarism—and of repeating someone else's mistakes. I scan the forewords, though, because there, if anywhere, is the environmental conscience. I regret to say that in the forewords I have scanned I haven't found any to speak of. Which is not to say there isn't any. But the absence points up the reason Ira and I got into guidebooking in the 1960s and why we're still at it.

You, dear reader, surely will concede that the Spring/Manning conscience never escapes your notice. We never get out of your face. Even within The Mountaineers, whose purposes proclaimed in 1906 include "preserving the natural beauty of Northwest America," there have been mutterings. It's rude, we are scolded, to intimate that tax-paying church-going free-enterprisers sitting at their corporation desks smoking big fat cigars, and duly elected, perpetually campaign-fund-raising public officials, and blindered bureaucrats focused on getting home to dinner on time and making no trouble that might threaten the pension might occasionally be ill-informed, ignorant, stupid, asleep at the switch, or, once in

a blue moon, greedy or corrupt. When moves have been suggested that we be cooled, the possibility has been aired that we find other publishing pastures greener.

"Greener" as in politics, not as in greenbacks. We eschew the strategies of prudent profit-maximizers: We do our research in the field, not in the library. We do not content ourselves skimming the easy cream, but as is demonstrated by *100* and *100* and *100,* etc., dip our spoons deep in the curds and whey. We do not trim sails to catch merely the big winds, but huff and puff to stir faint breezes to strong gusts, to gales; we love hurricanes. We do not step around gross and immobile obscenities blocking our feet but crank up and kick butt. We heartily wish the same would be done by the row upon row of newcomers to bookstore shelves. Why else are they there?

To return to the "why" of The Mountaineers Books . . .

• • •

In 1964 *The North Cascades* took every loose nickel in the Literary Fund just to print and bind, leaving nothing to "merchandise" the book. Dave Brower (the Sierra Club) stepped in, bought from us (at cost) cartons of copies, and sent them to (I believe) just about every newspaper in America known to carry book reviews. From the clippings I saw, this doubtless was the first the citizens of Louisiana, Florida, Maine, and waypoints between ever heard of the area that contains more glaciers than the rest of the old 48 states combined. Brower did not omit, either, every member of Congress who demonstrated the least interest in the public lands.

In 1972, the Literary Fund having accumulated a great many more nickels, we blew the whole wad on *The Alpine Lakes,* done in the grand-opera Brower style, including a foreword by him for good measure, and with legwork help from the Alpine Lakes Protection Society conducted a Brower-like mass distribution of free copies. The Washington Congressional delegation, Democrats and Republicans in harness, led the charge for establishment of the Alpine Lakes Wilderness. Passed by both houses and sent to the White House in 1976, the bill ran up against a seemingly hopeless roadblock, the U.S. Forest Service and the Bureau of the Budget, recommending veto.

The Republicans had the White House. The fate of the bill thus was in Republican hands. Busy hands they were. Congressman Joel Pritchard pled for and obtained five minutes with the president for Governor Dan Evans. Evans flew to Washington City barely in time to only just make the appointment. But how could he in five minutes controvert the powerful opposition? The book! He'd forgotten to bring it. A copy was rustled up from a Sierra Club member, Evans rushed to the White House, and the five minutes ran on to many, many more as President Gerald Ford insisted on turning every page, marveling at each photograph, exclaiming "Such beautiful country!" and concluding, "It must be saved!"

Dave Brower was often chewed on (and at length fired) by bean-counters distressed by the extravagance of page size and white space and color bleeds in his Exhibit Formats, and by

his largesse in broadcasting the gorgeous, costly volumes to all points of the compass. He mildly responded to the first of these Scroogeisms by saying that in an age when the eye is kept so busy by myriad public entertainments, if you have a message, you have to first take a two-by-four and hit the mule over the head. To the second criticism he answered that you never knew exactly which mule might be the one who could—and would—do something about the message. Ironically, none of his own Exhibit Formats ever so perfectly proved his method as our respectful emulation. We hit the Mule-in-Chief right between the eyes.

In 1984 the Conservation Division, under Chair Jo Roberts, sponsored and brought into being a handsome if not-quite-Brower-like volume, *Washington Wilderness: The Unfinished Work,* to serve the thirty-eight-member Washington Wilderness Coalition as a tool in working for the Washington Wilderness Act. The book effectively served its purpose.

But not by itself. Ira had taken to Jo copies of our two books (since expanded to four), *101 Hikes in the North Cascades* and *102 Hikes in the Alpine Lakes, South Cascades, and Olympics,* with all the unprotected trails redlined. Jo was so powerfully impressed she rounded up a work party to make sets of the redlined books, the "101" and "102" crossed off so the covers read *39 Hikes in the North Cascades* and *47 Hikes in the Alpine Lakes, South Cascades, and Olympics.*

Ira flew the books to Washington City and personally presented sets to each of our two Senators and seven Congressmen. They were as powerfully impressed as Jo had been; again in bipartisan unity they pushed the bill through Congress—and even through the White House, despite its occupant being so disgruntled that he signed the measure in secluded secrecy, no ceremony, no publicity. Was he ashamed to be caught in the act of doing a good deed?

So that's the "why" of the department of The Mountaineer Books in which Ira and I work.

—Harvey Manning

Mount Adams from Juniper Ridge, Hike 81

INTRODUCTION

The historian Eric Hobsbawm says in his *The Age of Extremes:*

> *. . . a catastrophe would seem to be unavoidable. Humanity reached its first billion about 200 years ago. The next billion took 120 years to reach, the third 35 years, the fourth 15 years. At the end of the 1980s it stood at 5.2 billions and was expected to exceed 6 billions by 2000. . . . If humanity is to have a recognizable future, it cannot be by prolonging the past or the present. If we try to build the third millennium on that basis, we shall fail. And the price of failure, that is to say, the alternative to a changed society, is darkness.*

The conclusion of this millennium and the beginning of the next will see whether our civilization slips off the bubble or, if the bubble should go "thip!," evaporates with it. The wilderness, once considered the antithesis, the enemy of civilization, but in the past century gradually recognized as an ally, a support of our efforts to remain (or become?) civil, is in the front lines of the contest between darkness and light.

As we here offer a selection of 100 "Classics" from the 100, plus 100, plus 100, plus etc., of our third of a century of hiking guides, a thumbnail summary is in order of the past century of wilderness preservation in Washington:

1899, Mount Rainier National Park. We like to think of it as a deed done by John Muir, who climbed The Mountain, praised it, and recommended it for a park, which it became, preceded in national glorification only by Yellowstone geysers and Sierra canyons and sequoias. The disillusioning reality is it was a "gift" of the Northern Pacific Railroad, which was pleased to exchange land-grant glaciers and flowers for the big fat trees lusted after by its confederates, notoriously Weyerhaeuser.

1916, National Park Act. Enacted to curb the free-wheeling amorality of capitalist materialism, to codify a morality of social idealism.

1931–1935–1942, Goat Rocks and North Cascade Primitive Areas and Mount Adams Wild Area. As the new National Park Service was hitching its wagon to the new automobile, the U.S. Forest Service, influenced by Aldo Leopold and the like, was birthing an anti-automobile concept of wilderness preservation.

1938, Olympic National Park. The proposal, blocked for half a century by the timber industry and the U.S. Forest Service, at last done and done. To name only one of the many responsible, credit our greatest conservationist president and, to date, our last such, Franklin D. Roosevelt.

1956, Wilderness Bill. First introduced in Congress, only to be bottled up year after year by logging, grazing, and mining industries and U.S. Forest Service, within which the Leopold spirit had withered with the death of Bob Marshall in 1939.

1960, Multiple-Use-Sustained Yield Act. The Forest Service's formal proclamation of its self-assigned mission of "converting old-growth timber stands to fast-growing young forests." In political fact, a Maginot Line erected to frustrate panzers of the wilderness movement. The use has been multiple only in the sense of grinding up steak and potatoes to make hash. The yield was sustained only until bookkeeping sleight-of-hand no longer could conceal the overcutting. Flim-flam from the same propaganda machine as "the greatest good of the greatest number in the long run."

1960, Glacier Peak Wilderness. The plans drawn up by Bob Marshall, then buried by the Forest Service, excavated by the citizenry, and at last grudgingly conceded—in niggardly part.

1964, National Wilderness Act. Wildernesses in national forests and other federal jurisdictions removed from administrative whim, protected by Congress and the president. In Washington gave guarantees to Glacier Peak, Goat Rocks, and Mount Adams Wildernesses.

1968, North Cascades Act. Established North Cascades National Park and complementary Ross Lake and Lake Chelan National Recreation Areas. Reclassified North Cascade Primitive Area's eastern portion as Pasayten Wilderness, placed the western portion in the park. Small additions to Glacier Peak Wilderness.

1976, Alpine Lakes Wilderness. Established.

1983, Mount St. Helens National Volcanic Monument. Established.

1984, Washington Wilderness Act. Sponsored by the thirty-eight organizations of the Washington Wilderness Coalition. Modest enlargements of four existing wildernesses (Glacier Peak, Goat Rocks, Mount Adams, and Pasayten), establishment of nineteen new wildernesses, several of some size (William O. Douglas, Henry M. Jackson, and Lake Chelan – Sawtooth), the others lesser to tiny (in the Olympics: Buckhorn, Colonel Bob, Mount Skokomish, The Brothers, and Wonder Mountain; in the South Cascades: Indian Heaven and Trapper Creek; in the Rainier area: Clearwater, Glacier View, Norse Peak, and Tatoosh; in the North Cascades: Boulder River, Mount Baker, and Noisy-Diobsud; elsewhere, Salmo-Priest and Juniper Dunes). More than 1,000,000 acres placed in the National Wilderness Preservation System.

But the measure drawn up by the Washington Wilderness Coalition encompassed 2,500,000 acres—and that was itself drastically reduced from the want-lists of member groups. Is the glass one-third full? Or two-thirds still empty?

Note the eight-year periodicity: 1960, 1968, 1976, 1984. By rights, the year for Washington Wilderness Act II should have been 1992.

We are six years overdue! Let's get crackin'!

●　　●　　●

This wildland is your land, and it is your obligation to be its advocate, by working for Washington Wilderness Act II and in other ways discussed in these pages, and to be its steward. When Ira and I were born, humanity totaled 2 billion; it has now passed 5 billion and is predicted in the lifetimes of our grandchildren to reach 10 billion. What sort of world that will be, who knows? We are certain, though, that if a sufficiency of the earth does not then merit the definition of "wilderness," however weakened that definition may have become by the sheer weight of human flesh, voracity of human appetite, and ravages of inhuman machinery, the definition, then, of "civilization" will equally have suffered from galloping entropy. The "galloping," too, will be different; the barbarian hordes who attack and loot and destroy will come not on horseback but on wheels and wings.

Are we, the conservationists-preservationists-environmentalists-birdwatchers, fiddling while Rome burns? Of course. But it does help take our mind off the conflagration where Lucky Pierre the billionaire is—in the words of John Kenneth Galbraith—" . . . engaged in one of man's oldest exercises in moral philosophy, that is the search for a superior moral justification for selfishness." Do keep in mind that the wilderness preservationist is not forbidden from taking time out to carry a bucket of water in the fire brigade.

Meanwhile, in the wildlands, the freedom of the hills we enjoyed even as late as 1960, when we published the first edition of *Freedom of the Hills,* is sadly diminished, and rattling tin cups on the cell bars will not avail, because we built the prison: "We have met the enemy and he is us." For the sake of the land and your joy in it, you will have to—and want to—obey rules of behavior made necessary by those "extra" billions of human beings.

The freedom of laissez-faire camping in which we so recently reveled is as obsolete as other amenities of a larger, because emptier, world, such as cherry bombs. Land-managers are proceeding with some due speed and much careful thought to cope with the backcountry population explosion. The National Park Act of 1916 was adopted "to conserve the scenery and the natural and historic objects and wildlife." Each visitor must therefore enjoy the parks "in

Sunrise on Mount Rainier from Klapatche Lake, Hike 63

such manner and by such means as will leave them unimpaired for the enjoyment of future generations." The National Wilderness Act of 1964 embraces areas where "the earth and its community of life are untrammeled by man, where man himself is a visitor who does not remain."

Management rules (and Nature, too) are in such flux that we cannot publish new editions of guidebooks fast enough to keep up. When in doubt, you do well to seek current information by telephone about roads and trails and permits. The Forest Service–Park Service Information Center listed in the Seattle telephone directory is worth a try if it's not a toll call for you. The staffers do their best but are so few (thanks to Congress) and the roads and trails so many that whatever you are told may be out-of-date. Far more reliable are the offices close to the scenes; toll calls though they usually will be for you, those are the numbers given in the data block at the head of each trip description. Call well ahead of your trip; the offices usually are staffed only during business hours on weekdays.

- Ask about camping (backcountry travel) permits; these are required at most national park sites and at more and more national forests.
- Ask about campsite availability; in popular areas, where the beaten-to-death laissez-faire "zoos" have been closed for rehabilitation, camping is permitted only at designated sites, often full-up.
- Party size is limited in many popular areas to a dozen or fewer members; ask about that.
- Pets always have been forbidden on national park trails and are increasingly being banned from national forest wildernesses. Where they are permitted, the leash is becoming the One Essential. A tight leash.
- Ask about bicycles and motorcycles; their presence or absence may well affect your choice of trip. Wheels are not allowed on trails of national parks or wilderness areas. They are, as well, excluded from many other trails. Absence will become more common as the muddle-headed "multiple-use" policy is flushed.

Most horse-riders do their best to be good neighbors and know how to go about it. The typical hiker, though, is ignorant of the difficulties in maneuvering a huge mass of flesh (containing a very small brain) along narrow paths on steep mountains. The first rule is the horse has the right-of-way. For his own safety as well as that of the rider, the hiker must get off the trail—preferably on the downhill side, giving the clumsy animal and its perilously perched rider the inside of the tread. If necessary, retreat some distance to a safe passing point. The second rule is, when you see the horse approaching, do not keep silent or stand still in a mistaken attempt to avoid frightening the beast. Continue normal motions and speak to it, so the creature will recognize you as just another human and not a silent and doubtless dangerous monster. Finally, if you have a dog along, get a tight grip on its throat to stop the nipping and yapping which may endanger the rider and, in the case of a surly horse, the dog as well.

The sketch maps in this book are for preliminary orientation, not travel guidance. Our good fortune is to have available to us the best maps in the history of the world, the topographic sheets produced by the U.S. Geological Survey (USGS), which are sold by map shops and sporting goods stores. Unfortunately, the USGS is so strapped for cash (the Congress problem, again) that revision is so occasional that information on roads and trails is always largely obsolete.

Fortunately, the USGS sells the data "separations" (from which its sheets are published) on a nonprofit, cost-only, public-service basis. This has enabled commercial publishers to buy the separations, add and delete information, and issue maps that are designed specifically for hikers and are kept up to date. Though the USGS base map is always available, for areas where they exist we recommend the maps in the Green Trails series, which covers virtually all hiking areas in the Cascades and Olympics, and the Custom Correct series for the Olympics.

Also excellent are the Forest Service maps for wilderness areas, available from ranger stations, map shops, and sporting goods stores.

Though we will not dwell here on clothing and equipment because it is almost certain, in this Age of Holy Stuff, you have far too much, we insist that you carry the Ten Essentials, found to be so by generations of members of The Mountaineers, often from sad experience.

1. Extra clothing—more than needed in good weather.
2. Extra food—enough so something is left over at the end of the trip.
3. Sunglasses—necessary for most alpine travel and indispensable on snow.
4. Knife—for first aid and emergency firebuilding (making kindling).
5. Firestarter—a candle or chemical fuel for starting a fire with wet wood.
6. First-aid kit.
7. Matches—in a waterproof container.
8. Flashlight—with extra bulb and batteries.
9. Map—be sure it's the right one for the trip.
10. Compass—be sure to know the declination, east or west.

Why take these "essentials"? To keep your margin of safety from thinning out to nothing. Inclusion of a trail in this book does not mean it will be safe for you. The route may have changed since the description herein was written. Creeks flood. Gravity pulls down trees and rocks. Brush grows up. The weather changes from season to season, day to day, hour to hour. Wind blows, rain soaks, lightning strikes, the sun sets, temperature drops, snow falls, avalanches happen.

A guidebook cannot guarantee you are safe for the trail. Strength and agility vary from person to person. You vary from decade to decade, year to year, day to day, morning to afternoon to dark and stormy night.

You can reduce backcountry risks by being informed, equipped, and alert, by recognizing hazards and knowing and respecting your limits. However, you cannot eliminate risk, and neither can the attorney hired by your next of kin. An old saying from the Alps is that when a climber is injured, he apologizes to his friends, and when a climber is killed, his friends apologize for him. It's a dangerous world out there. Perhaps you'd be happier as an armchair adventurer. But you may want to strap yourself in as a precaution against earthquakes.

Permits issued for backcountry travel and camping, and prominent posters at many trailheads, instruct in the "good outdoor manners" of today's civil wildland society, often summarized in the Golden Rule: "Take only photographs. Leave only footprints."

We are encouraged about the potential of humankind for saintliness when we see how clean the trails and camps are compared to the slums of the Good Old Days. We rarely have to bellow, anymore, "PACK IT OUT! PACK IT ALL OUT!" It's enough to politely remind folks that if you can carry it in full, you can carry it out empty.

The careless/carefree slums of those Good Old Days had at their warm and smiling hearts the wood fire, and for many of us our time of green-bonding might almost be more accurately called campfire-bonding. Forgive our damp eyes. Year by year the fires are being driven down the mountain—from the meadows to the forest to the ocean beaches, and even there, in the driftwood, restrictions now exist. We've made no attempt in this book to keep up with the year-by-year regulation changes, have omitted all references to "no fires" and "stoves only," and the like. You won't have taken many backpacks before you learn never to count on a wood fire to keep warm (that's what clothes and a sleeping bag are for) or to cook your meals (the stove). (Personally, having become a minimalist, hostile to equipment that is more than medium-tech, I live by the wisdom of Wolf Bauer, founder of the Climbing Course, "Though the food is cold, the inner man is hot.")

The other sine qua non of a reputable camp in the G.O.D. was water, and it remains as true as ever that without it you will get thirsty, dirty, and eventually die. Yet in the a-changin' times an ambivalence has developed toward the stuff of which we are mostly made. Fear haunts the wildlands, and though I personally consider it a sacrilege to pump the nectar of the gods through a $200 machine, where wood fire is allowed I may do a boil-up (10 minutes does in the filthy little blighters that used to stay in Eurasia and Africa but now are emigrating via jet to destroy American livers). I carry a small bottle of iodine compound for use when drinking from swamps and ditches and swimmable lakes, but generally take straight whatever nature puts on my table.

Nurse log in the Hoh River rain forest, Olympic National Park, Hike 95

Never having suffered the Boy Scout trots, I hypothesize that I am, as has been the majority of the human race since our eons in Africa, immune to giardiasis. Nevertheless, warned by epidemiologist doom-criers, on encountering wildlanders who have the smell (it's the money) of jet-trekkers, I don rubber gloves and gauze mask and boil my Kool-Aid because among the diseases they are importing will be, sooner or later, the Red Death.

Despite the hydrophobia brought home by the trekky from foreign trails, and the mechanophilia of the tekky, the love of water for its own plain and simple sake still holds our hearts. Backpackers are so fond of the creek's babble and the lake's wind-ripple they want to be close enough to easily and frequently trample their way from kitchen through the deliciously lush plants to bank and shore. But water-near camps not only are precisely where human impact on fragile ecosystems is most ruinous, they are where the novices crowd. The canny hiker pauses at creek or lake, fills collapsible water bags, and continues onward a half-hour or so to a wide-view ridge, to solitude, to the sound of silence.

You will, of course, in your "leave no trace" behavior, respect the purity and clarity of natural water. Don't wash dishes in streams or lakes, loosing food particles and detergent. Don't wash bodies in streams or lakes. Don't swim in waters being taken internally by others. Eliminate body waste in places well-removed from watercourses; first dig a shallow hole in the "biological disposer layer," then touch a match to the toilet paper (or better, use leaves), and finally cover the evidence.

Mention must be made of a final peril of life amid the billions, millions of whom are thieves. When Ira and I were Scouts and, later, Khaki Gangsters, theft from a car left at the trailhead was rare. Not now. Equipment has become so fancy and expensive and hikers so numerous that stealing is a high-profit industry. Not even wilderness camps are entirely safe, but the professionals mainly concentrate on cars. First and foremost, don't make crime profitable for the pros. If they break into a hundred cars and get nothing but moldy boots and tattered T-shirts they'll give up. Don't think locks help—pros can open your car door and trunk as fast with a picklock as you can with your key. Don't imagine you can hide anything from them —they know all the hiding spots. If the hike is part of an extended car trip, arrange to store your extra equipment, perhaps at a nearby motel. Be suspicious of anyone waiting at a trailhead. One of the tricks of the trade is to sit there with a pack as if waiting for a ride, watching new arrivals unpack—and hide the valuables—and maybe even striking up a conversation to determine how long the marks will be away.

Among such dark thoughts, not to be omitted is awareness of the swelling social discontent in a time when the rich get ever richer and the poor ever poorer. As common, perhaps, as theft is vandalism for the sake of—well, for the same satisfaction, maybe, as drive-by shooting. Many a fortune-favored hiker keeps his Beamer locked in a garage at home, and at the trailhead parks a beater.

As for myself, relatively non-criminal though I am, my circumstances place me in the growing underclass, offended and depressed by egregious wealth flaunted in the manner of Little Jack Horner and the plum on his thumb. As a veteran of the Great Depression and a charter member of the Khaki Gang, strutting in Mountain Trooper parka and paratrooper pants and Air Corps goggles, eating K rations and sleeping in a feather bag under a liferaft sail, I shared my brag with that of my generation—we were cheapskates.

Passing a camp of bubble tents, internal-frame packs, the stoves a-whispering and the water-machines a-pumping, the citizens gaudily resplendent in boutique fashions, nibbling freeze-dried strawberries and shrimp, pinpointing their location by satellite and chatting on the cell phone with Aunt Nelly, I bethink me of Ed Abbey and his judgment, "Americans carry too much stuff in the wilderness. I like to give Nature a fair crack at me."

Chapter 1

NORTH CASCADES

It had been a long shag from Sibley Creek Pass, that September day of 1949, and our sole views had been of the Inspiration Glacier underfoot and the insides of clouds all around. The summit register recorded only ten or so ascents of Eldorado since the first in 1933. Interesting. The most interesting thing there was in that day, in that cloud. Then a sudden hole opened and revealed Alaska. Another hole, the Alps. The Himalaya. The Mountains of the Moon. We asked our leader, a veteran of these wilds, the names, and he didn't know. Neither did the map. ("Toto, I don't think we're in Kansas anymore.")

The next July we made the fifth or so ascent of Challenger and the third or so of Luna, that peak being not a climb but a fearfully long walk, down into, going and coming, and up out of, going and coming, the deep dark hole of Luna Cirque. I remember calculating from the register that our nine-man party more than doubled the number of humans who ever had set foot in that deep dark hole. Next day we were about to go for Fury or Phantom when a July semi-blizzard blew in and blew us out of there, back over the Challenger and East Whatcom Glaciers to Whatcom Pass. Before leaving my one-sleeping-bag-wide ledge hanging in the air above the cirque I built a little cairn for a register book and quoted in it from Scott's journal entry at the South Pole, "Great God! What an awful place."

This was not a hike, it was an alpine traverse, and very very deep, especially in that age before the helicopter shallowed all the wild world and the overcommunication industry wired it all together. Bust some bones and it would be a week and more to the hospital; a ruptured appendix would

have been a death sentence. Deep. Maybe a bit too deep for sport?

But if the heart of the Pickets is climbers' country, there is deep a-plenty, too, for hands-in-pockets pedestrians. "Collectors" from around the nation "do" North Cascades National Park by walking across it from the Nooksack to Whatcom Pass (an edge view of the Pickets) to ancient cedars of the Big Beaver. The Boundary Trail spans the Pasayten Wilderness from the ice-sharpened (by the plucking of alpine glaciers) giants of the west to ice-rounded (by the over-riding of the continental ice sheet) tundras of the east. The Pacific Crest Trail along the Cascade Crest from Harts Pass to Castle Pass is, for me, a pair with the John Muir Trail through the High Sierra. The Chelan Summit Trail in the gentle wilderness high above Lake Chelan is—well, go walk it and phrase your own "is." These are a few of my favorite things . . .

As for the short and shallow, that description fits more than half our Classics. Need I (dare I) mention Cascade Pass? (To let you in on a secret, the best day hike in that vicinity is Hidden Lake Peak, with the serendipities that you can be alone on the summit and the granite can withstand any number of boots without damage.)

By no means look down your nose at Mount Baker just because it's a volcano, every-day stuff in the Cascades. For a person with the taste, volcanoes can be exciting. Hearts going pit-a-pat, volcanologists fluttered in helicopters from the world around for the Big Show. When the curtain rose, of course, this wasn't the stage and they all fluttered off to St. Helens. Still, standing atop Park Butte and watching the steam plume rise thousands of feet from dazzling white into blue sky fills one with—well—awe?

Airview of McAllister Glacier and Eldorado Peak, North Cascades National Park

1 | HELIOTROPE RIDGE

Round trip: 6½ miles
Hiking time: 5 hours (day hike or backpack)
High point: 5600 feet
Elevation gain: 2000 feet
Hikable: August through September
Map: Green Trails No. 13 Mt. Baker
Information: Glacier Public Service Center (360) 599-2714

Villages in the Alps were crunched by advancing glaciers, the Greenland Colony mysteriously vanished, and that echo of the Pleistocene, the "Little Ice Age," made life in northern lands generally miserable. Then came a global warming caused not by the exhalations of young mankind but by the whimsy of Old Nature. Kermit the Hermit, friend of the ice, mourned the disaster of shrinkage we saw all about us in the Cascades. But a peculiar thing happened. Did Kermit's prayers have anything to do with it? In the course of our climbing Mount Baker in 1948 he reoccupied stations set up in the 1930s to measure the retreat of the Coleman Glacier. The Coleman was not retreating anymore, it was

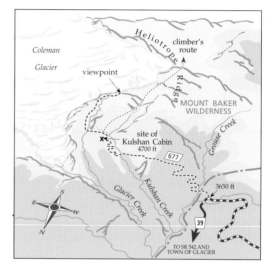

advancing! His capering and yodeling brought the faithful flocking, eager to see if Nature might, after all, be working on a solution to the Seattle problem.

The forest walk is splendid, and the moraines are an exuberance of flowers. The climbers, by the hundreds on summer weekends, are pleased as punch to strut their axes and ropes and helmets and hardware for a humble audience of pedestrian peasantry. As for me, having recovered from the need to climb mountains, my fondness for Heliotrope Ridge nowadays is as a safe and easy place to introduce kids to the geological power that converts hills to peaks. Our family also enjoyed, in the lifetime of dear old Tasha, watching the sheepdog with the piebald eyes dash this way and

Heliotrope Ridge and Coleman Glacier on the side of Mount Baker

Coleman Glacier

that, exercising the marmots to keep them in shape for dodging coyotes.

Drive Highway 542 to the town of Glacier and 1 mile beyond to Glacier Creek road No. 39. Turn right and continue some 8 miles to a parking lot at the sign "Heliotrope Ridge Trail," elevation 3650 feet.

Hike 2 miles to the site of historic Kulshan Cabin, 4700 feet, near but still below timberline. The trail climbs, crossing several streams which

on a hot day may be gushers from melting snowfields. Do not be confused by climber's routes going straight up the hillside. The way passes below steep flower-covered meadows and groves of alpine trees, over a rocky moraine to another moraine. Look down a gravel precipice to the blue-white jumble of the Coleman Glacier and up to the gleaming summit of ice-capped Mount Baker. Follow the moraine upward—stopping well short of the living glacier.

2 | SKYLINE DIVIDE

Round trip to knoll 6215: 6 miles
Hiking time: 4 hours (day hike or backpack)
High point: 6563 feet
Elevation gain: 2200 feet
Hikable: August through September
Map: Green Trails No. 13 Mt. Baker
Information: Glacier Public Service Center (360) 599-2714

A meadow as big and green as they get. An enormous white volcano—pound for pound, the iciest in the Cascades. Broad views of course. And—oh!—the sunsets and sunrises.

The trail has no real "destination." Always there is one more bend to peer around, one more knoll to climb over to see what the bear could see. For a kid's book, Ira named the first knoll "Lunch Box Hill." Who knows? Some surveyor, way back when, could have left his lunch box here.

Drive Highway 542 to 1 mile beyond the town of Glacier. Turn right on Glacier Creek road No. 39 and in a hundred yards turn sharply left on Deadhorse road No. 37. Follow the south side of the Nooksack River some 4 level and pleasant miles. The road then climbs abruptly. At 13 miles is the parking lot and trailhead, elevation 4300 feet. Find the trail at the upper end of the lot.

The trail, moderate to steep, climbs 1500 feet in 2 miles through silver firs and subalpine glades to an immense ridge-top meadow at 5800 feet and the beginning of wide views north. A little way trail leads to Lunch Box Hill. Open a lunch box and your eyes. The glaciers of the north wall of Mount Baker spread before you. Beyond forests of the Nooksack Valley are the greenery of Church Mountain and the rock towers of the Border Peaks and, across the border, the Cheam (Lucky Four) Range. On a clear day saltwater can be seen, and the Vancouver Island Mountains, and the British Columbia Coast Range. Eastward is Mount Shuksan and a gentler companion, little Table Mountain, above Heather Meadows.

Shut the lunch box, proceed ¾ mile along the ridge, and take the sidepath up the second knoll, 6215 feet. Second lunch? Sprawl and enjoy. For

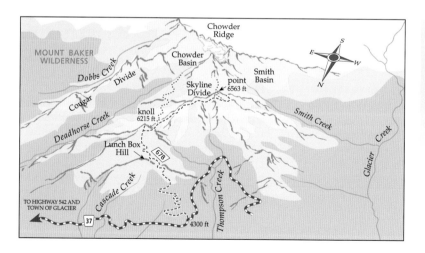

The trail has no real "destination," with always one more knoll to climb over to see what the bear could see.

Skyline Trail and Mount Baker

photographers, better a late breakfast or early dinner: The best pictures of Baker from here generally are taken before 10:00 A.M. and after 4:00 P.M.

Another ½ mile, at a 6000-foot saddle, the trail splits. The left contours a scant mile to a dead-end in Chowder Basin, headwaters of Deadhorse Creek, and campsites with probably all-summer water. Aside from that, the only drinkables likely on the ridge are from snowfield dribbles and the jug in your pack. The right climbs a step in Skyline Divide to 6500 feet and follows the tundra crest 2 miles to a 6300-foot saddle.

In benign weather the supreme overnight experience is atop the 6500-foot tundra, watching the setting sun turn Baker gold and the lights of farms and cities wink on, then awaking at dawn to watch Baker turn shocking pink. However, though the tundra is tough enough to withstand sun and frost and storm, it cannot take human abuse. Do not sack out on soft turf; lay your sleeping pad and bag on a hard rock or bare dirt.

3 | EXCELSIOR MOUNTAIN

Round trip from Canyon Creek road: 6 ½ miles
Hiking time: 4 hours (day hike or backpack)
High point: 5712 feet
Elevation gain: 1600 feet
Hikable: mid-July through September
Map: Green Trails No.13 Mt. Baker
Information: Glacier Public Service Center (360) 599-2714

Meadow summit views extend out from Nook-sack forests to saltwater and sweep from Mount Baker to the Border Peaks to the south-ernmost reach of the British Columbia Coast Range. Flowers in July, berries and colors in September. For the sake of early morning photos, Ira once spent a night in the deserted lookout building that stood from the mid-1930s to 1969. Several years later, after the building had been sloppily demolished, I and a friend spent a night for the sake of the stars; we tidied up the mess with a Hades of a blaze, the last fire the scene

Mount Baker from Excelsior Mountain

ever should see except by the wish of Nature, which always has the right.

Three trails lead to the cabin site; the easiest is recommended here. Drive Highway 542 to the Glacier Public Service Center and 1.8 miles beyond to Canyon Creek road No. 31. Turn left and continue 14.6 miles to the parking lot in a clearcut at the start of trail No. 625, elevation 4277 feet.

Climb through the forest a gentle ½ mile to the Canyon Ridge trail No. 689. Keep right a bit more to 4500-foot Damfino Lakes. (A ranger once was asked the names of the two ponds and shrugged, "dam-if-I-know.")

Climb another timbered mile and ascend a narrow draw. Cross a notch and sidehill through forest, then broad meadows, for ½ mile to 5300-foot Excelsior Pass, some 2½ miles from the road. (Pleasant camps at and near the pass when there is snowfield water—perhaps until early August.) Follow the trail another ½ mile, traversing under the peak, then go left ¼ mile to the 5712-foot summit. See the glaciers of Mount Baker across forests of the Nooksack. Half-turn to see more ice on Mount Shuksan and other peaks east. Full-turn to see the steep-walled Border Peaks and snowy ranges extending far north into Canada. Every which way see green meadows.

Two alternate routes up the peak have their purposes.

White paintbrush on Excelsior Mountain

Alternate No. 1. Eight miles east of Glacier at a small parking area (trail sign across the road), trail No. 670 switchbacks 4 miles, gaining 3500 feet on south-facing slopes that melt free of snow in May or June, thus offering good walking early in the year; turn back when snowfields so advise.

Alternate No. 2. Drive 11.5 miles east from Glacier and between mileposts 45 and 46 go left on a service road to Welcome Pass trailhead. It's 2½ miles to the pass and then 5 miles of simply swell ridge-walking to the mountain.

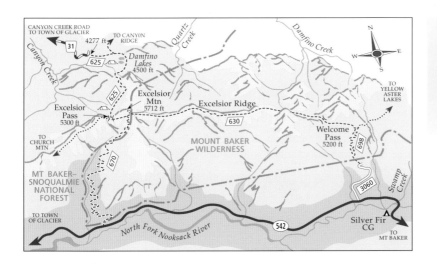

Three trails lead to a cabin site with views that extend out from Nooksack forests to saltwater.

4 | TWIN LAKES–WINCHESTER MOUNTAIN

Round trip to Twin Lakes from Tomyhoi Lake trailhead: 4 miles
Hiking time: 3 hours (day hike or backpack)
High point: 5200 feet
Elevation gain: 1600 feet
Hikable: July through September

Round trip to Winchester Mountain from Tomyhoi Lake trailhead: 9 miles
Hiking time: 6 hours (day hike or backpack)
High point: 6521 feet
Elevation gain: 3000 feet
Hikable: July through September

Maps: Green Trails No. 14 Mt. Shuksan
Information: Glacier Public Service Center (360) 599-2714

An easy and popular road/trail through alpine meadows to two delightful alpine lakes and on from there to a summit view of Baker, Shuksan, Border Peaks, and Tomyhoi, plus looks far down to Tomyhoi Lake and forests of Silesia Creek. Especially beautiful in fall colors. The lovely alpine waters, 5200 feet, and surrounding parklands are a superb basecamp for days of roaming high gardens, prowling old mines, and grazing September blueberries. Even if the upper road must be walked, access is easy for backpacking families with short-legged members.

Twin Lakes should be reached on easy and rewarding 2-mile trail, and for years Ira (and many others) has campaigned to "put to bed" the last 2 miles of road, impassable anyway for the average car, but grandfathered in by an ancient mining claim and thus kept open for the fun-trucks and incidentally macho SUVs (sports utility vehicles). Until sanity and justice prevail either grit your teeth and walk those last 2 miles or see how sporty your car is.

Drive Highway 542 east past Glacier Public Service Center 15.8 miles. Just beyond the highway

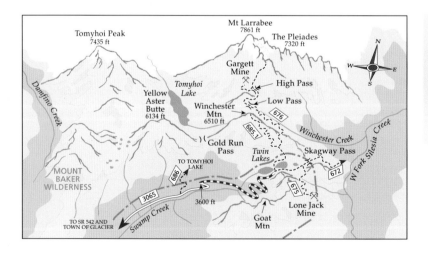

A trail through alpine meadows provides easy access for backpacking families with short-legged members.

maintenance sheds turn uphill and continue 4.5 miles on road No. 3065 to the Tomyhoi Lake trail sign, elevation 3600 feet (or as far as you want to drive). Parking is very limited.

The Twin Lakes road is not the work or joy of the Forest Service, which would love to put it to bed. The "mine-to-market" road was constructed by the county from pork-barrel funding and is maintained (only minimally) in the upper reaches solely by prospectors and then only sporadically.

The first 4.5 miles to the Tomyhoi Lake trailhead usually can be driven by the family car, but the final stretch to Twin Lakes, culminating in five wickedly sharp switchbacks, are something else. When the miners finally sell out, the road will be abandoned, returning Twin Lakes to the realm of trail country—where they belong.

Find the Winchester Mountain trail at the road-end between the lakes. Within ¼ mile is a junction with the High Pass (Gargett Mine) trail. Take the left fork and climb a series of switchbacks westerly through heather, alpine trees, and flowers. Near the top a treacherous snowpatch, steep with no runout, often lasts until late August. It may be possible to squirm between the upper edge of the snow and the rocks. Otherwise, drop below the snow and climb to the trail on the far side. Don't try crossing the snow without an ice ax and experience in using it.

In 1½ miles the trail rounds a shoulder and levels off somewhat for the final ½ mile to the summit, a fine place to while away hours surveying horizons from saltwaterways and lowlands to the Pickets and far north into Canada.

Winchester Mountain trail and Mount Shuksan in distance

5 | WHATCOM PASS

Round trip: 34 miles
Hiking time: Allow 3–5 days
High point: 5200 feet
Elevation gain: 5700 feet in, 2600 feet out
Hikable: late July through September
Maps: Green Trails No. 14 Mt. Chalkone, No. 15 Mt. Challenger
Information: Glacier Public Service Center (360) 599-2714
Backcountry use permit required for camping

Whatcom Pass in 1948 was the heart of solitude. Miners briefly had come a-rushing through on their way to the Caribou goldfields of Canada, then gone a-rushing somewhere else. The Forest Service had improved the old Indian-rusher-smuggler trail and maintained it, for a while. When our climbing party arrived there were fewer people around than grizzlies. But so classic a wildland of trees and flowers and rivers and glaciers was not to be denied. The North Cascades National Park was established in 1968 and the pass, as the high point on the unavoidably super-famous "Walk Across the Park," brought hikers a-rushing from all the nations of the world, and one fine day I gazed to the pass from a distant peak and was startled by a gabble of color, the glad-rags of a generation which knows not the meaning of khaki, forest green, field gray. But despite appearances, it is not a generation of vipers. I smile upon them.

Drive Highway 542 east from Glacier Public Service Center 13 miles to the Nooksack River bridge. Just before the bridge turn left on Nooksack River road No. 32. In 1.3 miles take the left fork, Ruth Creek road No. 32, and continue 5.4 miles to road-end at Hannegan Campground, elevation 3100 feet.

The trail enters Mount Baker Wilderness and ascends 4 miles to Hannegan Pass, 5066 feet. Forest switchbacks descend to the Chilliwack River and, at 4400 feet, Boundary Camp. The way gentles out in delightful forest to U.S. Cabin Camp at 10 miles.

At about 11 miles, elevation 2468 feet (2600 feet down from Hannegan Pass), the trail crosses the Chilliwack River on a cablecar and climbs moderately to the crossing of Brush Creek, 12 miles, and a junction.

Take the Brush Creek trail, which climbs steadily, gaining 2600 feet in the 5 miles to Whatcom Pass. At 13 miles is Graybeal Camp (hikers and horses), at 16½ miles the two sites of

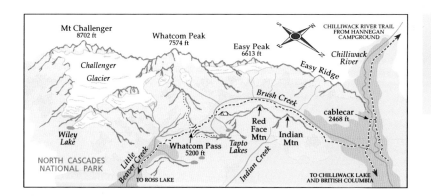

Views are superb from the pass meadows, but there is vastly more to do.

Whatcom Camp, and at 17 miles 5200-foot Whatcom Pass (no camping).

Views are superb from the pass meadows, but there is vastly more to do. First, ramble the easy ridge south to a knoll overlooking the gleam of Challenger Glacier. Tapto Lakes are next. Climb steep slopes north from the pass on a boot-built path in alpine forest. Where the hillside levels off continue left in meadows to rocky ground above the lakes.

In addition to the on-trail camps, cross-country camping is permitted at Tapto Lakes and on Whatcom Arm.

The "Walk Across the Park" from Hannegan Campground to Big Beaver Landing on Ross Lake covers 38½ up-and-down miles on easy trail beside wild rivers, through gorgeous forests, over three passes. Total elevation gain on the way is 5400 feet. To have time for sidetrips, a party should allow 7–9 days. From Whatcom Pass drop abruptly (fifty-six switchbacks!) to headwaters of Little Beaver Creek, an enchanting place where waterfalls tumble from cliffs all around. Camping here at Twin Rocks Camp, 3000 feet. At 6 miles from Whatcom Pass is Stillwell Camp and the 2400-foot junction with the Beaver Pass trail. To conclude the cross-park journey see Hike 13.

Mount Challenger from near Whatcom Pass

6 | LAKE ANN

Round trip: 8 miles
Hiking time: 6–8 hours (day hike or backpack)
High point (at the saddle): 4800 feet
Elevation gain: about 1000 feet in, 1600 feet out
Hikable: August through September
Map: Green Trails No. 14 Mt. Shuksan
Information: Glacier Public Service Center (360) 599-2714

A heaven of benevolent stars shone down on the five sleeping bags inert in the meadow. At the agreed hour four of the sleepers, veterans of the climb, silently and independently made the same decision. The fifth, a novice, slept on unawares until baked awake by the sun. He crawled out, donned boots, and stared at the experienced and inert four who were to guide him to the top.

"Hey fellahs, isn't it time to get going?"

Eyes of the four smiled open. Said one, "Too late!" Said another, "There are days to climb." Added a third, "And days to sit and look." Concluded the fourth, "No grander spot in the Cascades for sitting and looking."

The aspects of Mount Shuksan from Picture Lake and Artist Point are among the most-photographed mountain scenes of America. The view from Lake Ann is not more—possibly even less—esthetic. However, in that 4500-foot rise

from the lake are the Fischer Chimneys, the Lower Curtis Glacier, the cliffs down which avalanches rumble from Hell's Highway (the Upper Curtis Glacier), which extends from Winnie's Slide to the Hourglass to the Wind Cirque, which connects to the Sulphide Glacier leading to the Summit Pyramid. You don't have to have been all those places as a climber to enjoy the looking. But it helps.

Drive Highway 542 to the Mount Baker ski area. Continue on paved road about 1.5 miles upward to the parking lot at Austin Pass, elevation 4700 feet. Until August snow usually blocks the road somewhere along the way, adding ½ mile or so of walking.

The trail begins by dropping 600 feet into a delightful headwater basin of Swift Creek. Brooks meander in grass and flowers. Marmots whistle from boulder-top perches. Pause for a picnic.

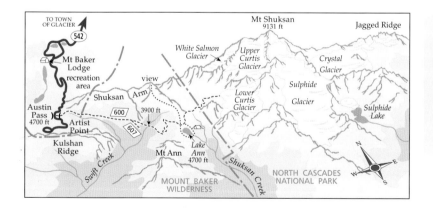

The aspects of Mount Shuksan from Picture Lake and Artist Point are among the most-photographed mountain scenes of America.

Lake Ann, Curtis Glacier, and summit of Mount Shuksan

The trail descends a bit more and traverses forest, swinging around the upper drainage of Swift Creek. At 2¼ miles, after a loss of 800 feet, reach the lowest elevation (3900 feet) of the trip in meadows by a rushing stream.

Now starts a 900-foot ascent in 1½ miles, first in heather and clumps of Christmas trees, then over a granite rockslide into forest under a cliff, to a cold and open little valley. If the way is snow-covered, as it may be until mid-August, plod onward and upward to the obvious 4800-foot saddle and another ½ mile to Lake Ann.

What to do next? First off, sit and watch the living wall of Shuksan. Then perhaps circumnavigate the lake, noting the contact between granitic rocks and complex metamorphics. In September, blueberry upward on the ridge of Mount Ann. If the time allows, go on longer wanders. Where? Anywhere. Just point your nose and follow it.

So much for the days. What about nights? To be perfectly honest, except in October midweek you're better off not trying to camp anywhere near the lake. Secluded nooks can be found at a distance and you'll be infinitely happier than in Babel.

7 | HEATHER MEADOWS

Round trip to Kulshan Ridge: 1 mile; to Table Mountain: 2 miles; to Chain Lakes: 5 miles; to Ptarmigan Ridge: 4 miles
Hikable: late July to mid-October
Map: Green Trails No. 14 Mount Shuksan
Information: Glacier Public Service Center (360) 599-2714

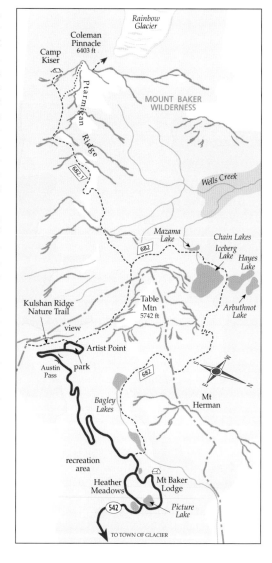

Photographers come from across the United States and around the world to Heather Meadows for the picture-perfect view of Mount Shuksan, which over the years has appeared on hundreds of calendars. Ira has seen it in travel brochures for Europe and South America (a sidetrip?). Brochures call it "The Land of Fire and Ice." The ice is in the glaciers on Shuksan and Baker. The fire is in the furnace of Mount Baker; when it steamed a bit in 1975 the threat of mud and meltwater rumbling down the Skagit Valley sent shivers through the lowlands. Views are so dramatic from the car they can't possibly get any better. However, only on two feet can flowers be sniffed, the chatter of birds and chatter of chipmunks be listened to, the magnificence of the scene be fully felt. Any of the four trails from the Artist Point parking area above Heather Meadows will do it for you.

From Bellingham drive Highway 542 through the town of Glacier to Heather Meadows and another 3 miles to the road-end at Artist Point, elevation 5100 feet.

No matter how gung ho, the visitor must start with the ½-mile Kulshan Ridge Nature Trail. Mount Shuksan and icefalls on its Curtis Glacier draw the eye one way, the gleaming glaciers on Mount Baker the other.

Not for the faint of heart is Table Mountain. Only 1 mile each way, the climb is made by hundreds of folks a day, but if they're not scared they should be on the stretch of trail that switchbacks up a cliff. Again, Shuksan is one way and Baker the other, and for a bonus there are the Border Peaks straddling the international boundary.

Nothing spooky about Chain Lakes, popular with day-trippers and backpackers. The farthest of the four lakes is only about 2 miles, but a 9-mile loop goes all the way around Table Mountain, through miles of heather and blueberry bushes. As a round trip or a one-way, elevation gain and loss are considerable.

Finally, the capper, Ptarmigan Ridge, a 2-mile walk over flower fields and rockslides to Camp Kiser, a climbers' bivouac below Coleman Pinnacle beside Rainbow Glacier. Ira especially likes the first rockslide for watching a colony of conies (pika, rock rabbit) stack hay to dry in the sun before packing it in the barn for winter snacking. The route begins with a mile on the Chain Lakes trail and then enters climbers' country. The tread is easy and safe when clear of snow but often remains white until mid-August and some years never does melt. When steep snow is encountered, leave it to the ice-ax people.

Mount Baker from Kulshan Ridge

8 | PARK BUTTE–RAILROAD GRADE

Round trip to Park Butte: 7 miles
Hiking time: 6 hours (day hike or backpack)
High point: 5450 feet
Elevation gain: 2250 feet
Hikable: mid-July through October
Map: Green Trails No. 45 Hamilton
Information: Mount Baker Ranger District (360) 856-5700

Recommending any one hike in the parklands of Mount Baker's southwest flank is like praising a single painting in a museum of masterpieces. But Ira sticks by what his camera says and votes hands down for Park Butte. There are days of memorable wandering here, exploring meadows and moraines, waterfalls and lakes, listening to marmots, and watching for mountain goats. The trail to Morovitz Meadow gives a good sampling of the country, with impressive near views of the glaciers of Baker, the towering Black Buttes (core of an ancient volcano), the Twin Sisters, and far horizons. This is the most popular hike on Baker's southern flanks. On weekends expect to meet hundreds of mountain climbers, hikers in street shoes and white shirts, little children, and—strangely enough—horses, encouraged by the Forest Service on the crowded trail.

Drive Highway 20 east from Sedro Woolley 14.5 miles and turn left on the Baker Lake–Grandy Lake road. In 12.5 miles, just past Rocky Creek bridge, turn left on Loomis–Nooksack road No. 12. In 3 miles go right on Sulphur Creek road No. 13 and follow it 6 miles to the end in a logging patch. Find the trail west of the road, near Sulphur Creek, elevation 3364 feet.

The trail immediately crosses Sulphur Creek into the heather and blueberries (in season) of Schriebers Meadow, passes frog ponds and enters forest. In 1 mile is an interesting area where meltwater floods from the Easton Glacier have torn wide avenues through the trees. The drainage pattern changes from time to time; the creek is crossed on a bouncing cable bridge.

Beyond the boulder—and gravel—area (find bits of sulphur crystal—this is a *volcano!*) the trail enters cool forest and switchbacks a long mile up a steep hillside (look out for horses). At the last switchback the Scott Paul Trail loop, an alternative return route, goes straight ahead. The grade gentles in heather fields leading to Upper Morovitz Meadow, 4500 feet.

At the next trail junction go left to Park Butte, climbing 1 mile to the lookout building on the 5450-foot summit. If the building, maintained by volunteers, is open, go in and get the feel of being a lookout. Views of Mount Baker glaciers (and much more) are magnificent. For the best

Mount Baker from tarn on side of Park Butte

Baker view, 200 feet below the lookout follow a path to a small tarn.

Morovitz Meadow offers much more to do. At the last junction go right on "the stairway to heaven," past little waterfalls and flower gardens, to 4962-foot Baker Pass, close to the snout of the Easton Glacier. Or ramble the elegant crest of Railroad Grade, a moraine built by the Easton Glacier in more ambitious days, higher and yet higher, in late summer perhaps to about 7000 feet before moraines, rubble, and polished slabs end at the glacier's edge.

9 | HIDDEN LAKE PEAKS

Round trip to Sibley Creek Pass: 6 miles
Hiking time: 5 hours (day hike)
High point: 6100 feet
Elevation gain: 2700 feet
Hikable: mid-July through October

Round trip to Hidden Lake Lookout: 8 miles
Hiking time: 8 hours (day hike or backpack)
High point: 6890 feet
Elevation gain: 3500 feet
Hikable: August through October

Maps: Green Trails No. 48 Diablo Dam, No. 80 Cascade Pass
Information: Marblemount Ranger District (360) 873-4590 ext. 37 or 39
Backcountry use permit required for camping at Hidden Lake

It is argued by some (whom I'll not name here lest I be reviled as a troglodyte with an attitude) that if Cascade Pass were restored to the deep wilderness of yore, they would have to "waste" a whole weekend to check it off their list of Things Every Cream-Skimmer Has Got To Get Done Before Summer Is Over. To which I

respectfully respond, let us behead the Cascade River and Stehekin River roads. Let their dust settle. When Edge wilderness is wanted, Sibley Creek Pass and Hidden Lake Lookout have the flower fields, heather meadows, ice-carved rocks, and snow-fed waterfalls—and a stupendous look across the Cascade River valley to Snow King, and a boggling panorama from Eldorado through the Ptarmigan Traverse to Dome Peak. I don't go to Cascade Pass much anymore. I'd rather remember it as it was, Deep. For edge wilderness (which I myself frequently need) Hidden Lake Peaks do the job.

Drive Highway 20 to Marblemount and continue east on the Cascade River road 10 miles to Sibley Creek road, signed "Hidden Lake Trail." Ascend the steep, narrow road 5 miles to the end, elevation 3600 feet.

Trail No. 745 begins in a 1950s clearcut, entering virgin forest in ¼ mile. The way switchbacks steadily up 1 mile, emerges from trees to lush avalanche-swath brush, and crosses Sibley Creek. More switchbacks ascend through alder clumps, deep grass, and flowers to a recrossing of Sibley Creek at 2½ miles, 5200 feet. Now the trail begins a long sidehill traverse of heather-and-waterfall-and-granite, rounds a corner of

Ptarmigan on trail to Hidden Lake Peaks

the ridge, and climbs to a precious little basin at 3½ miles. Atop cliffs the abandoned lookout cabin can be seen. A short bit above the basin is a 6600-foot saddle. Look down to 5733-foot Hidden Lake, out to Cascade Pass and a world of wild peaks. For most hikers this is plenty far enough, though it's only ½ mile and 300 feet more to the 6890-foot lookout. Slippery when snowy and always airy.

Personally, I prefer to leave the trail at the second crossing of Sibley Creek and amble-

scramble the goat path to Sibley Creek Pass. The views are better, in my opinion. And no fish, which is always a plus.

As for camping, the designated sites above Hidden Lake are minimally attractive, the several places along the trail where sleeping bags might be spread have a very limited capacity, and the terrain fortunately is too steep and granite-blocky to permit sprawl. Anyway, the wilderness here is sufficiently Edge to be satisfactorily absorbed on a day hike.

10 | BOSTON BASIN

Round trip to first high moraine: 7 miles
Hiking time: 8 hours (day hike or backpack)
High point: 6200 feet
Elevation gain: 3000 feet
Hikable: July through October
Map: Green Trails No. 80 Cascade Pass (trail not shown)
Information: Marblemount Ranger District (360) 873-4590 ext. 37 or 39
Backcountry use permit required for camping

When Forbidden Peak was included in a book as one of the "Fifty Classic Climbs of North America," Boston Basin became infested by pilgrims from several or more continents lusting for the Fifty Peak Pin. Well, not for me to sneer, having in my time earned a Six Major Peaks Pin, and a Snoqualmie Pass Ten Peak Pin, as well as the Blob Peak Pin awarded the elite few who knew what a "blob" was and where they were. Moreover, joking aside, the matterhorn architecture and splendid granodiorite of this "*Verbotengipfel*" exercised a fatal attraction for me and my bunch decades before the climb was hailed as Classic. But since I'm intimidated by the costly costumery of today's peakbaggers (all as

wealthy as the Sultan of Brunei), I avoid the summer and come for the autumn contrast of yellowing meadows and gray moraines and white glaciers. Late October. Tuesday or Thursday.

Drive Highway 20 to Marblemount and continue east on the Cascade River road 23 miles to the junction with an old sideroad built by long-gone "miners" to sell stock. Limited parking, elevation 3200 feet.

Walk 1 steep mile on the abandoned sideroad to a boot-built scramble-path which intersects an ancient prospectors' trail. Cross a ½-mile-wide jungle down which tumble Midas Creek and Morning Star Creek and, in season, climax avalanches. In forest again, switchbacks pass cabin

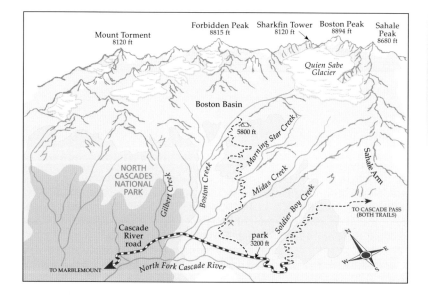

Climb over moraines and creeks to rich-green, marmot-whistling flower fields and waterfalls pouring down ice-polished buttresses.

Johannesburg from Boston Basin

ruins, emerge from timber, and swing around the foot of a naked moraine to a raging torrent; boulder-hop across and climb to a viewpoint.

Look up to the fearsome cliffs and spires of Forbidden Peak and Mount Torment, and to the glacier falling from Boston and Sahale Peaks, and across the valley to the mile-high wall of Johannesburg and its finger-like hanging glaciers.

For one exploration, traverse and climb westward over moraines and creeks to rich-green, marmot-whistling flower fields and the waterfalls pouring down ice-polished buttresses under Mount Torment. For another, find the intermittent tread of an old miners' trail that ascends a moraine crest to tunnels and artifacts close under Sharkfin Tower, right next to the glacier from Boston Peak.

Absolutely no camping is allowed in the meadows. You must stay at the 5800-foot "climbers' camp," three sites, bouldery and wretched, just above timberline between the forks of Boston Creek. For peace and quiet (and comparative comfort) carry your pack up onto the snowfields, the cliffs, anywhere but the climbers' slum.

11 | CASCADE PASS–SAHALE ARM

Round trip to Sahale Arm: 11 miles
Hiking time: 10 hours (day hike or backpack)
High point: 6600 feet
Elevation gain: 3000 feet
Hikable: mid-July through October
Map: Green Trails No. 80 Cascade Pass
Information: Marblemount Ranger District (360) 873-4590 ext. 37 or 39
Backcountry use permit required for camping

How many times has Ira hiked to Cascade Pass? He's lost count. He has photos of six-month-old Vicky being given a bath there, and of two-year-old John sliding on the snow. Twice he has camped on Sahale Arm in winter. One time he was awakened at daybreak by a family of ptarmigan quarreling outside his tent. Another time he met Supreme Court Justice William O. Douglas on the trail. Equally exciting was a blind man at the pass who vividly described what he "saw."

The Original Inhabitants crossed the Cascade Crest here from time immemorial. (The river on the east side of the pass is the Stehekin, a word meaning "the way through.") Explorers and prospectors arrived in the nineteenth century. A pork-barrel "mine-to-market" road (no honest mine, thus nothing to market, but plenty of gullible "investors") degraded the pass from deep wilderness to edge wilderness, bringing it world fame as one of the easiest high hikes in the North Cascades. But to focus on the beauty of the pass is to slight Sahale Arm, avenue to the sky through flowers and sparkling creeklets, and views that expand with every step.

Drive Highway 20 to Marblemount, cross the Skagit River and continue east 23.5 miles on the Cascade River road to the road-end parking lot and trailhead, elevation 3600 feet.

The 10 percent-grade "highway" climbs some thirty-three forest switchbacks to about 2 miles, where begins a long, gently ascending

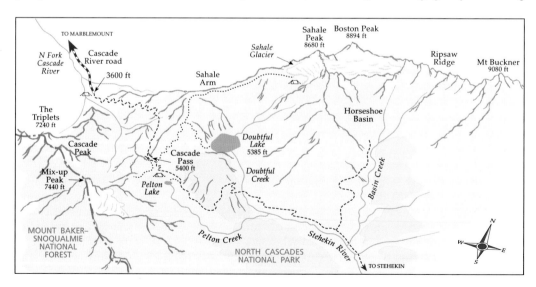

Trapper Peak and Magic Mountain from Sahale Arm

traverse through parkland and meadows to Cascade Pass, 3½ miles, 5400 feet. The scenery is spectacular even at road-end; exclamations are exhausted before the pass. Hardly an hour goes by that a large or small avalanche doesn't break loose from hanging glaciers on the 8200-foot mass of Johannesburg; several times a summer a terrifying roar sets the earth a-trembling as tons of ice cubes are delivered into greenery of the valley floor.

The beauties of Cascade Pass are easy. Too easy. During years of unsupervised overuse (compounded and aggravated by the Forest Service extension of the road past the "mine" to its present terminus) the meadows were loved nearly to death. A quarter-century of tender care by the Park Service has succeeded in rehabilitating the flower gardens. A few campsites are available below the pass to the east, in Pelton Basin, enabling a longer stay for extended sidetrips; several cozy pack-in sites at the road-end are as scenic as could be wanted.

Now, about that avenue to the sky: Climb north on a steep and narrow meadow path starting a few feet over the east side of the pass below a rock outcrop. In 1 mile and 800 feet the trail reaches the ridge crest and a junction. The right fork descends heather 800 feet in 1 mile to 5385-foot Doubtful Lake, a great hike in its own right, the shore cliffs riddled with old prospect holes. But Sahale Arm calls. Walk up and up the gentle ridge of flowers, and up some more. Look down the waterfall-loud cirque walls of Doubtful Lake, east into the Stehekin River valley, west to Forbidden Peak and the huge Inspiration Glacier on Eldorado, south to nine small glaciers on the first line of peaks beyond Cascade Pass. Walking higher, see range upon range of ice and spires, finally including the volcano of Glacier Peak. To see it all in sunset and starlight and dawn, continue on and camp in the rocks at the toe of the Sahale Glacier.

12 | THUNDER CREEK

Round trip to McAllister Creek: 12 miles
Hiking time: 5–7 hours (day hike or backpack)
High point: 1800 feet
Elevation gain: 600 feet
Hikable: April through November

Round trip to Park Creek Pass: 36 miles
Hiking time: Allow 3–5 days
High point: 6040 feet
Elevation gain: 5600
Hikable: late July through October

Maps: Green Trails No. 48 Diablo Dam, No. 49 Mt. Logan, No. 81 McGregor Mtn.
Information: Marblemount Ranger District (360) 873-4590 ext. 37 or 39
Backcountry use permit required for camping

Would 44½ miles be enough to give you the feel of the Deep Lonesome? I believe so. However, for that total the Stehekin River road would have to be reclaimed from wheels, unlikely until Deep is not automatically sacrificed for political purposes to the Quick. Nevertheless, the 18 miles of the Thunder Creek trail to Park Creek Pass, hitched to the 8 miles down Park Creek to the road, rank among the Deepest wildlanding available around here. Actually, those 26, done

in high summer, aren't as fulfilling as the 16 to the foot of Park Creek Pass in late spring. As intense a mountain night as ever I've spent was up there, alone, meltwaters roaring and grizzlies growling and ghosties and ghoulies dancing just outside the firelight circle.

Drive Highway 20 east to Diablo Dam and 4 miles beyond to Colonial Creek Campground and the trailhead, elevation 1200 feet.

The trail follows Thunder Arm of Diablo

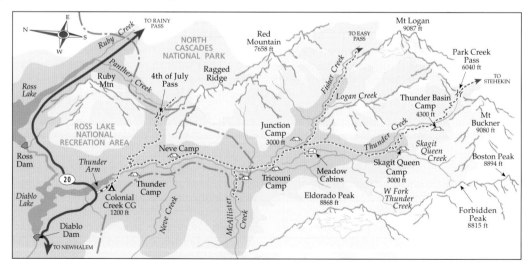

Thunder Creek trail

Lake about 1 mile, bridges Thunder Creek, and runs nearly flat for miles through big firs, cedars, and hemlocks, as well as young trees grown up after lightning fires in the early 1970s. At 2 and 2½ miles respectively are Thunder and Neve Camps, and at 6 miles the bridge to McAllister Creek Camp, a good turnaround for a day or weekend and open to travel early in the season and late.

At 7½ miles the trail crosses Fisher Creek to Tricouni Camp and in ½ mile more commences a 1000-foot ascent from the valley floor, which upstream from here is the Great Dismal Swamp, largest in the Cascades and forbidden (by Nature) to human entry. At 9 miles the trail levels out at Junction Camp, 3000 feet, in late spring (my favorite season) the limit of hikers who have no taste for the company of nobody but their own selves. In ½ mile a spur trail descends 1000 feet in 1 mile to the ancient Meadow Cabins at the edge of the Great Dismal; you can look all you want but mustn't touch. The main trail passes gasper views of the enormous Boston Glacier, Buckner and Boston thrusting above, drops steeply to the valley bottom at the upper end of the Great Dismal, 2200 feet, and climbs to Skagit Queen Camp, 13 miles, 3000 feet, near where Skagit Queen Creek joins Thunder Creek. The way climbs steeply, gentles out somewhat in a hanging valley; at 15½ miles, 4300 feet, is Thunder Basin Camp. The trail ascends steadily up and around the meadow flanks of Mount Logan to 6040-foot Park Creek Pass, 18 miles, a narrow rock cleft usually full of snow.

One dark spring afternoon as I returned to Colonial Creek Campground after a week up high a little girl on a nature walk spotted me and leapt shrieking into Daddy's arms. The park ranger had told the evening campfire audience that two grizzlies had been seen in the Lonesome and the kid didn't know exactly what a grizzly looked like but figured I was close enough.

13 | LITTLE BEAVER–BIG BEAVER LOOP

Loop trip: 26½ miles
Hiking time: Allow 3–5 days
High point: 3620 feet
Elevation gain: about 3500 feet

Round trip to Beaver Pass: 27 miles
Hiking time: Allow 2–3 days
High point: 3620 feet
Elevation gain: 2000 feet

Hikable: June through October
Maps: Green Trails No. 15 Mt. Challenger, No. 16 Ross Lake
Information: Marblemount Ranger District (360) 873-4590 ext. 37 or 39
Backcountry use permit required for camping

With all due (and very great) respect for J. D. Ross, champion of public power in the duel-to-the-death with the hated "Eastern bankers" of private power, Seattle City Light entered the 1960s as mindlessly smug as Galahad. Thanks to the valiant Ross it had, in the 1920s, snatched the Skagit River from the greedy privatizers, and all these decades later doggedly insisted in raising Ross Dam to increase the storage capacity of its reservoir, unavoidably drowning more wilderness. Their minds piously closed, his heirs preached that Ross's will must be done on the Big Beaver as it had been on the Skagit itself.

In August of 1967, when the Elderly Birdwatchers Hiking & Griping Society went tripping to the Northern Pickets via Little Beaver Creek and Beaver Pass, we chose to exit via the Big Beaver purely because as experts on the pending North Cascades National Park we felt the long valley deserved a look, though nobody we knew ever had suggested it did, nor saw anything terribly wrong with drowning it.

The next-to-the-last day we descended from the high country and partway down the Big Beaver. We were in no hurry the last morning, having plenty of time to make our boat pickup at Big Beaver Landing. Each of us set

out separately, I last for the sake of a third cup of coffee. I walked alone for hours, at first impressed, then entranced, and at last in such an epiphany as I'd not experienced since Marmot Pass in 1938. Arriving at the landing, I said not a word to my three companions, nor they to me. The beatific smile on each of their faces, which I knew was on mine as well, said it all. We had been to the Big Beaver and seen the cedars. And we went home to Seattle to spread the glad tidings.

This loop hike from Ross Reservoir to close views of the Picket Range and back to Ross Reservoir offers perhaps the supreme days-long forest experience in the North Cascades. The 27-mile trip up the Little Beaver Valley and down the Big Beaver Valley passes through groves of enormous cedars, old and huge Douglas-firs and hemlocks, glimmery-ghostly silver fir, lush alder, young fir recently established after a fire (in 1926 enormous acreages of the Skagit country burned), and many more species and ages of trees as well. And there are brawling rivers, marshes teeming with wildlife, and awesome looks at Picket glaciers and walls. While the hike is recommended as a loop, the Big Beaver trail to Beaver Pass makes a great

Big Beaver trail in a grove of ancient cedars

round trip—as does the much shorter hike up the Big Beaver to the Epiphany.

Drive Highway 20 east to Colonial Creek Campground. Go another 3.8 miles and park at the Ross Lake trailhead. Walk the trail to Ross Lake Resort (see Hike 14, Desolation Peak) and arrange for taxi service up the lake and a pickup at trip's end. The loop (or day or weekend hikes) can begin at either end; the Little Beaver start is described here.

After a scenic ride up Ross Reservoir, debark at Little Beaver Landing; a campground here, elevation 1600 feet. The trail starts by switch-backing 300 feet to get above a canyon, then loses most of the hard-won elevation. At 4½ miles is Perry Creek Camp, an easy ford-or-footlog crossing of several branches of the creek, and a passage along the edge of a lovely marsh. At 9 miles is Redoubt Creek; scout around for a footlog. At 11½ miles, 2450 feet, is a junction.

The Little Beaver trail goes upstream 6 miles and 2800 feet to Whatcom Pass (Hike 5). Take the Big Beaver trail and ford Little Beaver Creek (beware—the creek isn't so little in early summer), pass a sidetrail to Stillwell Camp, and climb a steep mile to Beaver Pass, 3620 feet. The trail goes nearly on the level a mile to designated campsites at Beaver Pass Shelter (emergency use only), the midpoint of the loop, 13½ miles from Little Beaver Landing and 13 miles from Big Beaver Landing.

An hour or three should be allowed here for an easy off-trail sidetrip. Pick a way easterly and upward from the shelter, gaining 500–1000 feet through forest and brush to any of several open slopes that give a staggering look into rough-and-icy Luna Cirque.

Passing Luna Camp on the way, descend steeply from Beaver Pass to the head of Big Beaver Creek; two spots on the trail offer impressive

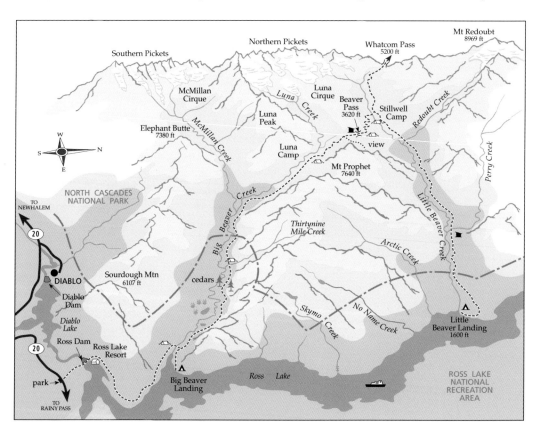

Big Beaver valley from side of Pumpkin Mountain

glimpses of Luna Cirque. At 6 miles from Beaver Pass Shelter (7 miles from Big Beaver Landing on Ross Lake), the Big Beaver tumbles down a 200-foot-deep gorge; a good view here of Elephant Butte and up McMillan Creek toward McMillan Cirque. The moderately up-and-down trail crosses avalanches that have torn avenues through forest, passes enormous boulders fallen from cliffs above, and goes by a marsh.

At 8 miles from Beaver Pass (5½ from Ross Lake), cross Thirtynine Mile Creek; a campsite here.

The way now enters the glorious lower reaches of Big Beaver Creek, a broad valley of marshes and ancient trees, including the largest stand of western red cedar (some an estimated 1000 years old) remaining in the United States. Seattle City Light planned to flood the lower 6 miles of the valley by raising Ross Dam, but after an epic fifteen-year battle, in 1983 the plans were permanently dropped.

Passing one superb marsh after another, one grove of giant cedars after another, at 3 miles from Ross Reservoir the trail for the first time touches the banks of Big Beaver Creek, milky-green water running over golden pebbles. Finally the trail reaches Big Beaver Landing, from which a ¼-mile trail leads left to Big Beaver Camp. (This is a boaters' camp. Hikers should use Pumpkin Mountain Camp, 100 yards south of the bridge over Big Beaver Creek on the Ross Reservoir trail.)

There are two ways to return to Ross Dam. One is by hiking the 6-mile Ross Lake trail, which branches right from the Big Beaver trail at a junction ¼ mile before the landing. The second is to arrange in advance with Ross Lake Resort to be picked up at Big Beaver Landing.

14 | DESOLATION PEAK

Round trip from Desolation Landing: 9 miles
Hiking time: 7 hours (day hike or backpack)
High point: 6102 feet
Elevation gain: 4400 feet
Hikable: mid-June through August
Map: Green Trails No. l6 Ross Lake
Information: Marblemount Ranger District (360) 873-4590 ext. 37 or 39
Backcountry use permit required for camping

A forest fire swept the slopes bare in 1926, giving the peak its name. A lookout built on the peak in 1932 was manned in 1939 by Ira's brother-in-law Ed Willgress, a University of

Crossbill in an old fire pit

Washington forestry student. Ed was transported by boat up the Diablo Reservoir, then by foot up the Skagit Valley trail through miles of virgin forest, past several waterfalls, to the Desolation Peak trailhead. Since Ed's time Ross Dam has been built, drowning the forest, and the North Cascades Highway has been built. Fame in literary circles came after a summer's residence by the late Jack Kerouac, "beat generation" novelist and occasional Forest Service employee. Some of his best writing describes the day-and-night, sunshine-and-storm panorama from the Methow to Mount Baker to Canada, and especially the dramatic close-up of Hozomeen Mountain, often seen from a distance but rarely from so near. Before and since Kerouac, the lookout frequently has been the summer home of poets. Guitars are common. Acoustic, of course.

The start of the Desolation Peak trail can be

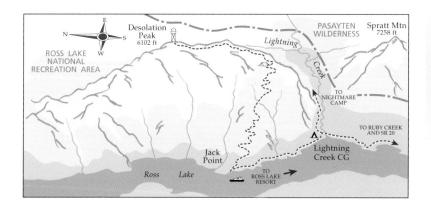

Before and since Jack Kerouac, the lookout frequently has been the summer home of poets.

Desolation Peak trail above Ross Reservoir, Jack Mountain on left

reached by walking 18 miles on the East Bank Trail (see Hike 15, Crater–Jackita Ridge–Devils Loop) or by riding the Ross Lake Resort water taxi. Drive Highway 20 east from Colonial Creek Campground 3.8 miles to the parking lot of the Ross Reservoir trailhead, elevation 2200 feet. Lose 450 feet walking down to the dam and boat dock opposite the resort; here the taxi-boat will ferry you to your destination and return to pick you up at a prearranged time. To learn the current price and make arrangements for the water taxi, telephone Ross Lake Resort, (360) 386-4437, in advance, either from home or while driving up the Skagit Valley.

The trail starts steep and stays steep, climbing 1000 feet a mile. It's a scorcher in sunny weather; carry a lot of water. Even better, sleep on the reservoir shore and hit the trail in the dim cool of dawn. The desolate-appearing hillside has a surprising amount of shade, the way often tunneling through dense thickets of young trees. But nary a drop to drink. Except for the flies, your blood.

The lookout still stands and is manned during high fire danger.

15 | CRATER–JACKITA RIDGE–DEVILS LOOP

Loop trip: 43 miles
Hiking time: Allow 5–9 days
High point: 6982 feet
Elevation gain: about 7300 feet
Hikable: mid-July through October
Maps: Green Trails No. 16 Ross Lake, No. 17 Jack Mountain, No. 49 Mt. Logan
Information: Methow Ranger District (509) 997-2131
Backcountry use permit required for camping at Ross Reservoir

Either end of the loop is a trip in itself, but what's the rush? Don't be a quick-dipper, dive in for the deep immersion, the whole 43 miles, meadow ridges and views from Canada to Cascade Pass, Pickets to Pasayten, while encircling rock walls and white ice of 9066-foot Jack Mountain, "King of the Skagit." Walk,

don't run. Speed kills the thing that makes wilderness wild.

An excellent argument for doing the loop clockwise is that the beginning 16 miles are less than purely wild (though good, very good) in forest just across Ruby Creek from the North Cascades Highway and then along the fluctuat-

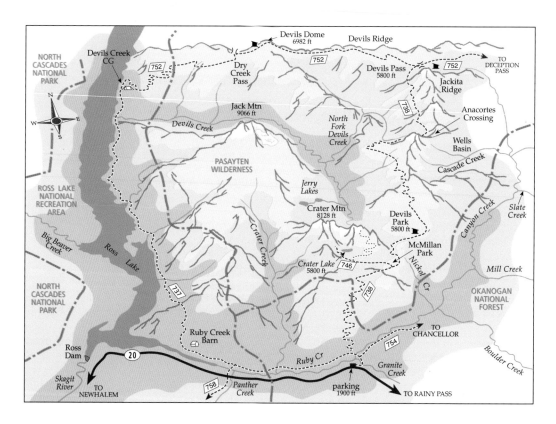

Crater Mountain from Devils Ridge

ing shore of Ross Reservoir, saving for last the 27 miles of the High Lonesome. That we describe the counterclockwise here is a concession to the popularity of Jack's by-no-means obsequious attendant, Crater Mountain.

Drive Highway 20 east from Colonial Creek Campground 11 miles to Jackita Ridge (Canyon Creek) trailhead, elevation 1900 feet.

After bridging Granite Creek and Canyon Creek, the trail gains 3400 feet in 4 miles, ameliorated by the shade of big trees, creeks just where the throat needs them, and glimpses of peaks. At 5280 feet is the junction that separates short-trippers from long-loopers.

To the left ¾ mile is the meadow-and-cliff cirque of Crater Lake, 5800 feet. Just before it, a 2-mile trail climbs eastward to a lookout site on the broad, 7054-foot easternmost summit of Crater Mountain. From the lake a 2½-mile trail climbs westward to an older lookout site on the 8128-foot main summit of Crater, abandoned because the final ½ mile is for trained climbers only; no matter, the panoramas are glorious long before difficulties occur.

The right fork, trail No. 738, descends McMillan Park to Nickol Creek, 4900 feet, ascends an old burn to Devils Park Shelter, 7 miles, 5800 feet, and continues up through clumps of pointy little trees and bleached snags and meadows to a larch-dotted basin at 8¾ miles, 6200 feet. Now commences a rollercoaster north along the garden path of Jackita Ridge—up to a shoulder, down to a basin, up and down again, to North Fork Devils Creek, 13¼ miles, 5500 feet, and Devils Pass, 15¼ miles, 5800 feet.

The loop turns west on Devils Ridge trail No. 752, near and on the ridge, to the trip's highest elevation, 6982 feet, at demolished Devils Dome Lookout, 20 miles. The great glacier in the marvelous big cirque scooped into the north face of Jack takes a long look. A descent into a basin of waterfalls and boulders and blossoms and a contour around slopes of Devils Dome leads at 21½ miles to a ¼-mile sidetrail to Bear Skull Shelter, 6000 feet. A descent of 4500 feet in 5½ miles concludes at the East Bank Trail, end of the 27 miles of perfection, start of the 16 miles of phased reentry into the mad mad mad world.

16 | MAPLE PASS LOOP

Loop trip: 7 miles
Hiking time: 5 hours (day hike)
High point: 6850 feet
Elevation gain: 1950 feet
Hikable: July through mid-October
Maps: Green Trails No. 49 Mt. Logan, No. 60 Washington Pass, No. 81 McGregor
　　Mtn., No. 82 Stehekin
Information: Methow Ranger District (509) 997-2131

Jewel-size flower fields, wide-screen views, and sky-mirroring cirque lakes pretty well sum up the loop. The Forest Service built the plush trail to Maple Pass (over the strenuous objection of the Park Service), intending it to go from there down Maple Creek as a segment of the Pacific Crest (Freeway) Trail. Only very belatedly did it concede what had been obvious to the Park Service, that the stomping of these fragile meadows by thousands of National Scenic Trail feet—and especially the hooves—would be catastrophic. The Park Service stubbornly held out and won a partial victory, managing to dead-end the freeway at Maple Pass and to get camping banned throughout the pass area.

Drive Highway 20 east from the Skagit Valley or west from the Methow Valley to Rainy Pass and park at the south-side rest area. Find trail No. 740, signed "Lake Ann–Maple Pass," elevation, 4855 feet.

Ira and I have a disagreement. Should the loop be done clockwise or counterclockwise? I insist the dessert must follow the main course and so say counterclockwise, starting on the easy grade and saving the best part (which is non-freeway and thus steeper) of the loop for last. Ira finds it easier on his eight-years-older knees to climb the steep part first (the dessert) and return by the gentler grade. Let your personal knees be your guide. However, since most hikers settle for the main course and skip the dessert, the trail is described my way.

A short bit from the cars is the junction of decision, the left aiming at Rainy Lake, the right at Lake Ann. Counterclocking, take the right. At 1½ miles, 5400 feet, is a spur left to Lake Ann, destination of most hikers. This ½-mile path goes along the outlet valley, nearly level, by two shallow lakelets, around marshes, to the shore.

Gaining elevation at the obnoxiously energy-wasteful 10 percent grade of the Pacific Crest Freeway (for the comfort of horses), the

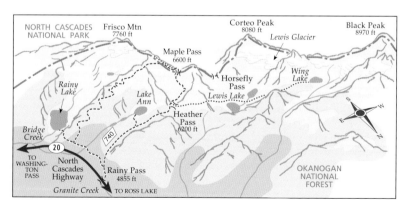

I insist the dessert must follow the main course and so say the loop hike must be done counter-clockwise.

Lake Ann from Maple Pass Trail loop

main trail ascends across a large rockslide high above the lake. At 2½ miles is 6200-foot Heather Pass. The eye is attracted to little Lewis Lake, and the imagination to Wing Lake, unseen in its cirque at the foot of Black Peak. A very difficult way trail takes off in that direction over steep heather, steep snowfields suicidal for the average hiker, and an ankle-twisting boulder field; many are called by Lewis and Wing but few go.

From Heather Pass the trail contours over the top of cliffs 1000 feet above Lake Ann to Maple Pass at 3⅓ miles, 6600 feet.

For the loop and more views, a decent enough but blessedly non-freeway trail follows the ridge crest eastward to a 6850-foot shoulder of Frisco Mountain and (my dessert) spectacularly descends the skinny ridge between the cirques of Lake Ann and Rainy Lake, joining the Rainy Lake trail ½ mile from the cars.

17 | GOLDEN HORN

Round trip: 23 miles
Hiking time: Allow 2 days
High point: 6900 feet
Elevation gain: 2700 feet in, 600 feet out
Hikable: August through September
Map: Green Trails No. 50 Washington Pass
Information: Methow Ranger District (509) 997-2131

When boundaries were being noodled for the proposed North Cascades National Park, Washington City experts took a quick look down from 10,000 feet and pronounced Hardy and Golden Horn and Tower and Cutthroat, and Methow Pass and Snowy Lakes Pass and Granite Pass to be "not of national park caliber." When I went walking there, as none of the City experts ever had, I swooned at the lovely pinkish-goldish hue of the Golden Horn granodiorite and moaned, "No, not of national park caliber." Beside the Snowy Lakes rippling in the wind on top of the world, my companion whimpered "Absolutely not of national park caliber." I guess in our days there we repeated the Washington City mantra a couple hundred times. At last, in leaving, we joined in a bellow to what-

ever Ear might be in the Sky, "Somebody in the National Park Service is not of national park caliber!" In the years since the park was created in 1968 we've launched salvos of letters to Congress demanding park and/or wilderness status. Eventually it will be done because it *must*. But in the 1960s there were no trails there, there was no constituency, no legion of green-bonded feet to cast ballots, write letters.

Drive Highway 20 to Rainy Pass and park in the north trailhead area, elevation 4800 feet.

At a grade that refuses to exceed the horse-beloved 10 percent, the two-horses-wide Pacific Crest Trail ascends through forest to big and bigger meadows. At 4 miles pass a campsite; at 5½ miles reach Cutthroat Pass, 6800 feet. The way continues up meadows and rockslides to a 6900-foot

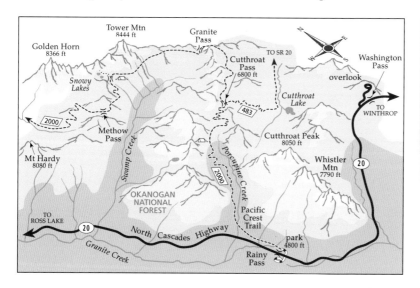

The view from Snowy Lakes Pass is straight up Golden Horn and Tower Mountain and out across Methow Pass to the spires of Mount Hardy.

Upper Snowy Lake, reflecting the green hillside, and the Golden Horn

high point with a view of needle-like Tower Mountain and the golden horn of Golden Horn, then drops 600 feet to Granite Pass; snow may linger on the tread until August in this vicinity, at a steepness that will force hikers lacking ice axes to turn around. From the pass the freeway-wide trail has been dynamited in cliffs and gouged out of steep unstable slopes for a long 2 miles across Swamp Creek headwaters. Due to slides this section is often impassable to horses and scared hikers. At about 2 miles from Cutthroat Pass the trail reaches Snowy Lakes Creek, 6300 feet, in a meadow flat.

An unmarked way trail climbs steeply ½ mile to Lower Snowy Lake, 6735 feet, and a bit more to Upper Snowy Lake, 6839 feet, miraculously located precisely at the summit of Snowy Lakes Pass. When we stumbled upon the lakes in the empty wilderness before the Crest Trail was built, the scene was the epitome of pristine. Returning several years after it was complete, we deconstructed approximately 125 fire rings at the lakes.

Cowboys and cowgirls, keep your horses on the Crest Trail. Pedestrians, spread your sleeping bags in the designated sites by the Crest Trail. If you don't show respect, you may soon find horses banned here. Sleeping bags, too.

The view from Snowy Lakes Pass is straight up Golden Horn and Tower Mountain and out across Methow Pass to the spires of Mount Hardy, above headwaters of the West Fork Methow River. The determined hiker can safely scramble some distance up the slopes of Golden Horn Mountain, but the feldspar crystals are just as stunning throughout the batholith.

18 | CUTTHROAT PASS

Round trip from Cutthroat Creek road-end to Cutthroat Pass: 12 miles
Hiking time: 6–8 hours (day hike)
High point: 6800 feet
Elevation gain: 2300 feet
Hikable: July through mid-October
Map: Green Trails No. 50 Washington Pass
Information: Methow Ranger District (509) 997-2131

The Springs have a special memory of Cutthroat Pass. Stopping there for lunch, they had just opened Ira's jar of gourmet peanut butter and laid out Pat's cheese and crackers when six mountain goats dropped by. A nanny and kid came in sniffing distance, sniffed, and turned up their noses. What, no pizza?

If transportation can be arranged, a hike can start at Rainy Pass and end at Cutthroat Creek, saving 400 feet of elevation gain. However, because a short sidetrip to the sparkles of Cutthroat Lake makes a refreshing rest stop, the trail is described starting from Cutthroat Creek. The upper regions are dry, so stuff the canteens full of sparkles.

Drive Highway 20 east from the Skagit Valley over Rainy and Washington Passes or west from the Methow Valley to Cutthroat Creek. Turn uphill on Cutthroat Creek road and continue 1 mile to the road-end and trailhead, elevation 4500 feet.

The trail crosses Cutthroat Creek and begins a gentle 1¾-mile ascent through open rain-shadow forest to a junction with the Cutthroat Lake trail. The lake, 4935 feet, has the last "official" campsites, ¼ mile away, but by filling a plastic water-carrier you can take your choice of scenic, lonesome, bugfree sites up high.

The next 2½ miles climb through big trees and little trees to meadows and a campsite (no water in late summer except what you bring). A final scant 2 miles lead to 6800-foot Cutthroat Pass, about 6 miles from the road-end, and the intersection with the Pacific Crest Trail.

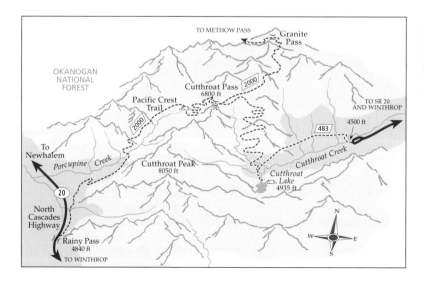

Climb through big trees and little trees to meadows and a campsite.

Mountain goat and kid at Cutthroat Pass

It is absolutely essential to stroll to the knoll south of the pass for a full course of one of the most scenic sections of the Crest Trail. Cutthroat Peak, 8050 feet, stands high and close. Eastward are the naked west slopes of Silver Star. Mighty Liberty Bell sticks its head above a nearby ridge. Far southwest over Porcupine Creek is ice-white Dome Peak.

If time and energy permit, sidetrip 1 mile north on the Pacific Crest Trail to a knoll above Granite Pass and striking views down to Swamp Creek headwaters and across to 8444-foot Tower Mountain, 8366-foot Golden Horn, and Azurite, Black, and countless more peaks in the distance. This portion of the Crest Trail may be blocked by snow until mid-August.

From Cutthroat Pass the Crest Trail descends Porcupine Creek, passing several campsites, a pleasant 5 miles to Rainy Pass, the first 2 miles in meadows and the rest of the way in cool forest by numerous creeks. The trail ends a few hundred feet west of the summit of 4840-foot Rainy Pass.

19 | WINDY PASS

Round trip: 7 miles
Hiking time: 5 hours (day hike or backpack)
High point: 6900 feet
Elevation gain: 500 feet in, 1000 feet out
Hikable: early July through October
Maps: Green Trails No. 18 Poseidon Peak, No. 50 Washington Pass
Information: Methow Ranger District (509) 997-2131

On the slope of a little meadow, screened from the big meadow by a grove of little trees, is a little snowbank and at its base a little pool. A troop of little children slides squealing down the snow and splashes screaming in the pool. When adequately blue they lie in the sun until pink. Then, dear friends, once more unto the snow, the pool! Ah yes, Windy Pass . . .

Drive Highway 20 west from Winthrop or east from Washington Pass to a junction 1.5 miles east of Early Winters Campground. Turn off the highway, cross the Methow River to the hamlet of Mazama, turn left, upvalley, on Harts Pass road, and continue for 20 miles to 6198-foot Harts Pass. Turn right on the Slate Peak road and go about 1.5 miles to the first switchback and a small parking area at the trailhead, elevation 6800 feet.

Meadows, meadows, meadows, nothing but meadows for miles and miles. The Pacific Crest Trail gently climbs the first ½ mile, contours steep slopes of Slate Peak, and drops into

lovely little Benson Basin. The way swings up and out to a spur ridge, contours to Buffalo Pass and another spur, and descends above gorgeous greenery of Barron Basin to 6257-foot Windy Pass.

Barron Basin is one of the most magnificent easy-to-reach glorylands in the Cascades, but it is mainly "private property" and the "owners" have raised havoc, gouging delicate meadows with bulldozers, dumping garbage at will. This hike is bound to convert any casual walker into a fierce enemy of the archaic, ultra-permissive federal mining laws.

Since the Forest Service can't or won't protect the land, what do *we* do? Those ancient letters of marque which license piracy must be revoked by Congress. Write! Howl! Stamp your feet! The tide of protest and righteous anger is rising. Join it. Our will be done. As for the "private" property, it must be reclaimed for the public domain. "This land is your land, this land is my land." The boundary of the Pasayten

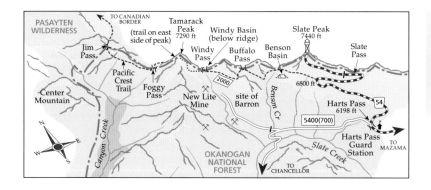

Meadows, meadows, meadows, nothing but meadows for miles and miles.

Pacific Crest National Scenic Trail below Slate Peak, Silver Star Mountain in distance

Wilderness, which follows the divide, must be extended west to take in the stock peddlars' manglings as well as the entire route thus far of the Pacific Crest Trail from Rainy Pass.

Views? They start with Gardner Mountain, the Needles, Silver Star, Golden Horn, Tower Mountain, and especially the near bulks of Ballard and Azurite. Westerly, Jack and Crater dominate, but part of Baker can also be seen, and many more peaks. Easterly is the Pasayten country, high and remote.

Explorations from Windy Pass? Wander meadows north to 7290-foot Tamarack Peak, or the Crest Trail a scant mile to Windy Basin. Hard to quit there. Around a shoulder of Tamarack Peak are Oregon Basin and Foggy Pass, and around the shoulder of Jim Peak is Holman Pass, and then come Goat Lakes Basin, Rock Pass, Cony Basin and Windy Pass, and around the side of Three Fools Peak, Lakeview Ridge, and then Hopkins Pass and Castle Pass and—what do you know? Canada!

20 | PARSON SMITH TREE–HIDDEN LAKES

Round trip to Big Hidden Lake: 35 miles
Hiking time: Allow 3 days
High point: 5400 feet
Elevation gain: 2200 feet in, 2700 feet out
Hikable: late June through September
Map: Green Trails No. 19 Billy Goat Mountain
Information: Methow Ranger District (509) 997-2131

I've roamed in many foreign parts my boys
And many lands have seen.
But Columbia is my idol yet
Of all lands she is queen.

— Parson Smith, June 8, 1886

From the middle of the nineteenth century, miners rushed through the Pasayten to Canadian goldfields. A few paused to poke around, notably Allen L. Smith, known as "Parson Smith," trapper, artist, and poet, who on a non-rushing return from Canada camped a few days by the Pasayten River. There, on a pine tree just 12 feet from the U.S.–Canada border, in what was then the Columbia Forest Reserve, he carved his poem.

Parson's verses were first reported in 1903 by the International Boundary Survey crew which cleared a 10-foot swath on each side of the border. They were rediscovered in 1913 by

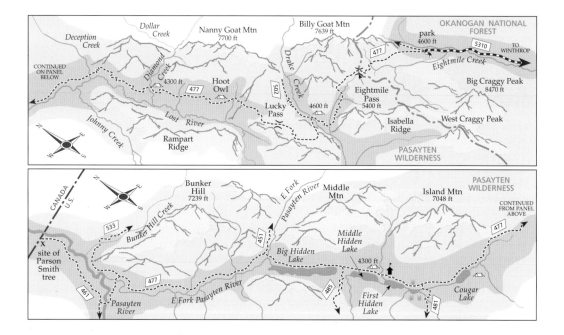

Forest Service rangers Frank Burge and George Wright and in 1926 by ranger Bill Lester. In 1965 the tree was found to be dead and a shelter was built over the stump. In 1971 the stump was placed on the National Register of Historic Places. However, the shelter wasn't protecting the wood from rot, which was found by a bear to be tasty chewing. In 1980 the stump was moved to the Winthrop Forest Service Visitor Center. Ira, not content with just looking at the carving, and intrigued by pioneers of the trackless wilderness, set out to track down the original site.

From Winthrop drive either the East or West Chewuch River road to where they join (and become road No. 51). Drive another 3.5 miles and go left on Eightmile Creek road No. 5130 some 16.7 miles to the end at the hikers' parking area, elevation 4600 feet.

The trail follows a mine road about 100 feet; keep right. In ¼ mile, at Billy Goat Pass junction, keep left on Hidden Lakes trail No. 477. At 1¼ miles is a good view of Eightmile Pass and the steep gully Parson Smith may have descended. At 1½ miles cross the 5400-foot pass and drop to a campsite and bridge over Drake Creek, 4 miles from the road, 4600 feet. This is the last campsite with reliable water for the next 6 miles. At 8 miles pass Hoot Owl Camp (doubtful water), cross over Lucky Pass, the highest point, and at 10 miles reach a campground at the crossing of Diamond Creek, 4300 feet, lowest point of the trip.

The trail climbs 300 feet, with ups and downs to dodge cliffs. Pass Deception Creek (underground most of the summer). At about 13 miles the way nears the Lost River and enters a fine old-growth forest that was spared by the great fire of around 1920. At 14 miles, 4300 feet, is lovely Cougar Lake and campsites. At 15½ miles is Island Lake (usually dry), and at 16 miles First Hidden Lake. Beyond are two Forest Service patrol cabins and separate campsites for horses and hikers. Next are Middle Hidden Lake and the crossing-over to Pasayten drainage. The trail soon reaches 1½-mile-long Big Hidden Lake, 4300 feet, 17½ miles from the road.

Most hikers are content to turn around here, but in 1½ miles, at the far end of Big Hidden

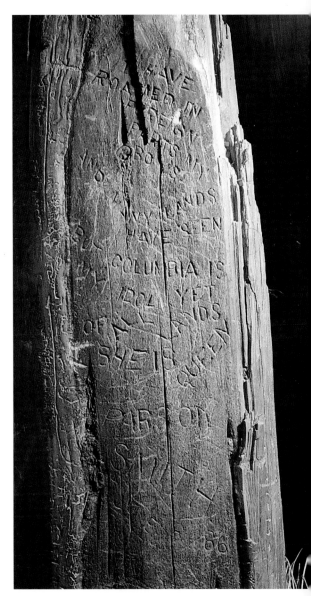

Parson Smith Tree in Forest Service's Winthrop Visitor Center

Lake, wonders are to be seen: a large shelter and a rusted grader. A final 7½ miles lead to the Canadian border, where Parson Smith carved his tree; however, to see it, go to the Winthrop Visitor Center.

21 | CATHEDRAL LAKES

Round trip: 42 miles
Hiking time: Allow 5–7 days
High point: 7400 feet
Elevation gain: 4900 feet in, 400 feet out
Hikable: July through September
Map: Green Trails No. 20 Coleman Peak
Information: Methow Ranger District (509) 997-2131

The most photographed scene in the eastern Pasayten Wilderness is Upper Cathedral Lake, in a rock bowl amid ice-polished slabs, beneath the cliffs of 8601-foot Cathedral Peak and 8358-foot Amphitheater Mountain. Cameras infest the place in fall, when the larch trees are bright gold, but also in summer, carried on hands and knees over the miles of lush herbaceous meadows and stony tundra which demand the close-up lens.

From Winthrop follow either the East or West Chewuch River road to where the two join and become road No. 51 (see Hike 22, Remmel Lake); drive roads No. 51 and 5160 some 17 miles to Andrews Creek trail No. 504, elevation 3050 feet.

The trail has a fit of steepness at the start but after crossing Little Andrews Creek and a little divide settles down, at about ½ mile dropping a bit into Andrews Creek valley. Alternating between long valley-bottom flats and short, abrupt steps, it proceeds patiently toward its remote destination. At 5½ miles pass the Meadow Lake trail. At about 8 miles begins an earnest climb to Andrews Pass, 6700 feet, 13 miles from the road. On one side rises the west face of Remmel Mountain, on the other the rounded dome of Andrews Peak.

The way now loses 400 feet into Spanish Creek valley, at 15 miles passing the Spanish Creek trail. The ever-expanding meadows submerge

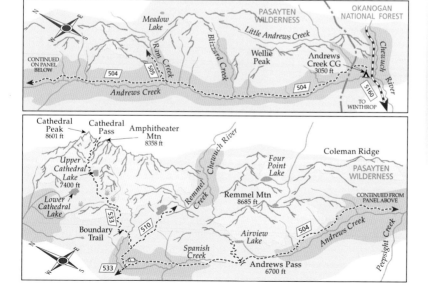

A very large proportion of the Cascades terrain that satisfies the technical definition of "tundra" is located hereabouts.

Cathedral Lake

memories of the long, sweaty, and usually fly-bitten miles. Choose a spot for a basecamp near the junction with the Boundary Trail, close by the tread or off in a secluded nook. But *camp*—the sites at Cathedral Lakes are few and small and probably full and those at Remmel Lake are very horsey.

Boundary Trail No. 533 climbs right, to Upper Cathedral Lake, 7400 feet, 21 miles from the road. My first time here we'd come farther than that on the Boundary Trail from Horseshoe Basin. After days in the rounder mountains of the far-eastern Pasayten, entering the humbling notch between Cathedral and Amphitheater I heard Wagner's Valhalla music. Though never having been a fan of that particular toy of the kineticists, had my pack included roller skates I'd likely have taken a spin on the ice-smooth slabs, and probably a spill, trying to jump an ice-dug groove. What's the proper glacier music? My favorite is Vaughn Williams' score for the film of Robert Falcon Scott in Antarctica. My special fascination with the Pasayten country is its Pleistocene past. This area has experienced both local alpine glaciation, from such cirques as that of the Cathedral Lakes, and continental glaciation from accumulation centers in Canada, which fed ice sheets that rode over and rounded the tops of all the peaks except a very few, including Cathedral.

Absorbed in the planing and gouging at the upper lake, I never got around to the sidetrail down to Lower Cathedral Lake. Anyway, we were soon off west, ascending the Boundary Trail to spend a night on Bald Mountain. The music we heard that night was, of course, Moussorgsky, his witches and warlocks accompanied by a chorus of were-coyotes serenading at the supernatural Northern Lights. So by all means do Bald, on the chance of catching the second show. Also wander up the hands-in-pockets amphitheater of Amphitheater, which didn't manage to keep its head above the rounding ice from Canada. A very large proportion of the Cascades terrain that satisfies the technical definition of "tundra" is located hereabouts. Sit amid the high-alpine blossoms and the lichen-covered stones and gaze to the Arctic Ocean.

22 CHEWUCH RIVER–FOUR POINT LAKE– REMMEL LAKE

Round trip: 40 miles
Hiking time: Allow 3–6 days
High point: 6871 feet
Elevation gain: 3400 feet
Hikable: July through September
Map: Green Trails No. 20 Coleman Peak
Information: Methow Ranger District (509) 997-2131

Meadows that in season are lupine blue and paintbrush red and sunflower yellow. Higher and drier meadows—true tundra, as in the Arctic—spongy and wet early in the season, buckled by frost heaves into small ridges and mounds, and peppered with innumerable holes of Columbian ground squirrels,"rockchucks," which behave in a most marmot-like manner, whistling alarms and diving into their homes

to escape ever-patrolling raptors, as well as the pistol-packing "plinkers."

Drive from Winthrop 30 miles on the Chewuch River road to its end at Thirtymile Camp and the start of Chewuch River trail No. 510, elevation 3500 feet.

Heavily stomped by horses, hikers, and cattle (the route is listed on the Forest Service inventory as a "stock driveway"), the trail starts wide

Remmel Lake and Remmel Mountain

and dusty and pretty much stays that way, except when it's wide and muddy. In 1 mile it enters the Pasayten Wilderness. Just 300 feet are gained in the scant 3 miles to Chewuch Falls. The way passes swampy Pocket Lake, reaches the junction with the Fire Creek–Coleman Ridge trail at about 5 miles, and at 8 miles Tungsten Creek trail, having gained thus far only 1100 feet. At 12 miles is the junction with the Four Point Lake–Coleman Ridge trail, elevation 5250 feet.

For a recommended sidetrip, go left, fording Chewuch River, easy when the water is low, and hike 3 miles to 6830-foot Four Point Lake, under a shoulder of Remmel Mountain. A horse trail once went to a fire lookout located atop 8685-foot Remmel Mountain from 1932 to 1956. The trail was abandoned and expunged from government maps, but hikers report the tread survives the official "disappearing." From the spur to Four Point Lake go uphill about ½ mile to a series of switchbacks, leave the trail and follow a stream up a few feet, and scout on the hillside for evidence of human and equine presence.

Back on the Chewuch River trail the tread grows tired, worn, and rocky, but the angle inclines upward only a little as forest thins to parkland. The rugged north face of Remmel appears and the path flattens to the shore of Remmel Lake, 6871 feet, 14 miles from the road.

If there were a market for horse apples, the

Paintbrush

harvest here would be bountiful. The lake is ringed with campsites but, unless one has grown up in a barnyard and *likes* that smell, finding a spot to eat supper is a problem. One would think that the Forest Service would keep horses at least 500 feet from camps and lakeshores or designate some campsites for hikers-only. For clean camps continue above the lake to a small creek. From Remmel Lake it is fairly easy to hike to Cathedral Lakes (Hike 21).

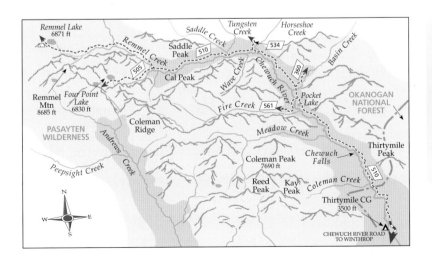

Columbian ground squirrels behave in a most marmot-like manner, whistling alarms and diving into their homes.

23 | HORSESHOE BASIN (PASAYTEN)

Round trip to Sunny Pass: 9 miles
Hiking time: 6 hours (day hike or backpack)
High point: 7200 feet
Elevation gain: 1200 feet
Hikable: late June through mid-October
Map: Green Trails No. 21 Horseshoe Basin
Information: Tonasket Ranger District (509) 486-2186

At the northeast extremity of the Cascades is a tundra wildland so unlike the main range a visitor wonders if he/she hasn't somehow missed a turn and ended up in the Arctic. Nobody I knew in the 1960s knew anything about the country. We were climbers, and maps showed a lot of high peaks but we heard they weren't genuine "peaks," that over there sheep grazed the summits of "eight-thousanders." When the North Cascades Act of 1968 was nearing passage, and among its provisions was converting the North Cascades Primitive Area to the Pasayten Wilderness, we were not perturbed that a large chunk of the extreme east was to be released to multiple-use.

At the last minute, as the bill was approaching the floor of Congress, a wail arose in the Okanogan. Our field man, Brock Evans, went for a look, returned raving, and I and my wife

and kids and friends went and came home raving, and Horseshoe Basin survived the cut. The lesson is, when in doubt, wail and scream and stamp your feet. Somebody might be listening.

Drive from Tonasket to Loomis and turn north. In 1.5 miles turn left at signs for Toats Coulee, cross the valley of Sinlahekin Creek, and start a long, steep climb up Toats Coulee on road No. 39. At 11 miles from Loomis is North Fork Campground and in another 5 miles is a junction. Go right on a narrow road, No. (3900)500, signed "Iron Gate." Turn right and drive 7 rough and steep miles to the road-end and beginning of Boundary Trail No. 533, elevation 6100 feet, at Iron Gate Camp (no water) on the edge of the Pasayten Wilderness.

The first ½ mile is downhill along the abandoned road to the old Iron Gate Camp (no water). The trail from here begins in small

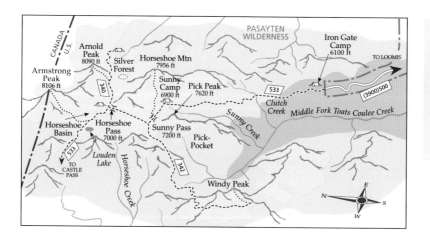

All around spreads the enormous meadowland of Horseshoe Basin, demanding days of exploration.

Shallow Louden Lake in Horseshoe Basin

lodgepole pine (most of this region was burned off by a series of huge fires in the 1920s) on the old road to Tungsten "Mine." The grade is nearly flat ½ mile to cool waters of Clutch Creek and then starts a moderate, steady ascent. At 3¼ miles the route opens out into patches of grass and flowers. After a brief steep bit, at 4 miles the way abruptly emerges from trees to the flowery, stream-bubbling nook of Sunny Basin and splendid Sunny Camp, 6900 feet.

The trail climbs ½ mile to 7200-foot Sunny Pass; be prepared to gasp and rave. All around spreads the enormous meadowland of Horseshoe Basin, demanding days of exploration. From the pass the trail goes right, contouring gentle slopes of Horseshoe Mountain to the wide flat of Horseshoe Pass, 7000 feet, 5¾ miles, and then continues on and on along the Boundary Trail to the Cascade Crest. All the summits are easy flower walks—7620-foot Pick Peak, 7956-foot Horseshoe Mountain, and 8090-foot Arnold Peak. The ridge north from 8106-foot Armstrong Peak has the added interest of monuments to mark the U.S.–Canada boundary.

24 | GOLDEN LAKES LOOP

Loop trip: 23 miles
Hiking time: Allow 3 days
High point: 8000 feet
Elevation gain: 4200 feet
Hikable: mid-July through September
Map: Green Trails No. 115 Prince Creek
Information: Methow Ranger District (509) 997-2131

The Enchantment Lakes have gained such wide and well-deserved fame that the Forest Service has adopted a long list of do's and don'ts to preserve the quality of the land and the recreational experience. Trembling on the brink of comparable fame is the Golden Lakes Loop through miles of meadows, past five lakes and looks down to three others, and to ridge tops with views from the Columbia Plateau to the Cascade Crest. The trip is a glory in summer, the grass lushly green and the flowers many-colored. In fall it's absolutely mystical, the larch trees turned to gold, giving the name by which this tour of High Sierra–like "gentle wilderness" is becoming a legend.

If I may be permitted, let me spotlight the

chief flak for the legend, the Grumbler, mainly responsible for the brink-trembling. Ira is on the Forest Service's back about this like an itchy fur coat on a bear trying to hibernate. He is the one who has discovered the paradox of the Golden Lakes, which is, that for all its wonders, the trails presently provide a surprising degree of solitude. How can that be? Motorcycles!

Yes, motorcycles. The loop has a link motorists cannot use, but hikers can. Motorcycles gobble up so many miles in so short a time the jockeys don't find it worthwhile to haul machines to the trailhead, which gives access to barely a

Larch tree in fall splendor

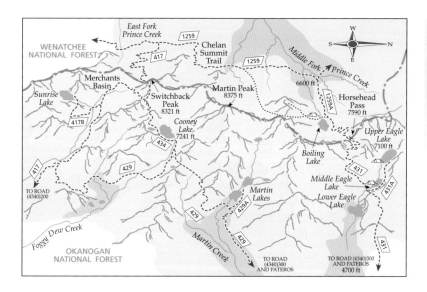

The Golden Lakes Loop travels through miles of meadows, past five lakes, and looks down to three others.

Cooney Lake

hundred or so minutes exercising their wheels. A happy situation for hikers? Yes, except they know the trails are "multi-use" and are kept away by the mere possibility of a mood-destroying encounter with the racket and stench and rude speed of sit-down travelers. Thus, solitude!

This is embarrassing to the multiple-users, whose dogged devotion to a discredited dogma has, here, resulted in the next thing to no use. The solution to their "solitude problem" requires money, but Congress has cut back trail funds drastically. However, access has been ob-

tained to an alternate sugar daddy—the state. Employing that financial backing, the Forest Service proposes to build a connector to hook together a 40-mile motorcycle loop, sufficient for a ride of 3 or 4 hours. *That* would bring a horde of ORVs a-roaring and a-fuming. And that would drive away the hikers—few now but potentially many, many—from a foot loop of three or four joyous days.

How do *you* feel about it? You probably haven't walked the loop because you've heard it's motorcycle country. Doesn't have to be. I remember when the Forest Service was converting the Chelan Summit Trail to a motorway. I got a hearty chuckle, after 1984, coming to the boundary of the new wilderness and proceeding into the sanctum on expensive wide motorway become wide trail, no oil slicks on the creeks, no fumes clinging to the flowers. Go walk the Golden Lakes Loop. Then come home and write strong letters to Congress (copies to the Forest Service), demanding to know how come the Enchantments are treated so tenderly as to exclude horses and dogs, yet in this companion wonderland the motorcycles are permitted—more accurately, officially encouraged, pampered.

From Pateros on the Columbia River, drive the Methow Valley Highway some 17 miles towards Twisp and turn left on the county road signed "Gold Creek Loop." In 1.5 miles go left on North Fork Gold Creek road No. 4340. (Coming from Twisp, drive 15 miles and go right on the Gold Creek Loop.) At 6.7 miles go left on (4340)300, signed "Crater Creek," and continue another 4.6 miles to the start of Eagle Lake trail No. 431, elevation 4700 feet.

The description here is counterclockwise; clockwise is just as good. Either way, start on the Eagle Lake trail, at 2 miles passing the Martin Creek trail, the final leg of the return loop. At 7 miles, 7110 feet, on a short spur from the main trail, is Upper Eagle Lake; camp here the first night.

Cross 7590-foot Horsehead Pass to Boiling Lake and from the lake drop a mile in forest to a junction, 6600 feet. Go left on the Chelan Summit Trail, climbing back to meadows, passing nice campsites, to a 7100-foot saddle. Contour from the saddle about ½ mile into the broad headwaters basin of East Fork Prince Creek and the junction with the trail up and over Switchback Peak. For a century this trail has served feet and hooves perfectly well, and still does; wheels, though, demand "improvements," and that's the proposed project to perfect the ORV loop. The junction may or may not be signed, but it is not difficult to find. As the mass of the peak rears up off your larboard bow, look for cairns and horse apples and bits of tread slanting up the lush sidehill meadows. The tread soon is definite and continuous.

The switchbacks ascend to an 8000-foot high point on the shoulder of 8321-foot Switchback Peak, tremendously scenic. The way sidehills above Merchants Basin to the ridge above Cooney Lake. Switchbacks drop (steep snow here may force the unequipped to turn around or die) to a campsite bench near the upper end of Cooney Lake, 7241 feet. The third day is mostly downhill. From Cooney Lake go left on the Martin Creek trail, switchbacking down into forest and a junction with the sidetrail to Martin Lakes. Stay with the Martin Creek trail down to the crossing of Eagle Creek and up the 500 feet to the Eagle Lake trail, just 2 miles from the trailhead.

Upper Eagle Lake

25 | CHELAN SUMMIT TRAIL

One-way trip: 38 miles
Hiking time: Allow 5–9 days
High point: 7400 feet
Elevation gain: about 6500 feet
Hikable: early July through September
Maps: Green Trails No. 115 Prince Creek, No. 83 Buttermilk Butte, No. 82 Stehekin
Information: Chelan Ranger District (509) 682-2576

To tell the knowing hiker that only twice before the final plunge to Stehekin do the 38 miles of trail dip as low as 5500 feet is to inform him that never is he out of the scent of flowers. To add that the scene is well east of the main range is to assure him that clouds drowning the Cascade Crest are, here, mainly empties. Oh, did I forget to mention the easy-roaming ridges, stupendous views across the air gap of Lake Chelan to the ice giants, sensational camps everywhere, and alluring sidetrips to lakes, passes, and peaks?

The route may be sampled via approaches from valleys on either side, but the dream trip is the whole thing, end to end, though this entails the obvious complication of arranging a drop-off by a friend at the southern trailhead. (The *Lady of the Lake* takes care of the pickup on the north and return to the friend; see Hike 26,

A bright flower from the Compositae family

Bryan Butte from Summer Blossom Trail

Chelan Lakeshore Trail.) There are in reality three southern trailheads; my emphatic recommendation is Summer Blossom. Cars can be driven here 23.5 miles from the Methow Valley Highway or 40 miles from Chelan; the latter route is my somewhat dubious choice, but be sure to call the Forest Service to make sure it's in good repair.

Drive the North Shore Road from Chelan past Manson and turn right on Grade Creek road, signed "Antilon Lake," at this point becoming road No. 8200. At 40 miles, 2 miles past South Navarre Campground, is Summer Blossom trailhead, elevation 6440 feet.

The wheelfree, horse-free, narrow, sometimes meager trail ascends 2½ miles to a shoulder just a quick stroll from the 7963-foot summit of North Navarre, descends tight switchbacks and a short bit of use-your-hands balcony to a luscious basin, and contours to a junction, 6 miles,

with the (official) Summit Trail at the 7400-foot pass between Horsethief Basin and East Fork Prince Creek. The bad news is that motorcycles may be met here, but Ira is working on the problem and with your help expects ultimately to prevail.

The way drops 700 feet to the broad meadow basin of the East Fork and makes a big swing around it, under 8321-foot Switchback Peak to a 7120-foot pass, 8 miles, to Middle Fork Prince Creek. Down and around another wide parkland, at 10 miles are the junction with the Middle Fork Prince Creek trail and a basecamp for sidetrips to Boiling Lake and Hoodoo Pass and all.

The trail climbs to Chipmunk Pass, the 7050-foot saddle, 11½ miles, to North Fork Prince Creek, and here enters the Lake Chelan–Sawtooth Wilderness, the end of motorcycles. It descends to a 5560-foot low point in forest, 14

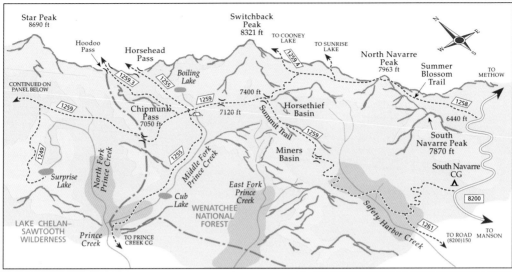

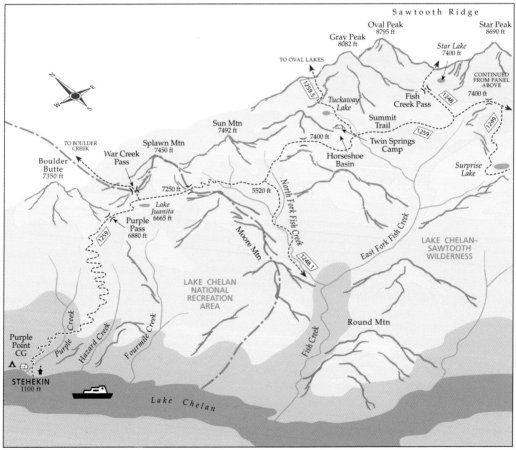

Shoulder of South Navarre Peak from Summer Blossom Trail

miles, and climbs to flowers again and the 7400-foot pass, 18½ miles, to East Fork Fish Creek.

A short, steep drop leads to a 6800-foot junction with the trail to Fish Creek Pass. From a camp here, sidetrips include a stroll to larch-ringed Star Lake beneath the great wall of Star Peak and scrambles to the summits of 8690-foot Star Peak and 8392-foot Courtney Peak. On the other hand, if camp is made after a meadow traverse to Twin Springs Camp in Horseshoe Basin, there are sidetrips to Tuckaway Lake, Gray Peak, and Oval Lakes.

The way ascends to the 7400-foot pass, 22 miles, to North Fork Fish Creek, descends into woods at 5520 feet, 24½ miles, and climbs gardens to a 7250-foot pass, 27½ miles, to Fourmile Creek. A descent and an upsy-downsy traverse lead to Lake Juanita, 6665 feet, 30 miles. The quick and terrific sidetrip here is to Boulder Butte, 7350 feet, a one-time lookout site.

At 30½ miles is 6880-foot Purple Pass, famous for the gasps drawn by the sudden sight—5800 feet below—of wind-rippled, sun-sparkled waters of Lake Chelan, seeming close enough for a swandive. Hundreds of switchbacks take your poor old knees down Hazard and Purple Creeks to Stehekin, 38 miles, the ice cream, and the dock of the *Lady of the Lake*.

26 | CHELAN LAKESHORE TRAIL

One-way trip from Prince Creek: 17½ miles
Hiking time: Allow 2–4 days
High point: 1700 feet
Elevation gain: perhaps 2000 feet
Hikable: late March through early June
Maps: Green Trails No. 82 Stehekin, No. 114 Lucerne, No. 115 Prince Creek
Information: Chelan Ranger District (509) 682-2576

Monkeyflower

My first trip was two days on the trail, an afternoon and a morning and the one night between. Each return has been longer as more and more delectable spots required me to sit beside the dancing waters, then lay my body down there overnight. About two or three trips from now, at a guess, the star-sparkle on the lake, the green lawns atop jutting buttresses, the groves of ancient ponderosa pine, the mystic glades of glowing aspen, the slot gorges of frothing waterfalls, just won't let me go, will keep me there in eternal spring, the sun dependable but not too weighty, the breezes cool, and the bloom rich: trillium, chocolate lily, glacier lily, spring beauty, yellowbells, Johnny-jump-up, red currant, and more; later, spring gold, prairie star, blue-eyed Mary, naked broomrape, primrose monkeyflower, death camas, balsamroot, miners lettuce, calypso, and whatever else is on special in April-May.

Drive to Field Point, up the lake from the town of Chelan, and board the *Lady of the Lake*.

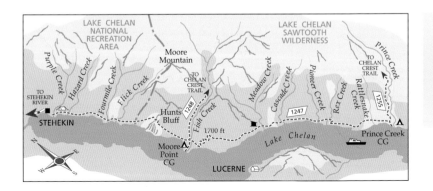

Each return has been longer as more and more delectable spots required me to sit beside the dancing waters.

Chelan Lakeshore Trail

(Call the Forest Service–Park Service Information Center for the current schedule.)

Debarkation at Prince Creek, about 11:00 A.M., allows an easy afternoon, hiking the 7 miles to a camp at or near Meadow Creek Shelter, after crossing Rattlesnake, Rex, Pioneer, and Cascade Creeks. The 10½ miles remaining to Stehekin are reasonably walked next day by boat time in early afternoon. That's the two-day plan.

My initial relaxation into Chelan indolence was a three-day plan, attaining on the second day the trail's high point at 1700 feet on a long, wide shelf then descending to Fish Creek, 3½ miles from Meadow Creek. A sidetrail ½ mile down the creek took me to a second camp at Moore Point, where I loitered through the ancient orchard and the deer pasture fenced by New England–like stone walls, then spread my sleeping bag under the cottonwoods and closed my eyes, lulled by waves slapping the shore.

The 6½ miles from Fish Creek to Stehekin are a sauntering morning for your three-day trip, climbing to 1600 feet on Hunts Bluff and its climactic views of lake and mountains. The trail then drops to the shore and never again climbs high, wandering the base of cliffs and through woods to Flick Creek, Fourmile Creek, Hazard Creek, and finally Stehekin.

Next year your trip will be four days, then five, then . . .

27 | HORSESHOE BASIN (STEHEKIN)

Round trip from Cottonwood Camp: 8 miles
Hiking time: 5 hours (day hike or backpack)
High point: 4800 feet
Elevation gain: 2000 feet
Hikable: July through October
Map: Green Trails No. 80 Cascade Pass
Information: North Cascades National Park, Stehekin District (509) 682-2549
Backcountry use permit required for camping

Nine or more waterfalls froth and splash and pound to the meadow floor of this great hole. Above are glaciers on Sahale and Boston Peaks, both nearly 9000 feet, and the teeth of Ripsaw Ridge. My first visit was on a high alpine traverse from Cascade Pass to Park Creek Pass; above the cliffs that half-ring the hole, we gazed to its depths. My next visit was with wife and little kids, hiking from a basecamp in the valley, gazing up from the flowers to the waterfalls and glaciers and peaks. An interesting encounter there: we were camped under blue skies, tattered rags of clouds scooting over the Cascade Crest from the west; a party of climbers I knew greeted us, telling how those tattered rags were, on the Crest, a hard-driving drizzle-rain that had kept them tented up a week before rumors of sunshine called them east.

The Horseshoe Basin trail can be reached from Cascade Pass, but not by me. The pass is properly on the way to Sahale Arm or Cache Col. The basin belongs to the Stehekin Valley and that is the respectfully ceremonious approach.

After leaving the *Lady of the Lake* (see Hike 26, Chelan Lakeshore Trail) at Stehekin Landing, take the Park Service shuttle bus up the Stehekin

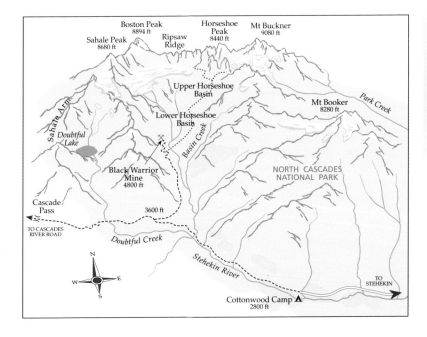

Impressive looks upward from flowery knolls to ice and crags, and a magical view and sound of white water on the glacier-excavated walls.

Waterfalls in Horseshoe Basin

River Road to Cottonwood Camp. From Cottonwood Camp, elevation 2800 feet, the trail (which believe it or not was, for a summer or two in the early 1950s, a "mining" road) proceeds upvalley 2 miles to a junction, 3600 feet. The Cascade Pass trail goes left, the basin trail right, climbing around and up the mountainside to enter the hanging valley (cirque actually) of Basin Creek. At 1½ miles the way emerges from brush and flattens out amid boulder-strewn meadows, 4200 feet. Impressive looks upward from flowery knolls to ice and crags, and a magical view and sound of white water on the glacier-excavated walls.

The road remnants continue ½ mile upward across the sloping floor of the basin to the Black Warrior tunnel at 4800 feet, close under the froth and splash of the falls. The Park Service has tidied up the prospect hole to make explorations safe; bring a flashlight.

The road to Cottonwood Camp deserves a few words. Cottonwood Camp for many years was the terminus of the Stehekin River Road. Or at least it used to be. Now and then. However, Nature is on the side of wilderness, and has so testified by regular anti-engineering. That road is *not wanted*, and in any given summer the trailhead may be at a washout any number of miles down the valley.

The more miles the better. On one trip or another, in one season or another, I have walked wheelfree (by virtue of snow or washout or collapsed bridge) from Lake Chelan to Cascade Pass, and can testify that the "road" is the grandest low-elevation trail in the North Cascades National Park. The National Park Service does not recognize the value of such a nonpareil trail. The National Park Service had darn well better change its mind. I'm sure not going to change mine.

28 | CASCADE LOOP–MONUMENT 83

Loop trip: 34 miles
Hiking time: Allow 2–3 days
High point: 6550 feet
Elevation gain: 4900 feet
Hikable: late June through October
Map: Green Trails No. 18 Pasayten Peak (U.S. only)
Information: Methow Ranger District (509) 997-2131

When built in the 1920s the fire lookout at Monument 83 was probably the most remote in the Cascades. It still is if approached from the United States via the Pacific Crest Trail from Slate Peak, a wilderness walk of nearly 30 miles, mathematically three times grander than the 10 miles from Trans-Canada Highway 3 across Manning (B. C., not Harvey) Provincial Park. The lookout came to Ira's attention in 1979 while researching a book on the subject. From the map, he could see that if the International Boundary could be crossed without too much red tape, the Canadian approach was his best bet for a photograph. To his surprise he discovered that the lookout lies on Manning Provincial Park's Cascade Loop, a very popular trail featuring miles of splendid forest, climaxes of alpine meadows, and the thrill of (technically illegal) international travel. Not only that, but he could get a U.S. Forest Service permit from the Canadians for the section of the loop in the Pasayten Wilderness (a permit required then but not presently). No red tape!

Drive Highway 3 from Hope across Allison Pass to Manning Provincial Park administration office, lodge, and visitors center (Nature House). Park here, at the end of the loop hike, in order to have your car waiting, or drive 1.8 miles farther

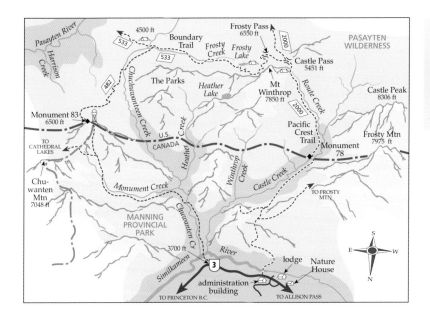

A very popular trail featuring miles of splendid forest and climaxes of alpine meadows.

Old lookout at Monument 83

to the Monument 83 parking lot on the right side of the road, elevation 3700 feet.

The "trail" begins as a rough, seldom-used service road, closed to public vehicles. In ¼ mile it crosses the Similkameen River and begins a gradual ascent in forest along Chuwanten Creek and Monument Creek. At about 9 miles pass a side trail signed "Cathedral Lakes" and continue on the service road to the flowery little meadow of Monument 83, 10 miles, 6500 feet. In the 1920s the U.S. Forest Service built the small log cabin on the highest point, which happens to lie in Canada. In 1953 the tower, tall enough to see over the foreign hill, was erected on the United States side. A grave marker memorializes a pack mule that broke its leg and had to be shot.

From the American side of the lookout the trail (a true one from here) crosses Chuwanten Creek (here with the American spelling, Chuchuwanteen) and descends to a campsite at the crossing of Frosty Creek and a junction, 4500 feet, with trail No. 533, 15 miles from Highway 3. Go right, upstream on Frosty Creek, to a camp ¼ mile past tiny Frosty Lake, 5345 feet. The trail steepens and switchbacks to meadows at 6550-foot Frosty Pass, 21 miles, then drops 1½ miles to Castle Pass, 5451 feet, and a junction with the Pacific Crest Trail. Head north, passing water and a campsite in ½ mile. The Crest Trail descends gently above Route Creek, then Castle Creek, 3 miles to the border at Monument 78, then 7½ miles more along Castle Creek to Manning Park headquarters.

Chapter 2

GLACIER PEAK

When conservationism awoke in the 1950s from years of coma, the Forest Service had thrust logging roads halfway up the White Chuck River and was planning timber sales to timberline. A car campground at Kennedy Hot Springs! A scenic road (and not so incidentally, juicy forests to chainsaw) up the Suiattle River past Image Lake to Suiattle Pass, down Agnes Creek to the Stehekin River! Were these "foresters" the same species as us? Where did they come from with their brutal dogma of "multiple use"—on flying saucers from Mars?

Glacier Peak, the last *wild* volcano, buffered from the turmoil of machinery by forest miles of trail country, was our rallying point. Forced to the wall, in 1960 the Forest Service conceded a Glacier Peak Wilderness—insultingly small (and still so after two subsequent additions), and thereby triggered the campaign which led in 1968 to the North Cascades National Park—insultingly small, and so the story has as yet no end.

To climbers, Glacier is less significant for its own considerable merit than as the boundary monument between gentler peaks to the south and those higher and tougher and icier to the north. However, intermingled with horn-and-kettledrum climaxes are violin-and-woodwind interludes. The most callous exclusion from the statutory Wilderness is the Mad River, parkland ideal for family rambling, for green-bonding of the very young. Precisely *here* the Forest Service is striving to establish a motorcycle gymnasium! (Fathers and mothers: When your kiddies go out in the meadows to play, make sure they look both ways for traffic.)

The day hikes of Glacier are Classics. So too, for the experienced, are the deeps, wherein many days and many nights are the warp and woof to be woven together in a single whole fabric. The circuit of Glacier is a Scout Classic. Totem-seekers of the nation are issued helmets and gaiters and axes and despatched by Outward Bound in bands of a dozen each from Trinity to Buck Creek Pass to High Pass and down the Napeequa and over Little Giant Pass to the Chiwawa River. Among the all-time favorite loops of the North Cascades is Trinity-Spider Pass-Lyman Lakes-Cloudy Pass-Image Lake-Buck Creek Pass-Trinity. No less popular is the loop whose middle is on the *Lady of the Lake* (Chelan, that is), hitching up Stehekin-Agnes Creek-Cloudy Pass-Lyman Lakes-Railroad Creek-Lucerne.

The Ultimate Classic of the long and the deep is no trail trip; it is a high alpine adventure, the Ptarmigan Traverse pioneered in the 1930s by the Ptarmigan Climbing Club. Perhaps something for you as a hiker to aspire to, train for. Something to dream on, surely, as we Scouts of the 1930s dreamt of Mount Everest. In 1953 five of my climbing buddies puzzled out, on the sketchiest of information, the route of the Ptarmigans north to Cascade Pass along the Cascade Crest. In 1957 Ira inveigled five photo subjects ("friends," he called them, the better to inveigle) into attempting a Third Traverse.

They made it. In weather so poor that poor Ira scarcely got out his camera. But he did so one dawn, moments before the clouds closed in, and his photo of White Rock Lakes on my living room wall would allow me no peace, as in Kipling's "Something lost behind the ranges. Lost and waiting for you. Go!" Twice I went, and twice was blasted out in fear of my life. Friends asked me to please let them know when I was going again so they could be sure to stay home.

White Rock Lakes and Dome Peak; Chickamin Glacier, left, Dana Glacier, right

29 | KINDY RIDGE—FOUND LAKE

Round trip to Found Lake: about 10 miles
Hiking time: 12 hours (backpack)
High point: 4800 feet
Elevation gain: 3500 feet in, 1100 feet out
Hikable: mid-July through October
Maps: USGS Sonny Boy Lakes and Snowking Mountain
Information: Mt. Baker Ranger District (360) 856-5700

A close view of seldom-approached Snowking Mountain, high meadows to explore, and six alpine lakes for camping and prowling. However, this is a boot-beaten route, not easy, recommended only for experienced cross-country travelers. Even when Ira was years younger and the road ended at 2500 feet instead of the present 1300 feet, he found this trip grueling. Ah, but worth it! Not that he makes it a habit.

Drive Highway 20 to Marblemount, cross the Skagit River and continue east 14.5 miles on the Cascade River road. Turn right on Kindy Creek road No. 1570, cross the Cascade River and follow this road to its end at a washout, elevation about 1300 feet.

Walk the road some 2 miles and find a straight-up boot path along an old fire line beside a 1970 clearcut. Eventually the way intersects the long-abandoned Found Creek trail, the lower end destroyed by the 1956 Found Creek Fire, which Ira photographed for a newspaper story.

The trail ends on a 4800-foot saddle. For wonderful views, leave the trail and climb the ridge 1000 feet to a 5791-foot viewpoint. Trees are few so the way is obvious; generally trend right for the easiest grade.

To see all there is to see, move about the broad summit—being careful of fissures, some deep, that split the rock. Snowking Mountain

Red heather

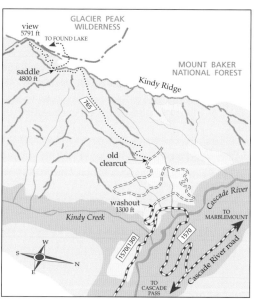

Found Lake below Snowking Mountain

and its glaciers are the big reward, but all directions yield dividends: Eldorado, Boston, Formidable, and Resplendent. Four lakes lie below. The water in two of them—Neori, the lower, and Skare, the upper—are clear blue. Snowking, the largest, and a nameless pond above are a striking turquoise. Two more lakes, Found and Cyclone, are out of sight.

Kindy Ridge is a splendid day hike for boggling views but no fit base for exploring the lakes, which cry out for it. A very rough route descends from the saddle 1 mile to Found Lake, 4000 feet, gateway to the other lakes and the slopes of Snowking Mountain. The lakes are connected by paths but to find them all requires close attention to the USGS map.

30 | GREEN MOUNTAIN

Round trip: 8 miles
Hiking time: 6 hours (day hike or backpack)
High point: 6500 feet
Elevation gain: 3100 feet
Hikable: late June through October
Map: Green Trails No. 80 Cascade Pass
Information: Darrington Ranger District (360) 436-1155

The name of the peak may seem banal, but few people ever have looked up from the Suiattle River valley without exclaiming, "What a *green* mountain!" The trail climbs through these remarkable meadows to a lookout summit with magnificent views to every point of the compass.

Drive Highway 530 north from Darrington or south from Rockport to near the Sauk River bridge and turn off on Suiattle River road No. 26. Continue for almost 19 miles to Green Mountain road No. 2680. Turn left and drive 6

miles to the road-end in a logging patch, elevation about 3400 feet. Find the trail sign above the road several hundred yards before the road-end.

The trail climbs a rather steep mile in mossy forest to a grubby hunters' camp with a year-round spring, then enters the vast meadow sprawl admired from below. First are fields of bracken fern and subalpine plants, then, on higher switchbacks, a feast (in season) of blueberries. Views begin—down to Suiattle forests and out to White Chuck Mountain and Glacier Peak. More meadows, and views of Mount Pugh and Sloan Peak beyond the intervening ridge of Lime Mountain.

At 2 miles, 5400 feet, the trail rounds a shoulder and in ½ mile traverses and drops 100 feet to a pair of shallow ponds amid gardens. Pleasant camps here, and all-summer water; please use established sites away from the ponds. No camping allowed beyond here.

A short way above the pond basin the trail enters a larger, wide-open basin. Please stay on the trail. The Forest Service is trying to restore the vegetation in erosion channels caused by hasty-footed hikers cutting switchbacks. (Ira faithfully observes such regulations but once was bullied off the trail by a belligerent marmot which was sunning itself in the tread and wasn't about to move.)

The summit can now be seen directly above, and also Glacier Peak. Climb in flowers to the ridge and along the crest to the lookout building at 6500 feet, 4 miles from the road. Look north along the ridge to the nearby cliffs and glaciers of 7311-foot Buckindy. Look up

Green Mountain trail and Glacier Peak

Downey Creek to peaks of the Ptarmigan Traverse from Dome north to Formidable. Look up Milk Creek to the Ptarmigan Glacier on Glacier Peak. Look in all directions to other peaks, too many to name.

The fire lookout was built in 1920s, rebuilt in 1931 and 1950. Unfortunately, the underpinnings have rotted and unless volunteers can be found to do repairs the building will be removed.

31 | IMAGE LAKE

Round trip: 32 miles
Hiking time: Allow 2–3 days
High point: 6100 feet
Elevation gain: 4600 feet
Hikable: mid-July through October
Maps: Green Trails No. 112 Glacier Peak, No. 113 Holden
Information: Darrington Ranger District (360) 436-1155

A 2-mile-high volcano, the image of its glaciers reflected in an alpine tarn. Meadow ridges for dreamwalking. The long sweep of Suiattle River forests. Casting ballots with their feet, hikers have voted this a supreme climax of the alpine world of the North Cascades and the nation. Ira often hears whining about the best views being locked up in wilderness. The art directors who buy his photographs say this is not true. Ninety-nine percent of mountain pictures used on calendars are shot from or near a road. Image Lake is the other 1 percent!

However, Volkswagen of America once did a magazine montage putting a Beetle by the shore against the background of Glacier Peak, and the advertising agency threatened to sue the North Cascades Conservation Council when it used the photo on the cover of its journal.

Drive Highway 530 north from Darrington or south from Rockport to near the Sauk River bridge and turn off on Suiattle River road No. 26 and continue some 23 miles to the end, elevation 1600 feet.

Walk abandoned roadway 1 mile to a Y; go left (straight ahead) on the Suiattle River trail, largely level, partly in ancient trees, sometimes with looks to the river, crossing small tributaries, to Canyon Creek Camp, 6½ miles, 2300 feet. At about 9½ miles, 2800 feet, is a creek with a small campsite but no water by midsummer. Just beyond is a trail junction; go left on Miners Ridge trail No. 785. The switchbacks are relentless and dry with occasional glimpses, then spectacular views, out from the trees to the valley and the volcano. At 12½ miles are two welcome streams at the edge of meadow country and at 13 miles, 4800 feet, is a junction; campsites here. Miners Cabin trail No. 795, to Suiattle Pass, goes straight ahead; take the left fork to Image Lake. Switchback up and up, into

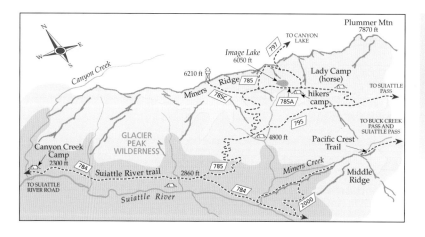

> Casting ballots with their feet, hikers have voted this a supreme climax of the alpine world of the North Cascades and the nation.

Image Lake at sunrise

blueberry and flower meadows to expanding views, to a junction atop Miners Ridge, about 15 miles, 6150 feet. A ¼-mile trail leads to Miners Ridge Lookout, 6210 feet, the wilderness ranger's headquarters. The main trail goes right ¾ mile, traversing then dropping a bit, to Image Lake, 6050 feet.

Solitude is not the name of the game here. Indeed, so dense is the summer population that to protect fragile meadows the Forest Service has prohibited camping around and above the lake; to keep the water pure it has banned swimming when the lake is low. Below the lake ¼ mile is a hikers' camp (the nation's greatest view from a toilet seat). A mile away at Lady Camp are accommodations for horses and mice. (On a bench above the trail look for the lovely lady carved in a tree by a sheepherder in about 1916.) From Lady Camp the trail drops some 500 feet in ½ mile to a junction with the Suiattle Pass trail, which can be followed 1¾ miles back to the Image Lake trail junction.

Exploring the basin, climbing the 6758-foot knoll above, visiting the fire lookout, walking the Canyon Lake trail into the headwaters of Canyon Creek—thus one may fill memorable days. By no means omit the finest wandering of all, along the wide crest of Miners Ridge, through flower gardens, looking north to Dome Peak and south across Suiattle forests to Glacier Peak.

Letters can and did make a difference here. Kennecott Copper Corporation planned to dig a ½-mile-wide open-pit mine 1 mile east of the lake at Lady Camp Basin. This blasphemy was prevented by violent objections from citizen-hikers who deluged Congress with anguish and rage.

32 | WHITE CHUCK GLACIER

Round trip to Glacier Peak Meadows: 24 miles
Hiking time: Allow 4 days minimum
High point: about 5400 feet
Elevation gain: 3100 feet
Hikable: late July through September
Maps: Green Trails No. 111 Sloan Peak, No. 112 Glacier Peak
Information: Darrington Ranger District (360) 436-1155

What the world needs now is more respect, long long trails that plumb the depths of wildness from low forests to high meadows, trails that are slow because the miles are many and the packs heavy, trips that are not one-day or weekend cream-skimmers but knit a number of days together with a number of nights. The White Chuck River, for paradigm.

My late friend Leo loved to tell of his introduction to wilderness on a long-ago ascent of Glacier Peak. He and his companions hitched a ride on the logging railroad from Darrington up the Sauk River to the mouth of the White Chuck and hoisted their packs. The second night they camped at Kennedy Hot Springs and the third below the White Chuck Glacier. Then, as it must to all wild travelers, came the rain, luckily only two days of it. They were thus five days and five nights deep in the wilderness before they set out for (and attained) the summit.

In 1948 Kermit the Hermit led several of us on a new route to the summit, directly up from Kennedy, which by then had been reduced by logging to 9½ trail miles; even so we had a three-day (and two-night) trip, still fairly respectful. Two decades later I gazed across the valley from Lake Byrne and plainly saw the boot-beaten trench over the glaciers, the route pioneered by Kermit having become the favorite of weekend cream-skimmers, the skimming the easier because logging had taken the road to within 5½ miles of Kennedy. (Until birdwatchers raised a howl heard in Washington, D.C., the Forest Service intended to put the boundary of the Glacier Peak Wilderness beyond Kennedy, which was to be a road-end auto camp!)

Drive the Mountain Loop Highway south from Darrington. At roughly 9 miles cross the Sauk River. Pass road No. 22 and in 0.2 mile beyond the bridge go left on White Chuck River

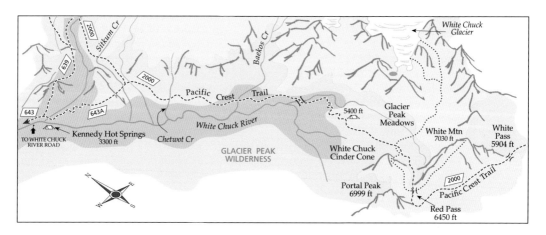

Wading the White Chuck River

road No. 23 then 10 miles to the road-end parking area and campground, elevation 2300 feet.

Begin in deep forest beside a loud river fed by frothing meltwater of Fire, Pumice, and Glacier Creeks. At 5½ miles is the large and crowded camp at Kennedy Hot Springs, 3300 feet. Across the river is the tublike pool just big enough for three or four people who don't believe in the germ theory of disease and delight in exchanging bodily fluids with strangers through the medium of hot water.

Ascend steeply then gently to join the Pacific Crest Trail at Sitkum Creek, 3850 feet, 7 miles from the road; climbers' camps here. The Crest Trail continues along the valley, passing the avalanche track and meadow-marsh of Chetwot Creek, fording Baekos Creek, and at 9½ miles, 4200 feet, crossing a high bridge over the rocky chasm and thundering falls of the White Chuck River.

Now the trail climbs a valley step. Trees are smaller and so is the river, assembling itself from snow-fed tributaries. A little meadow gives promise of what lies above. After more subalpine forest, the way enters the tremendous open basin of Glacier Peak Meadows. At 12 miles, 5400 feet, is the site of the long-gone Glacier Peak Shelter; magnificent campsites everywhere around.

As a base for easy hiker-type explorations, this highland valley of flowers and creeks and snowfields is unsurpassed in the North Cascades. On my favorite climb of Glacier, in 1953, when Kennedy was still 9½ miles from the snarl of chainsaws, four of us spent our first night there and our second near the shelter site. As for the summit, it had to wait.

One day had to be spent exploring the White Chuck Cinder Cone, remnant of a volcano smaller and newer than Glacier Peak, and scrambling meadows ever higher to the summit of 6999-foot Portal Peak. Another was devoted to following the Pacific Crest Trail 2 miles up a wintry, rocky basin to 6450-foot Red Pass, continuing on the trail to White Pass, then climbing to the ridge crest and wading knee-high flowers to the top of 7030-foot White Mountain.

Wherever we were was where we were supposed to be. Total depth of our wilderness (not counting the way home), six days and five nights. That's respectful.

33 | LAKE BYRNE

Round trip: 16 miles
Hiking time: Allow 2–3 days
High point: 5544 feet
Elevation gain: 3200 feet
Hikable: August through September
Maps: Green Trails No. 111 Sloan Peak, No. 112 Glacier Peak
Information: Darrington Ranger District (360) 436-1155

In olden times, when it took two full days of hiking up the White Chuck River just to get to Kennedy Hot Springs, pedestrians never devoted less than a week to the trip. The glorious forest was savored fully. The bathers being few the springs were enjoyed in relative safety from loathsome diseases. The cherry on the tip of the whipped cream was Lake Byrne. Sorry to say, nowadays backpacking to the lake can be something of a horror story. Better, camp at Kennedy and day-hike to the lake. Best, go beyond the lake to basecamp somewhere along Lost Creek Ridge.

Drive the Mountain Loop Highway south from Darrington. In 0.2 mile past the Sauk River bridge go left on White Chuck River road No. 23 for 10 miles to the road-end parking area and campground, elevation 2300 feet.

Hike 5½ miles to Kennedy Hot Springs and find a campsite (lots of luck) on either side of the White Chuck River, 3300 feet. On the far side of the river pass a sidetrail that goes left, to the

springs, which it is safe to look at but definitely not to touch unless wearing a protective garment. The main trail takes dead aim on the sky, gaining 2200 feet in 2½ miles, chinks in green forest wall giving glimpses of blinding-white Glacier Peak. At 2½ miles from the river, 8 miles from the road, is Lake Byrne, 5544 feet.

Pretty to look at it surely is, entirely ringed by steep heather meadows, rockslides, cliffs, and snowfields. To camp at, it's on the ugly side. When our family finally found a vacant knoll that hadn't been recently used as a toilet, later arrivals kept traipsing through searching for a spot, in desperation cuddling up to us uncomfortably close. The designation of allowable campsites has solved that. Of course, there may be no "allowable" open for you.

So much the better. At the lakeshore take the right fork and climb to the rocky basin of Little Siberia and a 6000-foot knob overlooking Camp Lake, 5650 feet, in a deep, cold little bowl where the sun rarely shines. Campsites become frequent,

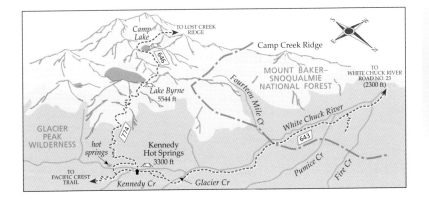

The way proceeds along Lost Creek Ridge, miles of green meadows and open basins and small lakes and big views.

Lake Byrne and Glacier Peak

delightful, and lonesome as the way proceeds along Lost Creek Ridge, miles of green meadows and open basins and small lakes and big views, one of the most memorable highland walks in the Glacier Peak region, 12 miles from Lake Byrne to a trailhead on North Fork Sauk River. However, the trail was built in ancient times when the practice was to build tread through patches of woods but leave travelers to find their own way across meadows. So don't get lost.

34 | BALD EAGLE MOUNTAIN AND DISHPAN GAP

Round trip to Bald Eagle Mountain: 12 miles
Hiking time: 8 hours (day hike)
High point: 5200 feet
Elevation gain: 2800 feet

Loop trip: 31 miles
Hiking time: Allow 3 days
High point: 6000 feet
Elevation gain: 4000 feet

Hikable: late July through September
Maps: Green Trails No. 111 Sloan Peak, No. 143 Monte Cristo, No. 144 Benchmark
Information: Darrington Ranger District (360) 436-1155

Dishpan Gap, at 5600 feet, is the hub of four spectacular trails; each is excellent and gives a unique perspective. Ira, partial to views and flower fields, has chosen the Bald Eagle trail for this book. The serendipity is that despite our ecstatic description in *100 Hikes in the Glacier Peak Region*, it's a lonesome lovely. A day trip can take the hiker to views of Pride Basin and Monte Cristo peaks. A several-day ramble can reward the soul with miles of subalpine trees and meadows on lonesome trails traveled by more deer and marmots than people. A backpacker must

be careful to plan to end each day at a campable ground with water, which is scarce on the high ridges. However, early summer normally has snowbanks which cook up nicely in a pot.

Drive south from Darrington 16 miles on the Mountain Loop Highway and turn left on North Fork Sauk River road No. 49. In 6.7 miles, pass road No. (4900)020 to the abandoned Sloan Creek Campground and the North Fork Sauk River trailhead, the end of the recommended loop trip. Drive another 2.5 miles to a junction and horse ramp and go right 0.5 mile more to the road-end

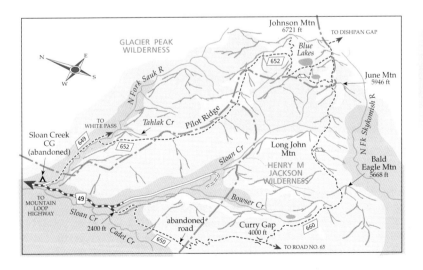

A several-day ramble can reward the soul with miles of subalpine trees and meadows on lonesome trails.

at Sloan Creek, the beginning of Bald Eagle Mountain trail No. 650, elevation 2400 feet, the start of the loop trip. If the loop is planned, unload packs here and park the car back near the trailhead, where you'll be coming out.

Walk 2½ miles on a road converted to trail. Enter forest on true trail and climb another sometimes muddy 1½ miles to Curry Gap, 4000 feet, and a junction with the Quartz Creek trail. Go left on Bald Eagle trail No. 660, climbing to the 5200-foot level of 5668-foot Bald Eagle Mountain, the turnaround for day hikers. Dig out the lunch stuff and soak in the views of Pride Basin and the glaciers on the north sides of Kyes, Monte Cristo, and Cadet Peaks.

For Dishpan Gap, pick up your pack and begin the ups and downs, past Long John Camp (often dry) at 8 miles from the road and Spring Camp (the first for-sure water) at 9 miles. The trail then climbs within a few yards of the crest of 5946-foot June Mountain. Be sure to take the short sidetrip to the summit for views of Sloan Peak, Monte Cristo, Glacier Peak, and valley forests. The tread on the north side of June Mountain may be covered by steep, hard snow. Take care.

At 12½ miles is a junction. The right fork proceeds 3 miles to Dishpan Gap, the Pacific Crest Trail, and the flower fields above Meander Meadows. The left fork is the looper, trail No. 652, which drops 500 feet to Upper Blue Lake at 5500 feet, usually frozen until mid-August; the best camps are near here. The trail then climbs 500 feet onto Pilot Ridge for more miles of some of the finest ridge-walking in the North Cascades. Finally it drops 3000 feet in an endless series of short, steep switchbacks to a ford and joins North Fork Sauk River trail No. 649, reaching Sloan Creek Campground at 11½ miles from Upper Blue Lake, 2½ miles from your start point.

Flower garden near Dishpan Gap, Sloan Peak in distance

35 | SILVER LAKE–TWIN LAKES

Round trip to Twin Lakes: 17 miles
Hiking time: 12 hours (backpack)
High point: 5400 feet
Elevation gain: 3500 feet in, 1000 feet out
Hikable: July through October
Map: Green Trails No. 111 Sloan Peak, No. 143 Monte Cristo
Information: Darrington Ranger District (360) 436-1155

Three beautiful lakes in the Henry Jackson Wilderness, especially lovely in fall colors. The nearest and easiest, Silver Lake, is tucked in a cirque of cliffs, waterfalls, and meadows. Twin Lakes, 3 grueling miles farther, are twin pools of deep blue beneath the great east face of Columbia Peak.

"The nearest and easiest," Silver Lake, was almost left out of the wilderness. While in Washington City lobbying for the 1984 Washington Wilderness Act, Ira was shown a map of the proposed boundaries of the Henry Jackson Wilderness. He pointed out that before Senator Jackson died he had written about his favorite hike as a boy—Silver Lake. The boundary was slightly expanded.

We authors don't want to hear any hikers whimpering about the December 26, 1980, flood that ripped up the road to Monte Cristo and forced them to walk 4 extra miles, each way. The Christmas flood was the best thing that's happened to this valley since the railroad shut down. The 4 miles now free of automobiles are the most scenic valley walk, forest walk, river walk in the area, with many excellent backpacker campsites, a terrific place to introduce little children to a life away from automobiles.

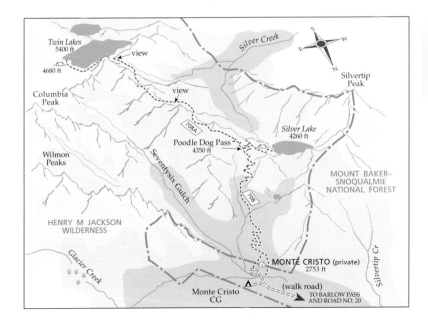

Silver Lake is tucked in a cirque of cliffs, waterfalls, and meadows.

Silver Tip Peak from Twin Lakes trail

Drive the Mountain Loop Highway east about 20 miles from the Verlot Public Service Center to Barlow Pass and park near the gated Monte Cristo road, elevation 2360 feet.

Hike the Monte Cristo road-become-trail 4 delightful miles to a junction. The left fork goes to a campground. Take the right toward Monte Cristo townsite, cross the Sauk River, and in a few feet reach the trailhead, elevation 2753 feet, signed "Silver Lake."

The trail is steep, eroded by water and boots, and cluttered by boulders, giant roots, and stumps from clearcutting on private property. It's only 1½ miles to Silver Lake; expect to spend 2 hours getting there. At 4350 feet the way crosses Poodle Dog Pass. Here the Silver Lake and the Twin Lakes trails separate.

For Silver Lake, go right from the pass ¼ mile to campsites near the shore, 4260 feet. For the best views and picnics cross the outlet and climb open slopes 700 feet to a shoulder of Silvertip Peak. Look down Silver Creek toward Mineral City and beyond Silver Lake to the Monte Cristo peaks. In season, graze blue fruit.

For Twin Lakes, go left on a boot-beaten track that follows an old prospectors' trail. The way is strenuous and rugged, gaining (and partly losing) 1500 feet in 2½ miles. Though the route is well-defined it would be easy to lose in snow, so don't go before August. In the first mile the up-down trail rounds a ridge with views out Silver Creek. After dropping under a cliff, at about 2 miles it climbs to a viewpoint over the deep hole of Seventysix Gulch to Wilmon Spires.

Walk on and scramble along above cliffs. Some 150 feet before the highest point of the ridge, the trail contours right toward an obvious pass and at 2½ miles reaches a viewpoint which is far enough for most hikers, 650 feet above the lakes, which lie at an elevation of 5400 feet. To reach the lakes go right, descending to the obvious pass and following the trail down a wide terrace to the lakes. Make a wrong turn and you're in cliffs.

36 | MOUNT PILCHUCK

Round trip: 4 miles
Hiking time: 4 hours (day hike)
High point: 5340 feet
Elevation gain: 2400 feet
Hikable: July to early November
Map: Green Trails No. 109 Granite Falls
Information: Darrington Ranger District (360) 436-1155

The first "Mount" I (and everyone else in Troop 324) climbed was the peak known in Scoutdom as Upchuck. Years later, under the spell of a book, *Nanga Parbat Adventure*, the more compelling because one of the adventurers, Peter Misch, was now a professor at our own University of Washington, climbing and geologizing our own North Cascades, the Mount was honored for its services to Boy Scouts by the title Nanga Pilchuck. On our way to peaks more relevant to mature alpine aspirations, always we gave a nod when passing dear old Nanga.

Drive the Mountain Loop Highway east 1 mile from the Verlot Public Service Center. Turn right on Mount Pilchuck road No. 42 and continue 6.9 miles to the trailhead, a bit short of the road-end, elevation 3100 feet.

This road, built to serve a phantasmal ski area promoted by fanatics and politicians who didn't bother to check out the long-term records of snow (skiable) accumulation, destroyed more than half the challenge of the Nanga. Troop 324 was already pooped when we had hauled our packs this far from the trailhead beside the Stillaguamish River, not many feet above sea level. What (temporarily) became the ski lodge area was known as Cedar Flats, and I recall our patrols shivering out of the rain into a big barnlike log cabin and weeping as we tried to learn to fry pancakes over billows of cold smoke.

The good news is that the upper half of the challenge remains pretty much as in days of yore. The trail sets out in a gorgeous relict of ancient forest, and though the mood is chilled by skirting the edge of a 1977 clearcut (have they, in the end, no shame?) and crossing the top of the joke of a tow hill, stripped naked for the sake of a miserable little yo-yo run, spirits are

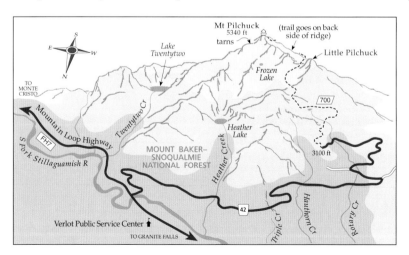

The views are unique because Pilchuck stands at the exact west edge of the high Cascades.

Lookout on top of Mount Pilchuck

restored while rounding Little Pilchuck and climbing heather and ice-polished slabs to a saddle. An infamous shortcut tempts the foolish directly up the rock-blocky ridge. The safe and sane trail drops under a cliff and switchbacks ½ mile to the summit.

The views are unique because Pilchuck stands at the exact west edge of the high Cascades, farms and towns and cities of lowland civilization underfoot in one direction, mountain wilderness at arm's length in the other. A serendipity is the fire lookout cabin, restored in 1989 by the Everett Mountaineers as a museum.

A climbing buddy of mine, in summers before beginning his advance to the magnificence of a deanship at the University of Washington, manned the lookout. Sunshine on Sunday always made him sad because he knew he'd be all day Monday and through the night to Tuesday searching for adventurers who had gone exploring to Frozen Lake, in the cirque below the summit, and the charming tarns along the ridge to the east. Adventurers still get lost, and stumble and tumble on the rocks, and body-toboggan down snow, but now it's Mountain Rescue and the helicopters that do the searching.

37 | MOUNT DICKERMAN

Round trip: 8½ miles
Hiking time: 8–9 hours (day hike)
High point: 5723 feet
Elevation gain: 3900 feet
Hikable: late July through October
Map: Green Trails No. 111 Sloan Peak
Information: Darrington Ranger District (360) 436-1155

All too few trails remain outside wilderness areas and national parks that begin in valley bottoms and climb unmarred forests to meadows. Probing the snow line on Dickerman in spring shapes up the muscles for summer; warms up a person, too, but the complete experience of life zones from low to high is worth every drop of sweat. The summit views are the frosting on the cake. Did somebody say "blueberries"?

Drive the Mountain Loop Highway east 16.6 miles from the Verlot Public Service Center to about 2.5 miles beyond Big Four Picnic Area, to a

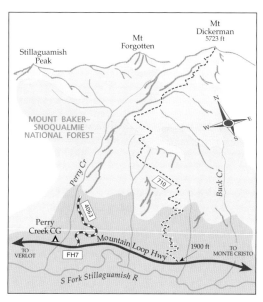

Paintbrush and phlox

small parking area and easily overlooked trail sign, elevation 1900 feet.

Trail No. 710 doesn't fool around. Switchbacks commence instantly, up and up and up through lovely cool forest, the tread varying from loose rocks to a smooth carpet but always steep. Tantalizing glimpses give promise of the scenery above. A bit past 2 miles lower-elevation trees yield to Alaska cedars and subalpine firs. Then the forest thins as the trail traverses under towering cliffs to flatter terrain. Near here, in a sheltered hollow to the west, is a snowmelt lakelet; the path to it is unmarked and faint.

The next ½ mile ranks among the most famous blueberry patches in the Cascades; in late

Big Four Mountain from Mount Dickerman trail

summer, grazing hikers may find progress very slow indeed. In the fall, photographers find the blazing colors equally obstructive. Now, too, the horizons grow.

The final mile is somewhat steeper, switchbacking meadows to the broad summit, as friendly a sackout spot as one can find. Abrupt cliffs drop toward Perry Creek forests, far below. Beyond are the green slopes of Stillaguamish Peak and Mount Forgotten. To the east rise Glacier Peak, the horn of Sloan Peak, and Monte Cristo. Across the South Fork Stillaguamiah River are rugged Big Four Mountain and the striking rock slabs of Vesper Peak.

A funny thing happened to Pat and Ira late one September. At timberline they caught up with a group from some outdoor club, obviously novices who had read a textbook (not my *One Step at a Time*, obviously) and learned everything but common sense. The day was very warm in spite of a sprinkling of snow yet everyone was wearing all the clothes they had, sweating like pigs in their heavy wool pants and down parkas. As Pat and Ira breezed by in shorts and light shirts, they got dirty looks and were lectured for wearing so dangerously little. The summit wind was freezing and the Springs quickly donned dry warm clothing. In half an hour the novices arrived, sweat-soaked and with nothing dry to wear, and so quickly did their wet clothes freeze they had to retreat with only a glance at the view.

38 | BLANCA LAKE

Round trip: 8 miles
Hiking time: 6–8 hours (day hike or backpack)
High point: 4600 feet
Elevation gain: 2700 feet in, 600 feet out
Hikable: July through October
Map: Green Trails No. 143 Monte Cristo
Information: Skykomish Ranger District (360) 677-2414

The rugged cliffs of Columbia, Monte Cristo, and Kyes Peaks above, the white mass of the Columbia Glacier in the upper trough, and the deep waters of ice-fed Blanca Lake filling the lower cirque make this a formidably popular day hike. Not so for backpacking—though new campsites have been hewn in the outlet area, the space is still too cramped to be recommended.

Drive US 2 to the Index junction and turn left on the North Fork Skykomish River road and continue for 15 miles. Just before crossing the North Fork is a four-way junction; turn left and go 2 miles on road No. 63 to the Blanca Lake trailhead sign and parking area, elevation 1900 feet.

Trail No. 1052 immediately gets down to the business of grinding out elevation, relentlessly switchbacking. At 3 miles the way reaches the ridge top at 4600 feet, the highest point of the trip, and enters the Henry M. Jackson Wilderness. In a few hundred yards is shallow little Virgin Lake, amid meadows and trees of a saddle on the very crest.

On a not-so-fine spring day Betty and I and friend Yorick came to this tiny "lake," identifiable as such because the snow was flat. We had no clue as to how the unseen trail got from here to Blanca. Betty sat under the tarp we'd rigged on a knoll. In a dense forest Yorick and I scouted for boot tracks in the snow to solve the puzzle. Lo! We came upon tracks so fresh the boots must be close by. We speeded up to catch them. They were joined by more fresh tracks! Was it a party? We invited ourselves. Still *more* tracks! Some sort of jamboree? Along about then the wires in my head connected and I gave Yorick such a look that he thought I'd gone suddenly stark staring mad. I told him what we'd been doing and his wires connected and *he* got such a look. When we returned rather sullenly to camp, Betty said we were out of sight the whole time but she had heard us chattering—around and around the knoll.

On a subsequent trip I and companions puzzled out where the trail would be when

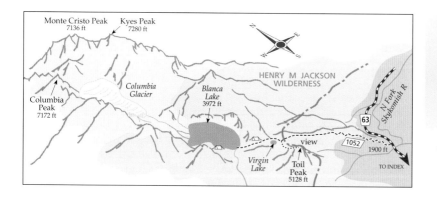

The best part is the braided stream channels and waterfalls and flowers at the head of the lake.

Blanca Lake, Columbia Glacier, and Kyes Peak on right

melted out, sidehilling steeply down in forest 600 feet in 1 mile to the Blanca outlet, 3972 feet. The ¾-mile-long lake was not at its best of wind-ripples and sun-sparkles, this visit also being in spring snow. However, the solid-frozen surface was much easier walking than would have been the rough west shore. But we missed out on the best part, the braided stream channels and waterfalls and flowers at the head of the lake. We did learn that mountain goats are not invariably sure-footed as we'd always supposed, coming upon one which had fallen from a cliff and lay there in the snow stone-cold dead. We were attracted by the "silver saddle"

between Columbia and Monte Cristo but didn't have time for both that and an ascent of Kyes.

Returning from the summit in twilight, we were treated to an awesome display of ice worms, which come to the surface only at night or on very dark days. Kyes (I prefer the older name of Goblin) is not a tough climb, but it is a climb. Hikers can be well content with the spectacular views from 5128-foot Toil Peak, the first of two wooded bumps between Virgin Lake and Troublesome Mountain. On the highest point of the trail above Virgin Lake find a faint path traversing heather meadows southward, climbing, at times steeply, to the summit.

39 | A Peach, a Pear, & a Topping (Meadow Creek Trail)

Round trip to Pear Lake: 16 miles
Hiking time: Allow 2 days
High point: 5200 feet
Elevation gain: 3200 feet in, 600 feet out
Hikable: July through October
Map: Green Trails No. 144 Benchmark
Information: Skykomish Ranger District (360) 677-2414

Tiling's monkeyflower (alpine yellow mimulus)

Savor flower and heather gardens ringing three alpine lakes and a spatter of ponds along the Pacific Crest Trail. And if all these sweet things seem to call for whipped cream, do as Ira did, stroll to a peak for the panorama of valleys and mountains.

To approach from the east, drive road No. 6701 from the Little Wenatchee River road (see Hike 41) and at 4 miles past the junction with road No. (6701)400 find Top Lake trail No. 1606. From the more popular west, drive US 2 to Skykomish and just east of town turn north on Beckler River road No. 65. At 7 miles turn right and go 4 more miles on Rapid River road No. 6530 to Meadow Creek trail No. 1057, elevation 2100 feet.

Beginning amid the ravages of the 1967 Evergreen Mountain fire and subsequent salvage logging, resulting in a mixture of silver snags

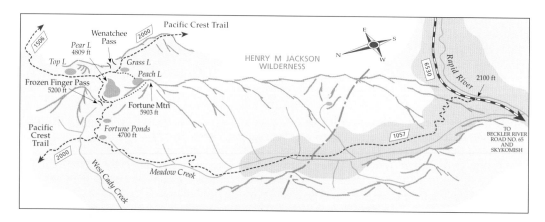

and saplings, the trail gains almost 1000 feet switchbacking out of the Rapid River valley. At about 1½ miles the burn is left, forest entered, and the grade moderates and contours into Meadow Creek drainage; cross the creek at 3 miles by hopping boulders (there aren't really enough). At 3¾ miles recross the creek and climb steeply into West Cady Creek drainage. At 6½ miles reach the lower of the two Fortune Ponds, 4700 feet, and an intersection with the Pacific Crest Trail.

Walk the Crest Trail south 1¼ miles, cross 5200-foot Frozen Finger Pass between West Cady Creek and the Rapid River, and drop to Pear Lake, 4809 feet, 8 miles from the car. Do not camp within 200 feet of the shores here or at Fortune Ponds. The meadows are so fragile, and so damaged, you really ought to sling a hammock in the trees.

Peach Lake, at the same elevation over the ridge to the south, is best reached by contouring off-trail around the ridge-end and below cliffs, passing narrow Grass Lake. Top Lake is attained via ½ mile more on the Crest Trail and another ½ mile on trail No. 1506. For the promised land of views, leave the trail at Fortune Ponds and ascend Fortune Mountain, 5903 feet.

Fortune Pond

40 | ROCK MOUNTAIN

Round trip: 9 miles
Hiking time: 6 hours (day hike or backpack)
High point: 6852 feet
Elevation gain: 3350 feet
Hikable: mid-July through October
Map: Green Trails No. 145 Wenatchee Lake
Information: Lake Wenatchee Ranger District (509) 763-3103

Forests, meadows, and switchbacks ascending to a skywalk along a tightrope of a ridge crest to the summit of Rock Mountain. Driving the highway east from Stevens Pass, often I've looked up there and wondered why Nason Ridge failed to make the cut for the Washington Wilderness Act of 1984. Two reasons, I'd guess. The multiple-use conspiracy always blurts a kneejerk "No" on constitutional principle, even though here and in many other wilderness-candidate areas they have no clue as to how to make an honest or dishonest buck exploiting the land. The other side of the coin is that too many hikers have been like me, looked up there and kept on driving and did nothing about it—until Ira came along and walked all the trails and wrote them up for our guidebooks. I truly believe a head of steam is building, powered by feet. Next

time, Washington Wilderness Act II, I predict it will be "Yea" for our side.

Two trails climb Rock Mountain. Masochists striving to purify their souls choose the south slope, where 95 switchbacks toil up the sun-blasted mountain stripped to the bones by fire and avalanche, and the only water is from chewing a few thousand of the flies which kamikaze into your gasping mouth. Okay for the young and stubborn or old and ornery. Me, I prefer the north, starting 900 feet higher and in cool forest shade when the other trail is so hot you can hear the ants sizzling.

Drive US 2 east 4 miles from Stevens Pass and turn left on Smith Brook road No. 6700. Cross Rainy Pass and about 5 miles from the highway, at a major switchback, go straight ahead on road No. 6705 another 3.6 miles to a crossing of Snowy

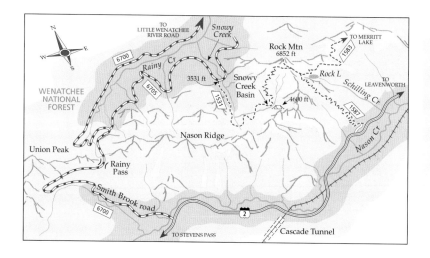

On the south-slope trail is cold little Rock Lake, set in blueberries and heather and snow bits and creeklets that implore you to come down and be happy.

Trail near the summit of Rock Mountain

Creek and the trailhead, elevation 3531 feet.

Snowy Creek trail No. 1531 heads into magnificent old-growth forest. At 2 long miles, 4600 feet, is a fine campsite in upper Snowy Creek Basin, a large meadow flat enclosed by a horseshoe of cliffy peaks. Tread vanishes in the meadow, then reappears halfway across, on the left. The next 2 miles (steep and dry) enter trees, leave them for flower fields, and gain 2000 feet to the summit ridge of Rock Mountain. Here is a junction with the Nason Ridge–Rock Mountain trail. Go left on the crest to the lookout site atop Rock Mountain, 6852 feet, and views south across the valley to the massive high bulk of the Chiwaukum Mountains and to the tip of Mount Rainier, rising above Mount Daniel, and north to Sloan Peak and Glacier Peak.

I've got to admit to being of two minds about the choice of trails, because on the south-slope trail 1000 feet below the summit is cold little Rock Lake, set in blueberries and heather and snow bits and creeklets that implore you to come down and be happy. Next trip I've just got to do that: allow an extra day to descend the steep mile of trail, stir up a pot of Kool-Aid, and carry it into the shade of a Christmas tree to read *The Rubaiyat* or the *Collected Zippy* aloud to my puppy dog.

41 | MEANDER MEADOW–KODAK PEAK–WHITE PASS

Round trip to Kodak Peak: 16 miles
Hiking time: 9 hours (day hike or backpack)
High point: 6121 feet
Elevation gain: 3100 feet

Round trip to White Pass: 24 miles
Hiking time: Allow 2–3 days
High point: 6121 feet
Elevation gain: 3600 feet in, 500 feet out

Hikable: July to October
Maps: Green Trails No. 144 Benchmark, No. 112 Glacier Peak
Information: Lake Wenatchee Ranger District (509) 763-3103

Perhaps the easiest way in the Lake Wenatchee area to sample the high country. A forest-and-meadow valley floor, a steep-and-hot struggle, and finally a superb little basin of grass and flowers and slow deep meanders of the headwaters stream. Above lie parklands of the Cascade Crest and endless wandering, views to everywhere.

Pacific Crest National Scenic Trail near White Mountain

Drive US 2 east from Stevens Pass for 19 miles and turn left toward Lake Wenatchee. Pass the state park, cross the Wenatchee River bridge, and go left to the Lake Wenatchee Ranger Station. From the ranger station drive 1.8 miles, then go left for 14.8 miles on Little Wenatchee River road No. 65 to its end at the Little Wenatchee Ford Campground and trailhead, elevation 3000 feet, and find Little Wenatchee River trail No. 1525.

The first 4 miles (in ¼ mile passing the Poe Mountain trail junction) are gently up and down for a net gain of only 700 feet, alternating between forest and glade and frequent stream crossings, to the edge of a vast meadow; here are a small creek and a campsite and the end of easy. The next 2 miles, gaining 1300 feet, require courage and fortitude in the heat of the afternoon sun in fly season. The way climbs grass and brush through sometimes-soggy greenery where at times the tread is hard to follow. Once above the meadow, in a mix of trees and avalanche paths, the tread is distinct but steep. Fortunately, as the flies grow angrier the views grow bigger. At 6 miles the trail drops a short bit to the basin of Meander Meadow, 5000 feet; the camps are splendid.

The trail crosses a meandering fragment of the Little Wenatchee River (which during one flurry of fly time held the entire Manning family and dog, Tasha, too, for a whole afternoon, just the tips of our noses exposed) and climbs another open mile and 500 more feet to the ridge crest and the Pacific Crest Trail. Flower stroll either way, south to Dishpan Gap or north toward Glacier Peak.

The junction with the Crest Trail gives the first view of Glacier Peak and marks the boundary of the Glacier Peak Wilderness. North ½ mile is a 5630-foot saddle on the east ridge of Kodak Peak. Climb a boot-beaten path through blossoms another ½ mile to the 6121-foot summit and start cranking film through the Kodak (no fair using a Nikon or Canon; if no Kodak, take your pictures elsewhere).

For more flowers, follow the Crest Trail northward, descend across a gorgeous alpine basin and down forest to mostly wooded Indian Pass, 5000 feet, so-so campsites, but usually no

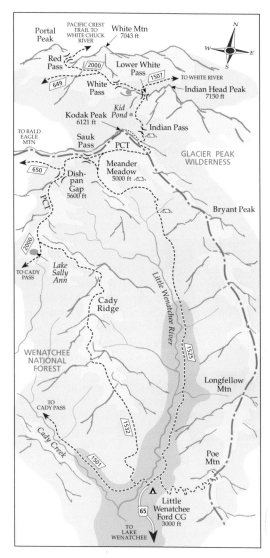

water except in early summer. Climb forest and gardens around the side of Indian Head Peak to tiny Kid Pond and beyond to 5378-foot (Lower) White Pass and a junction with the White River trail. The next 1½ miles have the climax meadows; go past Reflection Pond into flower fields culminating at 5904-foot White Pass. For dramatic views of Glacier Peak and the White Chuck Glacier walk the Crest Trail west another 1½ miles to Red Pass.

42 | LITTLE GIANT PASS

Round trip to the pass: 9½ miles
Hiking time: 9 hours (day hike or backpack)
High point: 6409 feet
Elevation gain: 4200 feet in, 300 feet out
Hikable: early August through September
Map: Green Trails No. 113 Holden
Information: Lake Wenatchee Ranger District (509) 763-3103

When Ira reached the top of Little Giant Pass, he wondered if this was "Little," what was "Big" like? He was fortunate to do the trail before the bridge over the Chiwawa River to the trailhead was lost. I came afterwards, and must say the thigh-deep wade was very refreshing. We nevertheless might have been willing to forego the pleasure, but were on the last day of a weeklong loop from Trinity to Buck Creek Pass to High Pass to Napeequa, and it was too far to retrace all that with the road just beyond the refreshing Chiwawa.

This is a climb to the famous view of the fabled Napeequa valley made famous as "Shangri La" by John Warth in a 1960s newspaper article he wrote while working as a summertime forest guard. Look down to the silvery river meandering through green meadows of the filled-in Pleistocene lakebed. See the gleaming relicts of the Little Ice Age on Clark Mountain and Tenpeak, glimpse a piece of Glacier Peak. But you gotta really want it. Strong mountaineers turn pale at memories of Little Giant in fly time. However, this route to Napeequa valley, though more grueling than the Boulder Pass entry, is 5 miles shorter, and that other entry has a sometimes fearsome and never trivial ford of the Napeequa River. At least on the Little Giant Pass route the ford is for most parties (though it wasn't for ours) at the beginning, so you get the bad news in time to choose another destination should a logjam be missing and the flood be boiling halfway up your Kelty.

Drive US 2 between Stevens Pass and Leavenworth and turn north on the Lake Wenatchee road. Cross the Wenatchee River

bridge and go straight ahead on the Chiwawa Loop road (county road No. 22). In 1.4 miles turn left on the Chiwawa River road and go about 19 miles to Little Giant Pass trailhead No. 1518, elevation 2600 feet.

Longingly inspect remains of the bridge taken out by a flood in 1972. Look around for a logjam. Finding nothing, try the wade, if fairly sure you can survive it, and if you do, follow abandoned roads through abandoned Maple Creek Campground toward the mountainside, and pretty soon pick up the trail. The straight-up sheep driveway of evil reputation has been partly replaced (the sheep are long gone from

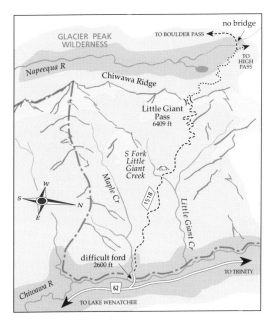

Napeequa Valley

here, too) by a trail that was nicely engineered, if steep, but is deteriorating rapidly from lack of maintenance. The way climbs the valley of Maple Creek in pretty pine forest, crosses a saddle, and drops to South Fork Little Giant Creek at about 2½ miles from the river, 4000 feet. Camps on both sides.

Now the way steepens and at 3 miles half-scrambles up a broad rib of bare schist that splits the valley in two and on a sunny day will fry your boots. But in ⅓ mile creeks begin. So do camps that get progressively better, the last on a scenic meadow knoll at 4 miles. A lovely ascent in greenery and marmots leads to the 6409-foot pass, 4⅔ miles from the river.

The trail down to the Napeequa has been abandoned for years, yet suffices for hikers—but not for horses or sheep, and bleached bones prove it. Watch your step—at spots a misstep could add you to the casualty list. The distance

to the 4200-foot valley floor is 2 miles, and if the views don't have you raving, the blossoms will. The abandoned trail proceeds upvalley 1⅓ miles to the site of the bridge that is gone and the ford that remains to cross the river to the Boulder Pass trail. The best camps hereabouts are on gravel bars—but watch out for sudden high water on hot afternoons.

You won't want to go down to the river from Little Giant Pass unless you've allowed plenty of time for explorations. Follow the trail up the wide, green valley floor 5 or 6 miles; good camps are numerous. In ½ mile look to glaciers on Clark Mountain. In 2 miles pass under the falls of Louis Creek. Wander on and on, higher and higher, better and better to moraines and creeks of Napeequa Basin, a deep hole half-ringed by dazzling glaciers, one of which, when I was last there, tumbled nearly to the basin floor.

43 | SPIDER GAP–BUCK CREEK PASS LOOP

Loop trip (including Image Lake): 44 miles
Hiking time: Allow 4–7 days
High point: 7100 feet
Elevation gain: 7200 feet
Hikable: late July to late September
Map: Green Trails No. 113 Holden
Information: Lake Wenatchee Ranger District (509) 763-3103; Chelan Ranger
District (509) 682-2576; and Darrington Ranger District (360) 436-1155

Valley-bottom forests and meadows, ridge-crest meadows, tumbling streams, quiet lakes, crags and glaciers—the supreme omnibus sampler of Glacier Peak Wilderness trails. Little wonder it's Ira's favorite. Don't you dare so much as think about doing it as a cock-a-doodle-doo marathon. The flowers! The sunsets! The blueberries! Take your time. Learn the difference between getting there and being there. Experience the nights that bind together the days; choice campsites abound.

The loop can be done in either direction. However, because the snowfield at Spider Gap may be unreasonably dangerous, counterclockwise is recommended to keep open a safe line of retreat if the party would rather live than be unreasonable.

Drive the Chiwawa River road some 22.5 miles from the Chiwawa Loop road (see Hike 42, Little Giant Pass), then go uphill on Phelps Creek road No. 6211 another 2.5 miles to a gate and trailhead, elevation 3500 feet.

Walk past the locked gate on Phelps Creek trail No. 1511 to the Glacier Peak Wilderness at 2¾ miles and at 5 miles to Spider Meadow. For a day trip or overnight, this broad valley-bottom meadow in a seeming cul-de-sac amid rugged peaks is a trip in itself. However, when the trail splits, at 6¼ miles, the loop calls. The left fork amazingly escapes the trap, breaks through the cliffs into a hanging trough with a little "glacier" and climbs over 7100-foot Spider Gap, the highest point of the trip.

From the gap, an unmaintained path, often buried in snow, descends to Upper Lyman Lakes. If the snow is hard and no safe detour is

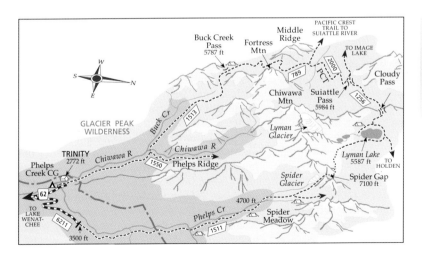

Experience the nights that bind together the days; choice campsites abound.

Lyman Glacier and Upper Lyman Lake

apparent, *turn back* and choose another trip. Your family and friends will thank you, Mountain Rescue will thank you. The three Upper Lyman Lakes are fed by the Lyman Glacier. The unmaintained path drops to forest and Lyman Lake, 5587 feet, some 13 miles from the Phelps Creek gate.

The next stage of the loop climbs to meadows of Cloudy Pass, 6438 feet, and at 2½ miles from Lyman Lake joins the Pacific Crest Trail at Suiattle Pass, 5984 feet. Glacier Peak will pop your eyes here, and keep them popping as the trip proceeds. A scant 2½ mile from the pass the Crest Trail comes to a junction where the loop goes left—but a sidetrip to the right is mandatory, a 7-mile round trip to Image Lake.

Back on the loop, follow the Crest Trail a long 1½ miles and turn left on trail No. 789, dropping to a crossing of Miners Creek. Having lost 1000 feet to get down in this forest hole, gain it all back climbing to meadows of Middle Ridge— and there's Glacier Peak again, right smack in the kisser. Descend a bit again, to Small Creek, and climb a bit again, past Flower Dome (yes, Glacier Peak once more, bigger than ever) to Buck Creek Pass, 5787 feet.

More sidetrips, a final goodbye to Glacier Peak, and the loop concludes in a 9½-mile descent to Trinity and (sob!) a 2½-mile road walk up Phelps Creek road to the car.

44 | MAD LAKE

Round trip from Maverick Saddle: 16 miles
Hiking time: Allow 2 days
High point: 5800 feet
Elevation gain: 1660 feet
Hikable: July to mid-October
Map: Green Trails No. 146 Plain
Information: Entiat Ranger District (509) 784-1511

When Ira sees what the Forest Service has done here, he finds the name most appropriate—Mad. That also is how he feels—upset! angry! MAD!

The Mad River country of the Entiat Mountains offers miles and miles of easy, pleasant, family-style roaming. Trails follow happy creeks through picturesque glades, trails cross broad meadows of flowers, trails round shores of little lakes, and trails climb mountains—a wealth of fun and peace for a weekend or a week-long vacation to be enjoyed by old and very young alike. But the Forest Service—stark staring mad—has dedicated the trails to motorcycles and is reconstructing and relocating routes to permit higher (noisier) speeds, deliberately converting trails ideal for the easy hiker to runways for the rough rider. That's the bad (dreadful) news. The little bit of good news is: wheels (and

horses too) are banned until the trails dry out, generally around July 15, leaving a small window between enough melting of snow to permit hiking and the roaring onslaught of motors.

It was here in 1980 that Ira first learned our state's tax dollars were paying for "improving" good trails into motorcycle roads. Because we revealed in our guidebook what was going on, for ten years all volumes in the *100 Hikes* series were banned from Forest Service shelves.

Drive US 2 to Coles Corner, between Leavenworth and Stevens Pass, and turn north, passing Lake Wenatchee State Park. Just beyond the Wenatchee River bridge go straight ahead on Chiwawa Loop Road. At 4.2 miles from US 2, just beyond the Thousand Trails sports facilities, and 0.4 mile past the Chiwawa River bridge, turn a sharp left on (unsigned) road No.

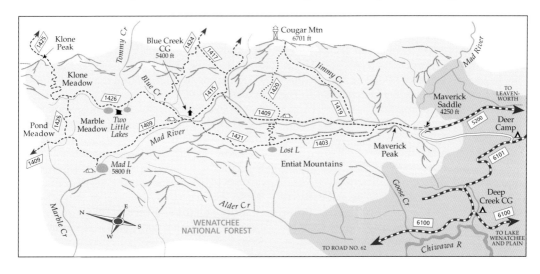

Mad Lake

6100. In another 1.5 miles, at Deep Creek Campground, go right on road No. 6101, signed "Maverick Saddle." At the first Y, 0.4 mile from Deep Creek, stay straight ahead. At 2.7 miles turn left at (primitive) Deer Campground. After a final steep and narrow (extremely scenic) 2.8 miles only a 4 x 4 could love is Maverick Saddle, 5.5 miles from Deep Creek. To the left a road drops 0.3 mile, to intersect Mad River trail No. 1409, elevation 4250 feet.

Upriver is your way to go. In 1 mile cross a bridge over the Mad River wide enough for a pair of motorcycles to race across side by side. At 3½ miles cross the Mad River. (Is there a log? Lucky you! During the "window" time I found it more than what Ira had told me was a "pretty creek." The wading was pretty dang invigorating.) At 4½ miles recross. At 5 miles is a broad meadow and at 5½ miles, 5400 feet, Blue Creek Campground, a splendid base for ramblings.

The guard station located here is the last remains of the Mad River Dude Ranch, popular in the late 1920s. The cookhouse stood near the present campground. The blacksmith shop and other buildings were scattered about.

The first ramble, of course, is to continue on the Mad River trail through a series of meadows. At 2 miles from Blue Creek Campground (8 miles from the road) go left a scant ¼ mile to Mad Lake, 5800 feet. On the west shore are excellent camps. As is true of most lakes hereabouts, this one is so silted-in that the bottom is too mucky for wading. However, the inlet stream has deposited enough sand to make a semi-solid beach suitable for cooling the feet.

The Forest Service map shows more trails. Loop yourself silly. And Mad enough to write letters! At Whistling Pig Meadow is an old hunters' cabin. The lookout site on Klone Peak has wide views.

45 | ICE LAKES

Round trip to Lower Ice Lake: 28 miles
Hiking time: Allow 3–5 days
High point (knoll above lower lake): 6900 feet
Elevation gain: 4200 feet
Hikable: August through September
Maps: Green Trails No. 114 Lucerne, No. 113 Holden
Information: Entiat Ranger District (509) 784-1511

Arriving at the two high lakes in cirques under cliffs of 9082-foot Mount Maude, I felt out of costume. Should have been wearing the Queen's red coat and one of those cute topees favored by officers of the Bengal Lancers on the Northwest Frontier. Yes, for movie purposes the scene would double very well for Khyber Pass. As for Maude, my first time to the top was in a fog so thick and the ridge so interminable that I kept looking for shining figures all in white, flapping huge wings and plucking harps. (Next time the sun was shining but I scarcely noticed the view, my eyes riveted on the incomparable show of those high-altitude flowers never seen in "alpine" meadows which really are merely subalpine.)

From Entiat on the Columbia River drive the

Entiat River road 38 miles to its end, 0.4 mile beyond Cottonwood Camp, elevation 3144 feet.

Hike Entiat River trail No. 1400 to a split at 8¼ miles, 4300 feet. I cannot omit brief mention of the right fork, going 7 miles from the split to the fade-out of tread in the fields of heather and flowers at 5500 feet in the miles-long Entiat Meadows, heading in cliffs of the huge cirque scooped from the mountain mass of Fernow, Seven-Fingered Jack, and Maude. The Elderly Birdwatchers Hiking and Griping Society combined the two splendid destinations, crossing over the ridge between them (easy and safe if you are properly equipped and trained, if not don't try it).

The left fork goes a short bit to a camp and

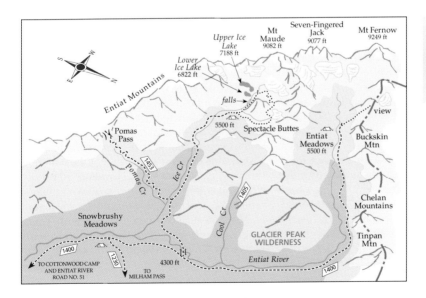

Follow the waters up to Ice Lake, beautifully cold and desolate.

Waterfall on Ice Creek near Ice Lakes

maybe (or maybe not—one strategy to enhance backcountry solitude is to utilize rushing rivers) a bridge. The way beyond the river climbs gradually in forest the first mile, then drops 400 feet to Ice Creek and begins alternating between meadows and clumps of little alpine trees. At about 3 miles is a crossing of Ice Creek; be prepared to wade. In another mile is another crossing; perhaps step over on rocks. At some 4½ miles from the Entiat trail, formal tread ends at a delightful meadow campsite, 5500 feet. The creek burble drowns the babble of a pretty waterfall tumbling from Upper Ice Lake.

A meager path follows the rocky meadow north to the valley head, passing the waterfall. Generally keep right of the creek, but cross to the left when the going looks easier there. The valley ends in a steep, green hillside; above, in hanging cirques, lie the lakes. From a starting point to the right of the creek, scramble up game traces, crossing the creek and climbing between cliffs to its left. The way emerges onto a rocky knoll 100 feet above 6822-foot Lower Ice Lake, 6 miles from the Entiat trail. Camp only at designated sites on pumice barrens, not the fragile heather.

Upper Ice Lake is a mile farther. Head southwest in a shallow alpine valley, below cliffs, to the outlet stream and follow the waters up to the 7188-foot lake, beautifully cold and desolate. Mount Maude cliffs are impressive; the safe and easy way around and through them has tricks to pull on innocent hikers and is best left to Elderly Birdwatchers who used to be doughty climbers.

46 | AGNES CREEK–LYMAN LAKE LOOP

Loop trip: 43 miles
Hiking time: Allow 5–9 days
High point: 6438 feet
Elevation gain: 4900 feet
Hikable: mid-July through September
Maps: Green Trails No. 82 Stehekin, No. 81 McGregor Mtn., No. 113 Holden
Information: Chelan Ranger District (509) 682-2576

Cloudy Pass is the high point of what experts hail as one of the classic loopers of the North Cascades, which in our expert opinion means, of anywhere, especially with the stupendous sidetrips thrown in. My main memory, though, is not the peaks and the flowers, but scurrying across the summit of the pass, head bent to evade the attention of the end-of-the-world blackness hanging heavy heavy above. Making breakfast in camp at Upper Lyman Lakes (we were doing the other classic loop of the neighborhood, from and to Trinity), we'd dodged

under the tarp during a brief crackle-boom and downpour, but the sky was blueing when we hoisted packs. By the time we descended to Lyman Lake the blue was graying and had we been more familiar with Mother Nature's electrical circuitry east of the Cascade Crest we'd have recognized our breakfast tempest as a squall-line advance agent of a Columbia Plateau three-ringer. The lesson was learned in the blackening; for a moment I stood in the famous Great White Light outside time, supposing we had for sure been struck dead. A miss is as good

Lyman Lake and Chiwawa Mountain from Cloudy Pass

as a mile. Not to worry about losing out on the scenery; I've seen Ira's pictures.

The loop entails interestingly complex transportation to and from trailheads. For the counterclockwise direction described here, the *Lady of the Lake* does the drop-off at Stehekin (see Hike 27, Horseshoe Basin, and Hike 26, Chelan Lakeshore Trail) where the Park Service bus takes you up the Stehekin River road, and also the pick-up at Lucerne, after you've ridden the Lucerne Resort bus 12 miles down Railroad Creek to the lake. The trip plan must take into account that hikers can't get on the trail until midafternoon the first day and must be off by early afternoon the last day to catch the boat. For the boat-and-buses schedule, call the Forest Service–Park Service Information Center in Seattle or the Chelan Ranger District.

From Stehekin Landing ride the bus 11 miles to High Bridge Ranger Station. About 500 feet beyond the bridge, on the left side of the road, is the Agnes Creek trailhead (Pacific Crest Trail No. 2000), elevation 1600 feet.

The trail drops a few feet, crosses Agnes Creek, and commences a long, easy grade in lovely forest with notable groves of cedar.

Glimpses ahead of Agnes Mountain and glaciers on Dome Peak; to the rear, McGregor Mountain. A good stop the first night is Fivemile Camp, 2300 feet. (For the first of the many noble sidetrips, if you can safely ford Agnes Creek—the old bridge is gone—day hike up West Fork Agnes to the monstrous hole at its head.) The valley forest is ever superb, featuring a fine stand of large hemlock and fir near Swamp Creek; another good camp here at 8 miles.

At Hemlock Camp, 12 miles, the trail splits. The new route of the Pacific Crest Trail crosses the river, climbs to high views on the side of the valley, and at 19 miles reaches timberline campsites at a junction, 5600 feet. (Sidetrip right 6 miles to Image Lake by way of 5983-foot Suiattle Pass.) For the loop leave the Crest Trail and climb over 6438-foot Cloudy Pass, 20 miles. (Sidetrip up meadows to 7915-foot Cloudy Peak.) Descend 2 miles to 5587-foot Lyman Lake. (Sidetrip to Upper Lyman Lake and Upper-Upper Lyman Lake.) Finish with 8½ miles down Railroad Creek to the bus stop. Good camps at Lyman Lake, Rebel Camp, and Hart Lake. Ice cream cones at Holden Village.

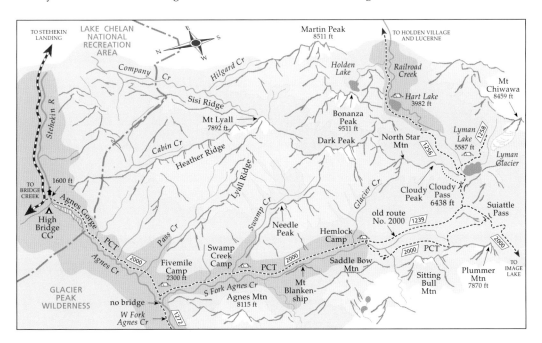

Chapter 3

ALPINE LAKES

To a lover of glaciers the Cascades immediately north of Snoqualmie Pass are rather sad. All those fine big holes in the mountains scooped by ice, and the ice—except mainly on Daniel—now long gone, the vacancies filled with water. Lakes. Big little and medium. Not to sound a sour note, lakes aren't all that the calendars crack them up to be. The water doesn't chortle and bubble as in a stream, it just lays there, ringed by smashed plants and bare dirt because like the summit of a peak, a lake is a "destination." A lake is where you take your picture and catch your fish and pat yourself on the back and start thinking about cheeseburgers and milkshakes.

For me the beauty of a lake is enhanced by distance. When I go to Spectacle Lake, for instance, I don't go *to* the lake, there to join the circus and dig out my iodine tablets because the clowns are swimming in my drinking water. I sit in lordly solitude high above on Spectacle Point and neither see nor hear the splashing contaminators.

Strike out the "Lakes" and the Alpine Wilderness would remain a national treasure. The tameness and fishiness of the waters are plentifully compensated for by the high drama of the Cascade Crest peaks from Lemah to Chimney to Summit Chief to Bears Breast to Daniel, and the Cashmere Crags of the Stuart Range. But strike out those, too, and there would still be . . .

I once met a hiker skipping down a trail in an ecstasy. "A dipper!" she burbled. "I just saw a dipper!" A native of New Jersey, long had she read about and literally dreamed about, but never before seen, John Muir's favorite bird. Another time a fellow from Illinois wouldn't let me by until I'd joined him in admiring the marmot atop a boulder. "It *whistled* at me!" he crowed.

Our "backyard wilderness," we call it, and it is that, just a step from home—though that 70 mph step along Interstate 90 gives a person a frazzlement that demands wilderness therapy, quick. And quick it is, for this is the supreme dominion of the shallow, the day hike, where the masses come for easy green-bonding.

How about the deep? The novice may not be able to find it right off, but a few bonding years in the shallow and he/she will know where to look and will then be ready. Recently I spent a week looping through high country above the Icicle, the valley which is the approach to the cosmos-famed, strictly rationed Enchantments. I saw only three people the entire week, all at the route's single lake, where I took care not to camp. I give you one clue: Big Jim.

Seek "solitude wilderness" and ye shall find, and we veterans of the Good Old Days of the High Lonesome tend to do that. Yet many of us are not shriveling into an old coot's cantankering, are learning to enjoy "sociable wilderness." During a recent week on the Pacific Crest National Scenic Freeway north of Snoqualmie Pass I passed tent cities at the usual spots—and every night spread my sleeping bag where never balloon tent billowed nor candle lantern glowed nor stove whispered nor guitar twanged. On the trail each day I socialized with "my sort," friends if we'd had more time together, from the nation. Because the Alpine Lakes have become not merely our but America's backyard wilderness. You can't really resent a person who has just seen her first dipper dip, heard his first marmot whistle.

Prusik Peak and Gnome Tarn

47 | LAKE SERENE

Round trip: 8 miles
Hiking time: 5 hours (day hike)
High point: 2550 feet
Elevation gain: 2000 feet
Hikable: mid-June to mid-October
Map: Not shown on any map
Information: Skykomish Ranger District (360) 677-2414

To Ira the lake is a jewel of the first order. He can sit there fascinated an hour or two or three photographing the reflection of Mount Index in the blue waters and the changing shadows on the 2000-foot East Face. But because of the walls that impress Ira, when you get there, there's no place to roam, and thus in my opinion the lake has at best modest appeal. Only twice have I hiked it, once upon coming down from the high and dry North Peak of Index, putting mouth to lake, and having to keep squirming forward on my belly

as the lake level fell, and the other time in a winter twilight when avalanches were magnificently dreadful. Whatever, the precipice of Mount Index above and the white ribbon of Bridal Veil Falls below so beguile the eye that the feet are compelled to climb up there to discover what unseen wonder lies between them.

Lake Serene used to be in *100 Hikes* but we dropped it in 1975, when it was decided by Powers Above that the eroded, boot-beaten scramble-path up cliffs, for half a century among the most popular hikes in the Cascades, was too dangerous for the mobs of novices who hadn't bought our guidebook and therefore didn't know what they were getting into.

During the interregnum when not in our books or on anybody's maps, the view from the Stevens Pass Highway continued to draw at least a thousand hikers a year to the awesome cirque and its miserable (my opinion, not Ira's) hole in the ground filled with water. The Powers finally capitulated and now an incredibly engineered trail has been built on slopes so steep that more than a hundred stair steps surmount difficult sections.

Drive US 2 east from Everett past Monroe, Startup, and the first Skykomish River bridge. At milepost 35, immediately before crossing the river the second time, go right on Mount Index (county) Road for 0.3 mile to a large parking area, elevation 600 feet.

Walk the abandoned road 1½ miles and just short of the end find the trail on the left side, leading downward. Within 1000 feet is a junction. The right fork climbs a scant ½ mile to a spectacular view of Bridal Veil Falls.

For the lake, stay straight ahead, losing a

Mount Index towering above Lake Serene

few more feet to a crossing of Bridal Veil Creek on a sturdy bridge. From here the way is up, up, and up as the trail zig-zags under and over cliffs, in occasional views north to the Monte Cristo peaks and down to the granite cliffs of the Index Town Wall. At a long 2 miles from the junction is the lake, 2521 feet.

Lake, cliffs, and brush leave little room for exploring. What's to do? Camping? Forget it. If you're a photographer, click click click. If you're an ex-mountain climber study the Fred Beckey route up the East Face and thank golly you're an ex.

48 | ENCHANTMENT LAKES

Round trip to Lower Enchantment Lakes: 20 miles
Hiking time: Allow 4–6 days
High point: 7000 feet
Elevation gain: 5400 feet
Hikable: late July through mid-October
Map: Green Trails No. 209S The Enchantments
Information: Leavenworth Ranger District (509) 782-1413
Backcountry use permit required

A legendary group of lakes in rock basins over 7000 feet high amid the Cashmere Crags of the Stuart Range. The area was discovered by A. H. Sylvester, U.S. Geological Survey topographer for some thirteen years and then, from 1908 to 1931, supervisor of Wenatchee National Forest. In his years of exploring he placed thousands of names on maps of the West. "Enchantment" expressed his reaction—and that of all who have followed. The one name covered everything until climbers arrived in the late 1940s and began assigning names to "The Crags." Then came Bill

and Peggy Stark, who over many years drew on various mythologies for names befitting the moods and auras they felt. A lake and its sword-like rock peninsula became Lake Viviane and Excalibur Rock. Other lakes and tarns they called Rune, Talisman, Valkyrie, Leprechaun, Naiad, Lorelei, Dryad, Pixie, Gnome, Brisingamen, Brynhild, Reginleif, Sprite, and Titania. And there is Troll Sink (a pond), Valhalla Cirque, Tanglewood, and many more.

Lower Enchantment Basin, at and around 7000 feet, is friendliest. Upper Enchantment

Little Annapurna and Snow Creek Glacier from Gnome Tarn

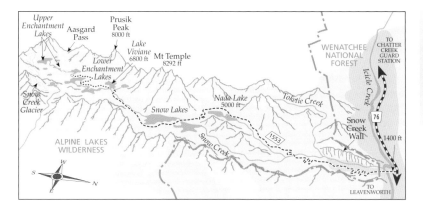

Upper Enchantment Basin is a splendidly raw desolation, the earth not yet fully created.

Basin, at and around 7500 feet, is a splendidly raw desolation, the earth not yet fully created. Some of its lakes are clear and some are rock-milky (jade-colored when the sun hits them right) and some are frozen solid all summer.

When I was here for a September week-plus of sometimes sun, bitter breezes, and snow flurries, the Manning family (including Cailin the Shelty) camped at the Stark's "guest room" below Merlin's Tower, above Excalibur, and roamed to all the Stark places noted above and more—the remnants of the Snow Creek Glacier, the summit of Little Annapurna, Aasgard Pass. That week will forever glow in memory, but I'll never go back. Not because the way is long, steep, and grueling, but because it's a *national* wilderness and I've had my share. And because it seems every American who owns a pair of boots wants his/hers. During our week-plus I tallied the daily population of both basins; it was (in addition to us) an average of a dozen. That seemed a crowd, since several years earlier the ordinary count was less than half that, usually named Stark. Several years later the population explosion was so noisy the Forest Service was forced to structure regulations as strict as any in American wilderness. Horses were excluded. Then dogs. And fires. Most campsites were closed. Parties were limited to six.

Finally came rationing, an absolute lid on the number of visitors, and permits obtained in advance—for the times in heavy demand, months ahead. "Red tape!" grouse the Sons of Freedom. "Bureaucrats!" But without such strict rules, the Enchantments would be as enchanting as Times Square on New Year's Eve. For details on how to apply for a permit, call the Forest Service–Park Service Information Center in Seattle or the Leavenworth Ranger District. If you're thinking of a trip next year, call now.

From US 2 on the west outskirts of Leavenworth, drive south 4 miles on Icicle Creek road and turn left into Snow Lakes trail parking area, elevation 1400 feet.

Snow Lakes trail No. 1553 crosses the river and immediately starts up—and up. At 5½ miles is Nada Lake, 5000 feet, and at 6¾ miles the passage between the Snow Lakes, 5415 feet. Follow the trail winding along the left shore. At the south end cross the inlet stream and proceed up the granite slot of Snow Creek. At 10 miles reach Lake Viviane, 6800 feet.

A concluding personal opinion: In recent years the Aasgard Fraud has been perpetrated. The innocent are suckered in by being told that climbing from Colchuck Lake to Aasgard Pass is "the easy way to the Enchantments." False. The fad-followers, the in-crowd wannabes, deem the Snow Creek approach demeaning, want to go the classy and sassy way, the route of the big kids.

A wilderness-mature adult ascends ritually and respectfully from the picturesque lower basin to the austere upper basin and at last to the cold snows and stern stones of Aasgard. To start with the ice cream and work through the meatballs and potatoes to the soup is not esthetic. Coming to the Enchantments by way of Aasgard is in very bad taste.

49 | LAKE MARY

Round trip to Lake Mary: 20 miles
Hiking time: Allow 3–5 days
High point: 6200 feet
Elevation gain: 3300 feet
Hikable: mid-July through October
Map: Green Trails No. 177 Chiwaukum Mountains
Information: Leavenworth Ranger District (509) 782-1413

If the Enchantments are the granite classic of the Alpine Lakes Wilderness, Snowgrass Mountain is the supreme green. This is the place for dreamlike wanderings along tundra ridges and through lake basins and around corners to magic surprises. But there is a price to pay: a gang of dreamers, hordes of dreamers, wandering everywhere.

From US 2 on the west outskirts of Leavenworth, drive south 17.5 miles on the Icicle Creek road to the edge of Rock Island Campground. Turn left to cross the concrete bridge and follow road No. 7600 for 1.9 miles to the end and Icicle Creek trailhead No. 1551, elevation 2880 feet.

The trail rolls through forest 2 miles to what used to be the start of the Frosty Creek trail, the easy entry to the "Mormon Lakes." Then in 1992 the bridge over the Icicle Creek

canyon collapsed. There, you see, is one method to make wilderness emptier, wilder. The bad news—which of course is also good, in its way—is that an entry has been restored. At 4½ miles up Icicle Creek, at 3000 feet, turn right on (new) Frosty Creek trail No. 1592. At 7½ miles, 4900 feet, emerge into Packrat Basin. At 8 miles a sidetrail drops to woodsy Lake Margaret, 5409 feet. At 9½ miles is Frosty Pass, 5800 feet, and the famous (super) meadows. Where to start?

Maybe not where you think you should. I've been to Lake Mary, 6100 feet, 1½ miles on Icicle Ridge trail No. 1570 from the pass, when no ears but ours were there to hear the gleeful shrieks of our little children. And I've camped under a tarp crowded by four Elderly Birdwatchers while the rain slowly invaded our sleeping bags and underwear, and lo but the country was lonesome.

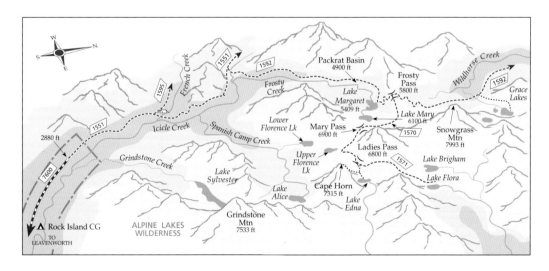

Late August snowstorm near Lake Mary

And, well, to sum up the history of the world and the wilderness, the landscape designer here was a genius, and you must come and admire. But don't count on finding an allowable place to camp.

So climb the garden-wall trail ¾ mile to Mary Pass, 6900 feet, and drop ½ mile to Upper Florence Lake, 6500 feet, with the most scenic camps of all. Probably full-up.

Just 1¼ flowery miles from Mary Pass is Ladies Pass, 6800 feet, above Lake Brigham and Lake Flora in headwaters of Chiwaukum Creek. In another mile, beyond the shoulder of 7315-foot Cape Horn, is Lake Edna, 6735 feet, a cold and rocky tarn.

Yet should all the world come to revere Mother Nature at her loveliest, there still would be peace and solitude. If you're clever. One tip: at Frosty Pass, go the other way. An unsigned, unmaintained trail contours northwest from the pass to an excellent camp and continues sketchily onward—ultimately to Doelle Lakes. The Wildhorse trail sidehills north from the pass, giving off-trail (meadow) access to Grace Lakes. The hottest tip: Fill your water jugs (gallon size) and climb high to the no-trail panorama country and find a hideaway.

You'll want the high panoramas anyway. For example, from Mary Pass ascend a way trail to the 7500-foot ridge of Snowgrass Mountain and views from Cashmere and Stuart to Monte Cristo and Glacier to Index and Baring. We explored several other routes to the ridge, but they're for us to know and you to find out. The several summits of the 4-mile-long mountain, the highest 8000 feet, require climbing experience and equipment, but easy hiking takes a person high enough to feel on top of the world.

NAVAHO PASS

Round trip: 11 miles
Hiking time: 5 hours (day hike or backpack)
High point: 6000 feet
Elevation gain: 3000 feet
Hikable: mid-June through October
Map: Green Trails No. 209 Mount Stuart
Information: Cle Elum Ranger District (509) 674-4411

In July the massed buckwheat blossoms will blind you, in mid-October the yellow leaves of cottonwood and the scarlet of vine maple and the maroon of dogwood, backlighted by a low autumn sun, will rend your heart. In any season the moonwalk across the serpentine barrens will awe and the views over the gulf of Ingalls Creek to the Cashmere Crags inspire. Plentifully Classic, to be sure, but the same can be said about many Teanaway trails. What I find uniquely remarkable here is the procession of conifer communities from low to high, a textbook display.

Drive County Road 970 north 5 miles from Interstate 90 and turn west on the Teanaway River road. Follow "North Fork Teanaway" signs 13.5 miles to a major junction at 29 Pines Campground. Go right for 1.3 miles on road No. 9737, then right on the Stafford Creek road, in 2.5 miles crossing Stafford Creek to Stafford Creek trail No. 1359, elevation 3100 feet.

A sign commands "NO VEHICLES," a restriction necessary to keep scofflaws from invading the *wheelfree* Alpine Lakes Wilderness—into which, indeed, this entire trail ought to be placed. The trail ascends moderately in airy forest of big old Ponderosa pine standing tall above copses of snowbrush and lawns of pinegrass. The next stars are enormous Douglas-fir. Many are more than ancient, are elderly. Many are nearing death, their bark charred, tops silvered or missing, testimony to a lethal crown fire of some recent decade, a blaze that opened up the forest, giving breathing room to young silver fir and lodgepole pine.

The trail swings up and away from the creek into lodgepole and western white pine, western hemlock and silver fir and Engelmann spruce—and still more of the Douglas-fir relics. At 4 miles,

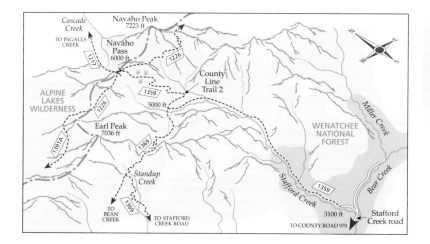

In any season the moonwalk across the serpentine barrens will awe and the views inspire.

Mount Stuart Range from Navaho Pass

5000 feet, Standup Creek trail No. 1369 joins from the left, crossing Stafford Creek from a campsite. A sign points to the right, "County Line Trail 2."

A long switchback ascends in growing down-valley views. Giant firs continue to 5500 feet, their seed-time up here dating to the warmer climate preceding the Little Ice Age. They finally yield to a sparse scattering of spindly-short lodgepole and shrubby subalpine fir in parched meadows. At 5600 feet, something completely different—a squishy-lush meadow-bog! What appears to be the main trail (but is not) veers left to the site of a vanished prospector's cabin by a tasty little creek. Forge straight ahead into treadless meadow and soon spot ducks on the far side.

The way emerges from forest into naked soil a-glitter with blue-green slickensides, one of the largest and finest of the area's many serpentine barrens. Subalpine firs clothe the final short slope to the boundary of the Alpine Lakes Wilderness at Navaho Pass, 5½ miles, 6000 feet— and the coda to the forest symphony, a stand of western larch, a sun of yellow flame in October. (The pass is not signed, nor is the trail down Cascade Creek to Ingalls Creek, nor the County Line Trail west.)

The views across Ingalls Creek to Little Annapurna and McClellan Peak are fine, and the day hiker may be content to snap shots of the Crags and check off the trip as "done." But for me three days are too few. My strategy is to fill a water jug that lets me camp in a private nook up high, saunter from the pass to the east summit of Navaho Peak, 7223 feet, lollygag west on the County Line Trail toward the saddle in a ridge of Earl Peak leading to Hardscrabble Creek and Fourth Creek, and spend a day simply brooding over the barrens.

GALLAGHER HEAD LAKE

Round trip to Gallagher Head Lake: 8 miles
Hiking time: 5 hours (day hike or backpack)
High point: 5600 feet
Elevation gain: 1800 feet
Hikable: late June through October

Loop trip through Esmerelda Basin: 15 miles
Hiking time: 10 hours (day hike or backpack)
High point: 5600 feet
Elevation gain: 3000 feet
Hikable: July through October

Map: Green Trails No. 209 Mount Stuart
Information: Cle Elum Ranger District (509) 674-4411

Idyllic, that's the word for the little lake ringed by brilliant flowers of subalpine meadowmarsh, its basin secluded from the brutality of economics by Mount Hawkins on one side and Esmerelda Peak on the other. Why, oh why, then, is it not (not *yet*) in the Alpine Lakes Wilderness? Because once upon a time prospectors roamed witlessly in quest of gold, precious jewels, the Holy Grail, or the philosopher's stone. Because the Forest Service used this as excuse for allowing today's fun-truckers to spin wheels and spew fumes. Let us pray that when we decent folk get to Heaven we do not find it administered by the dogma of multiple-use.

Nevertheless, snowbanks that linger into summer exclude the 4WD and the ORV, and post-melt weekdays they're mostly gassing up and laying in six-packs and chips, and the lake

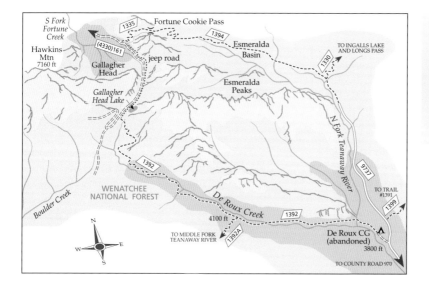

The way gentles out in forest, walks a log over the creek, here sedately meandering, and enters a meadowy vale.

Gallagher Head Lake and tip of Mount Rainier

basin then is tranquil. However, for my money it's merely the appetizer for the Teanaway's most sumptuous banquet.

Drive North Fork Teanaway Road 22.1 miles from County Road 970 and turn left on a road signed "Trail 1392." In 0.3 mile, near the far end of abandoned De Roux Campground, find unsigned Boulder–De Roux trail No. 1392, elevation 3800 feet.

In a scant ¼ mile cross the North Fork Teanaway on the bridge, if any, or maybe a log, or if snowmelt is roaring, perhaps not at all. At ¾ mile cross De Roux Creek on a log or however. Shortly beyond, at 4100 feet, the trail forks. Keep right, following the waterfalls, the way steepening to gain 800 feet in the next long mile. The way gentles out in forest and at about 2¼ miles walks a log over the creek, here sedately meandering, and enters a meadowy vale, 5000 feet. From the head of this ½-mile-long valley switchbacks ascend to the lake basin at 4 miles, and how sweet it is.

One moderately energetic day I continued on the loop around Esmerelda Peak—and afterward kicked myself for frittering away all that energy. More than 150 species of flowers were in bloom and in my hyperkinetic rush I could do no more than nod in passing.

So, next time I loaded up the Kelty and took a week: from the lake basin northward on a jeep track 1 mile, losing 450 feet; turning right on trail No. 1335 to climb a scant 1000 feet to Fortune Cookie Pass, finally loitering 3½ miles down Esmerelda Basin to the road and 1½ more miles to the Boulder–De Roux trailhead. Sidetrips: County Line Trail to Lake Ann and Van Epps Pass; Longs Pass. Camps, five. Could've used 2–3 more days, for Ingalls Lake and Iron Peak.

To make your world larger, go slower.

52 | CATHEDRAL ROCK–DECEPTION PASS LOOP

Loop trip: 14 miles
Hiking time: Allow 2–4 days
High point: 5500 feet
Elevation gain: 2300 feet
Hikable: July through September
Map: Green Trails No. 176 Stevens Pass
Information: Cle Elum Ranger District (509) 674-4411

The basic ramble around the head of the old Cle Elum Glacier trough, in meadows and by waterfalls and tarns, can be done in a couple of easy days. However, two or three more should be allowed for sidetrips to some of the region's most eye-bugging scenery.

Leave Interstate 90 on Exit 80 and drive 15.5 miles from Roslyn City Hall to Salmon la Sac and 12.5 miles more on road No. 4330 to the end at the Hyas Lake–Deception Pass trailhead, elevation 3350 feet.

As is axiomatic of loops, the trip can be done from either end, and it must be noted that most of the numerous cars usually parked here are those of day hikers and backpackers headed for some of the nicest family picnics and campsites around, an easy 1½ flat miles to mile-long Hyas Lake, especially popular

Columbia tiger lily

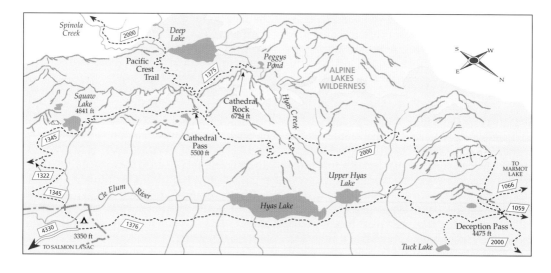

among novices trying out new gear and parents trying out new kids. In the following, however, we loop you clockwise.

From the parking area walk the road back a short bit to the last Y, go west a similar distance to the start of Cathedral Rock trail No. 1345, and follow it to Cathedral Pass, 4½ miles, 5500 feet. On the way, at 2½ miles, 4841 feet, is Squaw Lake, the last good camp that has summer-long water. From the intersection at Cathedral Pass the Pacific Crest Trail drops left to Deep Lake, the first of the possible sidetrips. To the right it heads for Deception Pass. Also from the intersection starts the second possible sidetrip, on a risky semi-path to Peggys Pond.

My first two visits here were to climb Cathedral and Daniel, but on the second I gave my Daniel companions a blessing as they set out up the miserable hot not-worth-it rock of Cathedral and spent a solitudinous day lollygagging around the Pond, actually a very respectable and exceedingly scenic tarn. There was not, in those days, even a semi-path contouring the slopes of Cathedral; two of our party, failing to make the Pond by nightfall and being forced to bivouac, named the route "the Lhotse Face," an inside joke only a fairly aged climber can appreciate. On my most recent visit I guided two Shelties to the Pond and, next day, nearly to the top of Daniel, but had to give up the climb when Eliane, the timid one, couldn't follow Myfy, the daring one, as she danced up the buttresses and clifflets.

The 4½ miles of the Crest Trail between Cathedral and Deception Passes are scenery all the way, views extending from the alpine gardens to the ground-down-at-the-heel glacial trough and its characteristic marshy lakes, Hyas and Fish. At places the Crest Freeway was dynamited in cliffs. (*Note:* Two stream crossings are formidable to the point of suicidal in the high water of snowmelt season. Many a party has been forced to turn back and make a long detour via the Cle Elum valley floor; when in doubt, call the Cle Elum Ranger District before setting out.)

At one of the "suicidals" I had to do an invigorating, mostly naked wade—three times—to deposit my pack on the far bank, then return

Pacific Crest Trail on side of Mount Daniel

to carry whimpering Eliane, Myfy meanwhile giving me a fit, dancing back and forth at the brink of a falls on a skinny, slippery log.

At 9 miles from the road the loop reaches Deception Pass, 4475 feet, and intersects the Marmot Lake trail, the third good sidetrip. Down the Hyas Lake trail ½ mile is the Tuck and Robin Lakes trail, the fourth sidetrip. The loop is completed with a quick descent to the floor of the trough and a passage along the shore of Hyas Lake to the road.

53 | TUCK AND ROBIN LAKES

Round trip to Robin Lakes: 14 miles
Hiking time: Allow 3–4 days
High point: 6250 feet
Elevation gain: 3200 feet
Hikable: August through mid-October
Map: Green Trails No. 176 Stevens Pass
Information: Cle Elum Ranger District (509) 674-4411

Ptarmigan

Since the requirement of permits to visit the Enchantment Lakes, Robin Lakes have what often seems the largest alpine population this side of the winter Olympics. The Forest Service tried to discourage use by canceling plans to build a real trail. We cooperated by removing the trip from our book. But in our age of wildland (and world) overpopulation there's no keeping a secret. The new management goal is not to hide the place but to keep it from being pounded and burned and polluted to death.

Drive from Salmon la Sac to the Hyas Lake–Deception Pass trailhead, elevation 3350 feet (see Hike 52, Cathedral Rock).

Walk the valley trail to Hyas Lake at 1½ miles, 3448 feet. At a scant 4 miles the trail turns steeply up, switchbacking. At some 4½ miles, 4300 feet, while still a long ½ mile short of Deception Pass, the way gentles. Watch for a trail sign.

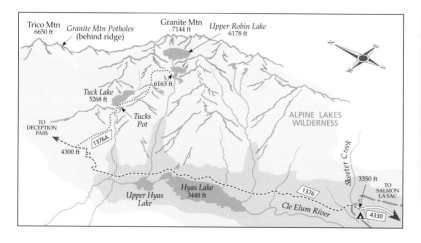

Roam as you please in the wide-open parkland. Sashay the long up-and-down ridge. Gaze down upon and/or prowl around nearly two dozen lakes.

Upper Robin Lake and Mount Daniel

An ancient firemen's track, unbuilt, unmaintained, dips to cross two small creeks, bumps against the forest wall, and begins an ingenious alternation of contours to get above or under cliffs and straight-up scrambles to get through them.

A short bit past a rock promontory in an old burn (stunning views), 6 miles, 5268 feet, the path levels out to Tuck Lake, surrounded by cliffs. Every square foot of flat ground is either an "established camp" or an "established toilet"—and is in the middle of a path to somewhere—and on a fine weekend is occupied.

From the lake outlet take any of the paths along the divider ridge and when it leaps upward ascend to the crest at 5800 feet. Cairns and tread lead along the crest, down and up the side of the ridge to its merger into the mountainside at 6000 feet, then up heather and

slabs to a 6250-foot shoulder, and at 1 mile from Tuck, down to Lower Robin Lake, 6163 feet, which connects to Upper Robin, 6178 feet.

Roam as you please in the wide-open parkland. With contour map in hand, go either way around Upper Robin to easily ascend 7144-foot Granite Mountain. Sashay the long up-and-down ridge to 6650-foot Trico Mountain. Gaze down upon and/or prowl around nearly two dozen lakes.

Now, the reason we returned the trip to the book: the sermon. What's good for the Enchantments is good for the Robins—maybe not good enough, the area being much smaller. Do not camp in the middle of the zoo; fill your water jug and find privacy in nooks on ridges or in adjacent basins. Better, camp in this neighborhood of Heaven only when essential to your soul, and not too often; don't be a hog.

RACHEL LAKE–RAMPART RIDGE

Round trip to Rachel Lake: 8 miles
Hiking time: 6 hours (day hike or backpack)
High point: 4650 feet
Elevation gain: 1600 feet

Round trip to Rampart Lakes: 11 miles
Hiking time: 8 hours (day hike or backpack)
High point: 5100 feet
Elevation gain: 2300 feet

Hikable: mid-July through October
Map: Green Trails No. 207 Snoqualmie Pass
Information: Cle Elum Ranger District (509) 674-4411

A cool and green valley forest, a large alpine lake walled by glacier-carved cliffs that drop straight to the water, a heaven of rock-bowl lakelets and ponds, gardens of heather and blossoms, and ridges and nooks for prowling.

Drive Interstate 90 east from Snoqualmie Pass 12.5 miles, take Kachess Lake Exit 62, and follow signs 5 miles to Kachess Lake Campground. Turn left and go 4 miles on Box Canyon road No. 4930 to a junction. Turn left 0.2 mile and hope to find space for your car in the enormous parking lot at the Rachel Lake trailhead, elevation 2899 feet.

The hike begins with a mile of moderate ascent to a rest stop by water-carved and potholed and moss-carpeted slabs. The trail levels out along the creek for 1½ miles. At 2½ miles the valley ends in an abrupt headwall and rough tread proceeds straight up, gaining 1300 feet in a cruel mile, ameliorated by cool-breeze rest-stop waterfalls. Suddenly the angle eases and forest yields to meadows and at 4 miles, 4650 feet, is Rachel Lake.

For the higher country, turn right at the shore on a path climbing above the cirque, with views down to the lake and out Box Canyon Creek. After a steep ½ mile the trail flattens in a wide parkland saddle, 5100 feet, and comes to a junction.

Go right 1 mile to 5200-foot Lila Lake (actually two lakes, or maybe six, plus ponds, scattered about a many-level basin). Go left an

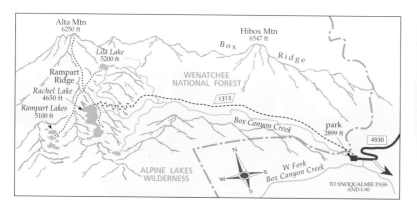

A heaven of rock-bowl lakelets and ponds, gardens of heather and blossoms, and ridges and nooks for prowling.

Lila Lakes and High Box Mountain

up-and-down mile to 5100-foot Rampart Lakes. Little lakes and tiny ponds, buttresses and waterfalls. Snoop into a flowery corner, climb a heather knoll, and before you know it, arrive on the crest of 5800-foot Rampart Ridge and views down to Gold Creek, west to Snoqualmie Pass, south to Rainier and Adams, east to Stuart, and north to Three Queens and Chimney Rock.

Camping? My first there was in early May, having parked at Lake Keechelus, climbed a little highway-side clearcut into snow, kicked steps near the top of Mount Margaret, and contoured to Lake Lillian, where we thatched together a king-and-queen-and-courtiers four-person bough bed, the Age of Aquarius not yet having dawned. Next morning we followed fresh goat tracks across the frozen Rampart Lakes and up the tightrope ridge to the summit of Alta. We next came years later, in September, with the kids, harvesting mushrooms in the valley as appetizers to be fried up by the lakeshore in evening, and blueberries to boil up into syrup for pancakes in morning. We came again, and again, saw many a sunset color the waters, and at last realized our good-time era had passed. The nation's population has swollen to double the size which can tolerate the easy-going ways of the Olden Days. All our elbows have got to be pulled in. The golden rule now is to come direct from home or camp in the valley forest, day hike to the high country.

55 | KENDALL KATWALK–SPECTACLE POINT

Round trip to Kendall Katwalk: 10½ miles
Hiking time: 8 hours (day hike)
High point: 5400 feet
Elevation gain: 2700 feet in, 300 out

Round trip to Spectacle Point: 33 miles
Hiking time: Allow 4–5 days
High point: 6700 feet
Elevation gain: about 6000 feet in, 2500 feet out

Hikable: mid-July through September
Map: Green Trails No. 207 Snoqualmie Pass
Information: North Bend Ranger District (425) 888-1421

The bag of superlatives is quickly exhausted on this, one of the most spectacular parts of the Cascade section of the Pacific Crest Trail, and the most accessible and popular. Wonderful as it is, should the trail have been blasted through this fragile area? Blasted it was. Ira has a contractor friend who was so concerned about the location he refused to submit a bid. Not only was he worried about crowds trampling fragile meadows, but he predicted hikers would be killed on the Kendall Katwalk. He was right on both counts.

However, the trail is in place and the Kendall Gardens are as gorgeous a color show as you'll find so near a freeway, so either put on your smiley face and mingle sociably with folks who can't be so bad (after all, they share your good taste in mode of travel) or go on a weekday. In any event, never cross the Katwalk when icy or blocked by a snowbank.

Drive Interstate 90 to Exit 52 at Snoqualmie Pass (Exit 53 from the east). Exit the freeway on the Alpental road and continue several hundred feet to the Pacific Crest Trail parking lot, elevation a bit above 3000 feet.

The trail ascends forest for 2 miles, loses 250 feet to avoid a boulder field, enters the Alpine Lakes Wilderness, and at 2¾ miles passes the Commonwealth Basin trail. Flattening briefly, the way switchbacks endlessly upward, at 4300 feet crosses an all-summer creek that may be the last water until Ridge Lake, and at 4700 feet attains the wooded crest of Kendall Ridge. On a long traverse around the mountain, the path opens out in Kendall Gardens, the start of alpine color that is virtually continuous to Spectacle Point. At 5¼ miles, on a 5400-foot bump overlooking the Katwalk, is a happy turnaround for a day hike.

To continue involves stepping carefully along the Kendall Katwalk, blasted across a cliff in solid granite. In my climbing days we never dreamt of going that way to climb Mount Thompson—it would have required ropes and belays. The Crest Trail could very simply have been located along the ridge route we used to take. When snow free the dynamited lane is wide and safe enough, though not recommended for acrophobes. When snowy, forget it. Beyond, the mountainside moderates to heather meadows. At 6½ miles is the 6270-foot saddle between tiny Ridge Lake and large Gravel Lake, the last trail camp until Mineral Creek Park.

Overnighters based here typically day trip to Alaska Mountain, 7¾ miles, 6746 feet, or to the

Kendall Katwalk and Pacific Crest National Scenic Trail

Trail on side of Kendall Peak

Huckleberry–Chikamin saddle, 10¼ miles, 6620 feet (due to ups and downs, a gross elevation gain of 1100 feet from Ridge Lake). On the way the trail swings around the basins of Alaska Lake and Joe Lake, both 1000 feet below and lacking sidetrails. The saddle is a precinct of Heaven but so fragile that to camp would be a mortal sin, or at least a capital crime. (It was not even a venial sin when we camped there in 1949 to climb Huckleberry and Chikamin. No trail, not even a game trace. Deep wilderness in sight of US 10.)

The upsy-downsy Pacific Crest Trail (Freeway) swings across the cliff-and-meadow face of Chikamin Peak and Four Brothers to a pass on the Cascade Crest at 6700 feet, 14 miles. The path descends the alpine basin of Mineral Creek Park to a designated and very pleasant meadow camp at 6200 feet, 14¼ miles, then dips farther to a 4970-foot pass near Park Pond and a junction with the Park Lakes trail. A final ascent of benches and swales tops out at 5475 feet, 16½ miles, on a shoulder of 6800-foot Three Queens Mountain. Sit on the prow

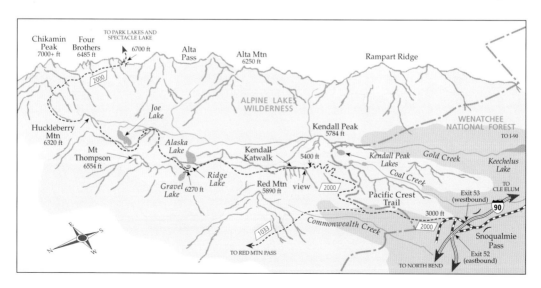

of Spectacle Point jutting out in the sky. Beneath your feet sprawl the octopus tentacles of Spectacle Lake, 4350 feet, 2½ miles down the Crest Trail and then a sidetrail. Across the valley Glacier Lake snuggles in a cirque. Above rises the long rough wall of Four Brothers, Chikamin, Lemah, Chimney Rock, and Summit Chief.

Pacific Crest National Scenic Trail and Ridge Lake

56 | SNOW LAKE

Round trip: 7 miles
Hiking time: 8 hours (day hike or backpack)
High point: 4400 feet
Elevation gain: 1800 feet in, 400 feet out
Hikable: July through October
Map: Green Trails No. 207 Snoqualmie Pass
Information: North Bend Ranger District (425) 888-1421

Snow Lake is the largest alpine lake (more than a mile long) near Snoqualmie Pass. Rock cliffs rise from one shore to Chair Peak, and forested cliffs fall from the other to the broad, deep gulf of the Middle Fork Snoqualmie River. The trail and lake are overwhelmingly popular—some 15,000 pairs of boots a year, 500 and more on a fine summer Sunday. If it's the sound of silence you're seeking, wear ear plugs.

More people does not have to mean more garbage or more degradation. More people can mean more friends, more green-bonded caretakers. Thanks to education in good manners and cleanup by rangers and volunteers, Snow Lake is in better shape now than on Ira's first visit in 1964. (The trash seen there now is a tiny fraction of what I saw in 1946.)

Drive Interstate 90 to Exit 52 (Exit 53 from the east) at Snoqualmie Pass and go north 2 miles on the Alpental road to the trailhead, elevation 3100 feet.

Trail No. 1013 ascends gradually, sometimes in forest shade, sometimes on rockslides, with views to Denny Mountain, The Tooth, and Chair Peak. Be prepared to take a pretty slow pace; the several hundred thousand feet that have passed through here over the past fifteen years, and many fewer dollars than that for trail maintenance, have resulted in badly "worn-out" tread, rocky and stumbley and ankle-twisty. At about 1½ miles switchbacks begin a steep mile in heather and flowers to the parkland saddle above Snow Lake, 3 miles, 4400 feet. (Not until *here* is the Alpine Lakes Wilderness entered! The commercial

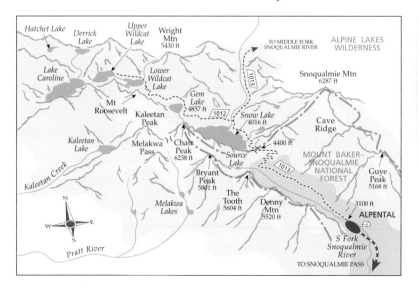

Day hikers may well be content to sit amid blossoms and blueberries and views, and get out their peanut butter and celery.

Snow Lake

ski area operators wanted the whole of Source Creek—and got it, though most of it is of no earthly use to them. However, hikers fought the good fight to save Commonwealth Basin for wilderness, which the operators also wanted.)

Day hikers may well be content to sit on a rock buttress at the saddle, amid blossoms and blueberries and views, and get out their peanut butter and celery. The trail drops sharply ½ mile to meadow shores of the lake, 3½ miles, 4016 feet, and rounds the east side.

Now, about the camping. Ira's advice is don't, not here. The Forest Service doesn't say that (not quite yet). However, to preserve the highest possible quality of experience without limiting the number of visitors, it has devised a management plan that instructs hikers in "the responsibility of freedom." You say you yearn to camp just as you dang well please and the heck with rules? Yearn someplace else.

More lakes lie beyond. Walk the shore ½ mile to the outlet, cross on a footlog, and proceed 1½ miles to Gem Lake, 4857 feet. The path circles the east shore, climbs a 5000-foot pass, and drops 1000 feet to the two Wildcat Lakes. Enough lakes? For peace and quiet, *avoid* lakes. Get off the trail. Snoop around for private nooks. Learn to hide. Take a vow of silence.

57 | GRANITE MOUNTAIN

Round trip: 8 miles
Hiking time: 8 hours (day hike)
High point: 5629 feet
Elevation gain: 3800 feet
Hikable: June through October
Map: Green Trails No. 207 Snoqualmie Pass
Information: North Bend Ranger District (425) 888-1421

The most popular summit trail in the Snoqualmie region, and for good reason. Though the ascent is long and in midsummer can be blistering hot, the upper slopes are a delightful garden of granite and flowers and a panorama to Mount Rainier south, to Mount Baker and Glacier Peak north, to Chimney Rock and Mount Stuart east, and infinitely more in-between peaks, valleys, and lakes.

Ira's first climb was not a happy one, called out by Mountain Rescue to search for two men caught in an avalanche. Their tracks ended less than 200 feet from the top of the slide, near the summit of the mountain. Two days were spent searching from that point down. No luck. Months later, when the snow melted, the bodies were found at the bottom of the mountain, only 500 feet from I-90.

They were not the first, nor the last, to fall into the Granite Trap. In spring the sunny southwest shoulder melts free of snow very early, deceptively seeming to provide bare-trail access to the heights. But the trail doesn't stay on the shoulder; it crosses a gully where snow lingers

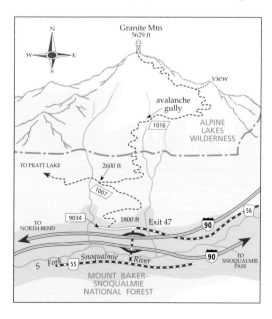

Alpine blueberry bushes in fall color

Granite Mountain trail with Mount Rainier in distance

late and where climax avalanches thunder to the very edge of the freeway. Hikers "rushing the season" are better advised to climb Bandera or Mailbox.

Drive Interstate 90 to Exit 47, cross north over the freeway, and turn west 0.6 mile to the trailhead parking lot, elevation 1800 feet.

The first steep mile on the Pratt Lake trail gains 800 feet in cool forest to the Granite Mountain junction, 2600 feet: The creek here may be the last water. Go right, traversing in trees ½ mile, then heading straight up and up in countless short switchbacks on an open south slope where fires and avalanches have inhibited the forest growth. (On sunny days, start early to beat the heat.)

At 4000 feet the trail abruptly gentles, swings east across the gully called "Granite Trap," and sidehills through rock gardens. Switchbacks climb steeply amongst grass and flowers to the summit ridge at 5200 feet. After a westward ascent in meadows above cozy cirque-scoop benches, more switchbacks finish the way to the fire lookout, 5629 feet, 4 miles.

Chapter 4

MOUNT RAINIER & THE SOUTH CASCADES

My first ascent of Rainier was Thanksgiving Day, 1931. The afternoon was unseasonably hot and we'd been climbing above Paradise a good long while and came at last to a big rock. I asked if this was the top and the folks said yes and for years I bragged of my conquest and got mad when I was laughed at and finally decided the folks had been kidding, the really truly Rainier most likely was that huge white heap in the sky.

My second ascent was mid-July of 1948, on an Experience Climb of The Mountaineers Climbing Course. The era's most famous mountaineer (due to his and twin brother Bob's photo spreads in the Sunday rotogravure) had led his rope team way off on the left wall of the Kautz Ice Chute that the rest of us were climbing straight up the center. "That's Ira for you," people were laughing. "Always wandering off for a picture."

Born and raised where there never was a clear day without that huge white heap filling a major part of the sky, for me The Mountain was as unavoidable as the moon—another fine piece of scenery I never aspired to put boot to. But in the Climbing Course it was what you did, if you could.

I confess to being impressed years later, on my first flight from New York, that I had done it. After a lengthy day crossing the nation from sea to sea, descending to Seattle in twilight, the DC-6 passed close enough to Columbia Crest that I could in mind's eye see myself standing there atop the most prodigious freestanding hunk of the American earth. But half a dozen times was enough of that.

The commonplace has it that a mountain is best seen not from the top but from the bottom, or somewhere near. Again, I had to get well away from Rainier to fully understand why.

North in the British Columbia Coast Mountains, I found peaks so submerged in ice, vastnesses of ice, little room was left for flowers. South in the High Sierra, from Desolation Valley to Mineral King I scarcely took a step without stopping to soak up summer colors—except white, because there was next to no ice.

Not too far north, not too far south, fortuities of latitude and maritime climate combine with elevation to give Rainier the largest single-peak glacier system of the old 48 states and—cheek-by-jowl with the white—as gaudy a rainbow panoply as brightens any place in the world. At this precise point in North America is the optimum coincidence, side by side, of glaciers and flowers.

The second guidebook we did, *50 Hikes in Mount Rainier National Park*, was at the request of park rangers who needed help in managing the growing throngs of all-American pilgrims. Ira jumped at the chance and walked (largely, re-walked) every mile of every trail in the park. Since pre-War II summers at Paradise Valley, janitoring and tourist-photographing, he'd wanted to do it but never until now had a justification acceptable to the IRS for deducting his peanut butter as a business expense. Take away Rainier and the South Cascades treasury of Classics nevertheless would be full. Mount St. Helens—well, I'd always yearned to see one of our volcanoes blow, and am glad it was St. H. I'd have hated to lose that quantity of Mount Adams, whose Round-the-Mountain Trail is more to my tastes than the Wonderland Trail. The Goat Rocks embody the virtues of being old, worn-out, and eroded to the roots, no more fretting and fussing, just relaxing, beautiful and serene forever, like some people we know. For a volcano that has more to say to the informed mind than show-biz superstar St. H, try Tumac.

Sunset on Mount Adams

PARADISE FLOWER TRAILS

Round trip: 1–5 miles or more
Hiking time: 1–5 hours (day hike)
High point: 5940 or 6900 feet
Elevation gain: 500 feet or 1500 feet
Hikable: mid-July to mid-October
Map: Park handout
Information: Mount Rainier National Park (360) 569-2211 ext. 3317

"Where the flowers and glaciers meet" is aptly applied to this Classic of blossoms, stupendous views of icefalls, a delightful waterfall, and friendly marmots sunning themselves along the trail or grazing themselves fat before hibernating. In late July or early August, when the meadows are a riot of color, as many as 3,000 people a day walk the paved trails at Paradise. But Ira still enjoys solitude on his favorite flower fields, and so can you. Seek and ye shall find.

In 1937, when Ira worked as a night janitor in Paradise Inn, the ground was still snow-covered the last days of June. By July 10 the snow was gone but the ground was white again with avalanche lilies, some so impatient to bloom they had forced their way through the snow to sunlight. Then came the blue of lupine, and by late July a rainbow of penstemon, daisy, aster, heather, paintbrush, columbine, and half a hundred more.

Paved trails shown on Park Service handouts radiate from the Paradise parking lot. One is a steep ½ mile to Alta Vista. A 1½-mile Skyline Trail to 6900-foot Panorama Point gives a look over the crest of the Tatoosh Range to Adams, St. Helens, and Hood in Oregon, then with a bit

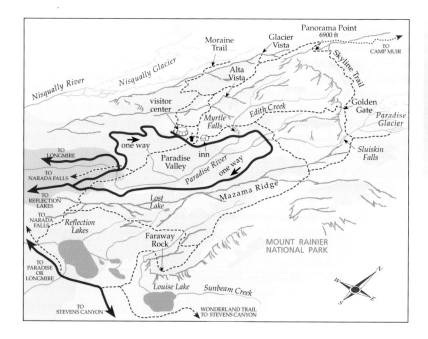

Blossoms, stupendous views of icefalls, a delightful waterfall, and friendly marmots sunning themselves along the trail.

Marmot on side of Panorama Point

more climbing loops back by way of Edith Creek flower fields.

A long, arduous, and potentially hazardous ascent—not a trail hike—leads to the overnight cabin at Camp Muir used by summit climbers. Much of the way is on snow. Or glacier? Beware of crevasses! Also keep an eye on the sky. The Mountain is notorious for "making its own weather"—mostly bad. Without warning, clouds may materialize from a clear sky, enveloping hikers in blowing fog and wiping out landmarks. The temperature may drop abruptly, the wind rise, and a balmy afternoon become a killing night. Take Ira's word, he has climbed to Muir several dozen times. Once a freezing rain turned the snowfield to a block of ice and instead of four hours to get back to the car he was two treacherous days creeping down.

Want to get away from people? Try the moraine trail beside the Nisqually Glacier, Ira's favorite for flower pictures. On many many trips over many many years, never has he met anyone there. The trail is maintained but looks muddy and goes downhill, so everyone passes it up. Too bad for them.

In 1937 the Stevens Canyon Road had not yet been built. A trail led to Reflection Lakes, a refreshment stand, and rental rowboats. During his day's "sleep time" Ira the night janitor often walked that trail as far as Artist Pool at Faraway Rock, but rather than dropping to Reflection Lakes, he'd follow a trail through flower gardens along the crest of Mazama Ridge, gazing across the valley to The Mountain. One time, straying from the trail, he discovered his "secret" lake, ideal for swimming and never mind a swimming suit.

Years later, on a photo assignment for Paradise Inn to promote the newly opened Stevens Canyon Road, he overheard two college-age waitresses (his models) talking about a "hidden" lake where they went skinny-dipping. They were taken aback when he exactly described the location.

9 | PINNACLE SADDLE

Round trip: 3 miles
Hiking time: 3 hours (day hike)
High point: 6000 feet
Elevation gain: 1150 feet
Hikable: August through September
Map: Green Trails No. 270 Mt. Rainier East
Information: Mount Rainier National Park (360) 569-2211 ext. 3317

Columbine

A grand view of The Mountain from a point distant enough to see it all in a single wide-eyed look, close enough to see fine detail of glaciers and lava cliffs. The location, south of Mount Rainier, is a photo-textbook example of studio lighting on a grand scale. By moving lights in a studio, a photographer can give an object a third dimension. By timing the sun's location to the subject, the same third-dimension effect is possible. Spend a day at or near the saddle. Early morning's eastern sunrays skim the mountain, highlighting ridges and glaciers. By 10:00 A.M. the sun has moved to the south; the view is still stupendous, but the shadows that give the mountain roundness are lost. By 4:00 p.m. the sun is far enough to the west that the ridges are once again highlighted and the roundness restored.

Drive the Stevens Canyon Road west 17.5 miles from the Stevens Canyon entrance of Mount Rainier National Park or east 1.5 miles

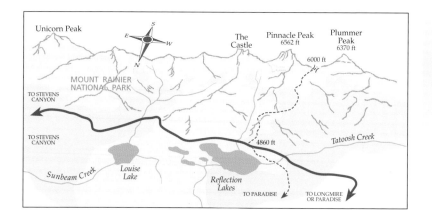

The view of Rainier grows steadily more impressive with every inch of elevation gained.

Small tarn near Pinnacle Saddle

from the Longmire–Paradise road to the Reflection Lakes parking area, elevation 4860 feet. The trail starts on the uphill (south) side.

The path is gentle at first but soon turns steep and remains so. In July several hazardous snowfields must be crossed. Use extreme caution; hikers lacking boots would do better to give up and try again later in the season, when the snow has melted.

The view of Rainier grows steadily more impressive with every inch of elevation gained; at the 6000-foot saddle is an almost equally impressive view south—across miles of forest, the village of Packwood, and the Goat Rocks, to Mount Adams.

The trail ends at the saddle. Though trained climbers consider 6562-foot Pinnacle Peak an easy ascent, most of the hikers who continue to the summit, many of them in street shoes, have no business on the steep, unstable rock. They are a hazard to themselves—and a hazard to others below, kicking down loose stones.

50 | NACHES PEAK LOOP

Loop trip: 4½ miles
Hiking time: 3 hours (day hike)
High point: 6000 feet
Elevation gain: 700 feet
Hikable: mid-July through October
Map: Green Trails No. 270 Mt. Rainier East
Information: Mount Rainier National Park (360) 569-2211 ext. 3317

Want to give visiting relatives the best look at The Mountain? No, not via an elevator up the Space Needle. Do what Pat and Ira always do— take them on the Naches Peak Loop, circling one of the guardians of Chinook Pass, through rich flower fields and beside two lakelets. In addition to Rainier there are blueberries (usually) by September, succeeded by a magnificence of flaming autumn color that will send your New England visitors back home crestfallen.

The loop is among the most popular hikes in the Park. Even more popular, and a pleasure for anyone who can walk at all, no matter how slowly, are the two beginning and ending segments, which in a few hundred feet or any longer distance offer as nice a combination of flower-sniffing and mountain-gazing as one can find anywhere.

Drive east from Enumclaw on State Route 410 to Chinook Pass, elevation 5040 feet, and continue 0.2 mile to the Pacific Crest Trailhead.

The loop can be done in either direction, but clockwise keeps Mount Rainier in front more of the time and thus is recommended. However, until late July or early August the trail along the east slopes of Naches Peak is quite snowy; counterclockwise may be preferred, turning back when the country becomes too white and wet for personal tastes. In such case park at Tipsoo Lake just before the Pass.

From the trailhead head south across the highway on a wooden overpass. Small paths branch off left and right; stay on the main trail along the east side of Naches Peak, leaving the National Park and entering the William O. Douglas Wilderness.

The way traverses a steep sidehill above a green little valley, crossing several small waterfall tumbling creeks—which, however, generally dry up in August. Flowers are at their prime roughly from late July to early August,

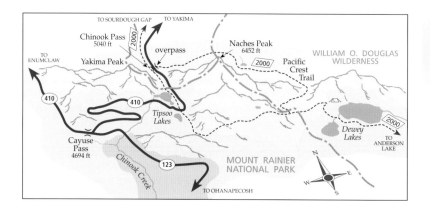

Blueberries are succeeded by a magnificence of flaming autumn color.

Beargrass and Mount Rainier from Naches Peak loop trail

but some bloom earlier, some later. About 1 mile from Chinook Pass is an unnamed lakelet. The trail ascends gently over a ridge, the highest point of the loop, enters the Park, and at 2 miles reaches a junction. The Pacific Crest Trail goes left, dropping to Dewey Lakes.

The loop goes right, over a small rise to another nameless lakelet reflecting Rainier. The way winds to high meadows on the west side of Naches Peak, Mount Rainier always in full view, and drops back to the highway near Upper Tipsoo Lake, ½ mile from the starting point.

For a whole new experience of high meadows and The Mountain, do the loop on a moonlit night in late August or early September. Listen for the bugling of bull elk.

61 | MORAINE PARK

Round trip from Ipsut Creek Campground: 12 miles
Hiking time: 6 hours (day hike)
High point: 6004 feet
Elevation gain: 3500 feet
Hikable: mid-July to mid-October
Map: Green Trails No. 269 Mt. Rainier West
Information: Mount Rainier National Park (360) 569-2211 ext. 3317

A close look at the snout of the Carbon Glacier, lowest-elevation glacier in the old 48 states, flower meadows and high ridges for roaming, and a near view of enormous Willis Wall. Watch for avalanches that seemingly float down its 3600 feet. You've got to keep your eye on the Wall because the sound is delayed and you may not know the show is happening until after it's over.

Drive to the Carbon River entrance of Mount Rainier National Park, the present (1998) start of walking, elevation 1744 feet. The road may or may not be reopened the 5 miles to its former end at Ipsut Creek Campground, elevation 2350 feet. Find the trail at the upper boundary of the camp.

The first 3 miles of trail lie on the valley floor close to river elevation. Pass the Northern Loop junction at 2 miles, the Seattle Park junction at 3 miles, and shortly beyond cross the Carbon River on a suspension bridge to another junction. Go right.

The trail now steepens, gaining 1700 feet in 2 miles. The first portion on rubbly and cliffy slopes above the Carbon Glacier is very rough. Here are close views of the glacier snout; though

Mount Rainier and small lake at Moraine Park saddle

some glaciers in the Park have receded almost a mile in the last forty years, the Carbon has held its own. A tumbling creek makes a good rest stop. Then the trail enters forest and in the final stretch emerges in parkland and flattens out.

The portion of Moraine Park traversed by the trail is pretty enough, especially in flower season, but the best is yet to come. Follow the trail upward a steep 1 mile to a 6004-foot saddle, 5½ miles from Ipsut Creek Campground. Either drop a long ½ mile to Mystic Lake or—better— hike up along Curtis Ridge for dramatic close-ups of Willis Wall and views over the Winthrop Glacier to Steamboat Prow.

My last time there (I've been visiting since 1946 and feel I've had my share of Mount Rainier, leave some for the next guy) was the Labor Day that all the National Forests of the state were closed by fire danger, only the National Parks were open, and a major percentage of the area's backpackers was camped at Mystic Lake. Campfires were still permitted then and the entire shoreline was ablaze at night, a ring of fire, spooky, as if all the covens were assembled for a festival of black magic. The lake was the only campsite officially open, but the Manning party included a little boy (the one we now know as Herr Doktor Professor) whose legs were too short to get that far in one day. So we left the trail and snuck off in meadows overlooking the Carbon Glacier, on the way passing marmot holes which meltwater had doubled and tripled in size. The boy wondered what they were. Child psychologists blanch, now, on

Crevasses in Carbon Glacier

hearing I informed him they were "monster holes." Our camp was comfortable under the clear skies of sunset, but very exposed. At midnight a presentiment woke me and I looked up to a darkness on The Mountain, flowing down Willis Wall. I signaled an emergency retreat to sheltering trees. The boy came awake screaming and we had to drag his unwilling feet until safely past the Monster Holes—into which, it turned out, he had gone to bed fully expecting to be stuffed.

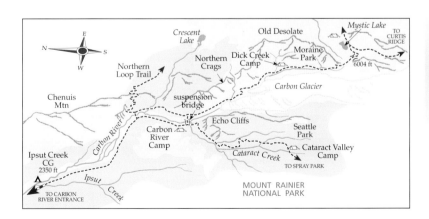

Here are close views of the lowest-elevation glacier in the old 48 states.

62 | GROVE OF THE PATRIARCHS

Round trip: 1½ miles
Hiking time: 1 hour (day hike)
High point: 2200 feet
Elevation gain: none
Hikable: June through October
Map: Park handout
Information: Mount Rainier National Park (360) 569-2211 ext. 3317

This Classic may have only trees and water, but WOW-OH-WOW, what trees!

The name paints the picture: a community of Douglas-firs, western hemlocks, and western red cedars that were already ancient when the Normans conquered England. The walk is short and easy, but many visitors have been known to drop to their knees, and not from weariness. Humility is what it is.

Drive to the Stevens Canyon entrance of Mount Rainier National Park and continue 0.25 mile on the Stevens Canyon Road to a large

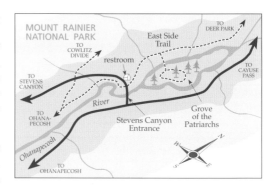

Indian pipe, a saprophyte

parking lot beyond the Ohanapecosh River bridge. Trail starts behind the restrooms, elevation 2200 feet.

The way goes upstream ½ mile to a junction. The nature trail turns right, crosses a suspension bridge onto an island in the Ohanapecosh River, and passes through small trees, to a split. Go either way; it's a loop. Signs identify plants and describe features of the ecological community.

Isolated on the island and thus protected from fire, the trees, estimated to be nearly 1000 years old, have grown to gigantic proportions. In this small area are 20 western red cedars more than 25 feet in circumference; among them is the largest cedar in the Park. Ten Douglas-firs are over 25 feet in circumference; one is 35 feet.

The rangers having promised to look the other way, to give a misty feeling to the forest Ira lit a smoke bomb. In black-and-white, the smoke appeared to be genuine fog, but was too blue for convincing color.

Grove of the Patriarchs

63 | THE WONDERLAND TRAIL

Complete loop: 93 miles
Hiking time: Allow 10–14 days
High point: 6750 feet
Total elevation gain and loss: 20,000 feet
Hikable: mid-July through August
Maps: Green Trails: Mount Rainier West No. 269 and 270
Information: Mount Rainier National Park (360) 569-2211 ext. 3317
Backcountry use permit required for camping

The Wonderland Trail encircling Mount Rainier, built in 1915, passes through every life zone of the National Park from valley forests to alpine meadows to high barrens of rock and snow. Along the way are trees, flowers, animals, and glaciers. And views: so different does Rainier look from various segments, it's difficult to recognize as all the same mountain. As the summit of Rainier is to a climber, so the Wonderland Trail is to a hiker—the experience of a lifetime.

In the 1930s plans were drawn up to use Works Project Administration (WPA) funding for a Wonderland Highway, permitting tourists to "do" The Mountain in 3 hours, seeing a lot and experiencing little. Happily, the emerging wilderness movement and sanity prevailed. Highway it was not, never a wheelway, nor even a horseway, strictly for feet and backs willing to spend ten days or two weeks to see The Mountain on its own terms.

A strong hiker can do the entire trail in a week, but 10–14 days are about average and much more enjoyable. To allow full appreciation of scenic highlights and opportunity for sidetrips, a party should spend two weeks or more—not forgetting extra time for sitting out several or so days of rain. Other hikers spread the hike over two or three years, hiking a portion of the trail each year. Transportation must be arranged to avoid doubling back.

Supplies for the entire trip can be carried from the beginning, but this makes for hard, slow walking the early days. A better plan is to arrange to be met at one or two intermediate points by friends bringing supplies. There is no place along the route to buy staples except the concession at Longmire; meals can be purchased at Sunrise, Paradise, and Longmire for a change from backpack menus.

Be prepared for rain by carrying a tent or tarp. Few parties are lucky enough to complete the entire trip without a few days of mist, downpour, or perhaps snow—which can and does fall on the high meadows throughout the summer. The few, small shelter cabins cannot be counted on; they are frequently reserved for groups.

Camping along the Wonderland Trail is allowed only at designated backcountry campsites and only with a backcountry camping permit for each night. There are eighteen designated trail campsites and four car campgrounds. Since campsites are not evenly spaced at the 9- to 10-mile intervals the average hiker covers in a day, some days a person may wish to do 13–14 miles, passing several campsites. When planning the itinerary and judging where to camp, take into consideration the elevation gains between campsites as well as the distances.

The Wonderland Trail is described here starting at Longmire solely because that point has bus service; no need to drive your car from Chicago to do this American Classic. There is no best starting point; they are all good. It makes no difference which way one hikes the

A field of avalanche lilies in Spray Park, and Mount Rainier

Eunice Lake and Mount Rainier

Wonderland Trail, counterclockwise or, as described here, clockwise. The views are great no matter which way the eyes are pointed.

The following is a very abbreviated trail description abridged from *50 Hikes in Mount Rainier National Park.*

Part 1   Longmire to Mowich Lake

One-way trip: 32½ miles
Hiking time: Allow 4–7 days
High point: 5800 feet
Elevation gain: 9900 feet
Hikable: mid-July through September

The Wonderland Trail begins at Longmire in forest, climbs to flower fields at Indian Henrys Hunting Ground, crosses a dancing Tahoma Creek suspension bridge, climbs over Emerald Ridge beside the Tahoma Glacier, past St. Andrews Park and more flowers to Klapatche Park, location of the only designated campsite from which to watch a sunset. After dropping to the Puyallup River, the trail again climbs to gardens at Golden Lakes, descends into forest, and climbs out again to Mowich Lake. The seven

designated campsites are at 3 miles, 5 miles, 11 miles, 14½ miles, 17½ miles, 22½ miles, and 29 miles. Before starting, be certain you can handle the suspension bridge at Tahoma Creek; there is no alternate route.

Part 2   Mowich Lake to White River

One-way trip: 30½ miles
Hiking time: Allow 3–6 days
High point: 6700 feet
Elevation gain: 5200 feet
Hikable: mid-July through September

The second and most remote section of the Wonderland Trail rounds the cold north side of The Mountain. From Mowich Lake to Ipsut Creek Campground the trail is fairly level to Ipsut Pass, then drops steeply to the campground, an easy and quick 5¼ miles with plenty of time for a sidetrip to Eunice Lake and Tolmie Peak. A more strenuous but very rewarding alternate route to Carbon River goes by way of Spray Park and Seattle Park, traversing miles of alpine flower fields before descending to the Carbon River Backcountry

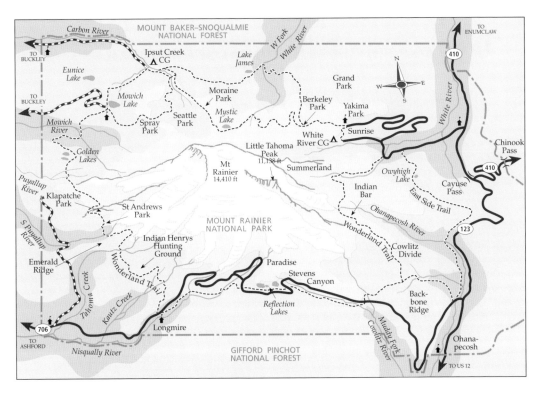

Campsite in 8 miles, the elevation gain 1700 feet and loss 3200 feet. From the Carbon River the trail climbs above the Carbon Glacier, to Moraine Park under looming Willis Wall, drops to Mystic Lake and below the Winthrop Glacier. The way climbs over Skyscraper Pass to ice cream cones at Sunrise Lodge. Then downhill again to the White River Campground. The six backcountry campsites along this section are at 5¼ miles, 8¼ miles, 12½ miles, 16 miles, 21½ miles, and 27½ miles. *Note:* Winthrop Creek bridge below the Winthrop Glacier is gone. Check with the ranger for crossing difficulties.

Part 3   White River to Longmire

One-way trip: 31 miles
Hiking time: Allow 6 days
High point: 6700 feet
Elevation gain: 5700 feet
Hikable: mid-July through September

The third and final section of the Wonderland Trail rounds the east side of The Mountain to Longmire. From the White River Campground the way climbs to the flower fields of Summerland and Panhandle Gap, the highest portion of the circuit and the most likely place of all to see mountain goats. The trail descends through meadows of Indian Bar to cross the Cowlitz River, ascends to Reflection Lakes, and finishes with a descent in forest to Longmire. The five backcountry campsites along the way are at approximately 7 miles, 11½ miles, 16 miles, 19 miles, and 27½ miles.

The hiker who arrives back at Longmire, having hiked 93 miles plus sidetrips, having gained some 20,000 feet or more, can take pride in an accomplishment as impressive as climbing to the summit of Rainier. In many ways he has known The Mountain more intimately than any climber, and will be far more aware of the many ways in which man and mountain and plants and animals are interrelated. The hiker will see, as John Muir did, that "when we try to pick out anything by itself, we find it hitched to everything else in the universe."

64 | PACIFIC CREST NATIONAL SCENIC TRAIL

One way trip from Columbia River to Allison Pass in Canada: about 500 miles
Elevation gain: about 85,000 feet
Hiking time: Allow the rest of your life
Hikable: for the most part mid-July through September
Maps: the Green Trails library
Information: Forest Service–Park Service Information Center in Seattle (206) 470-4060

Four volumes in our *100 Hikes* series treat the Pacific Crest Trail, which was famous under that name long before Congress bestowed on the entire Mexico-to-Canada route the international renown that now draws dogged "end-to-enders" like bees to honey, deer flies to hikers' sweat. With all due respect for the clearcuts of Oregon, the chaparral of Northern California, and the Mojave Desert, in our opinion the two portions of the journey most worth doing as

Cutthroat Pass

more than entertainment for local residents or mortification of the flesh to purify the soul are those through the High Sierra and along the Cascade Crest of Washington. Also in our opinion, though doing the whole of the latter provides an experience that is greater than the sum of its parts, some of the parts are (as on Animal Farm) more equal than others. For a sketchy end-to-end we refer you to our series and other books with more lavish detail. For a selection of Classics between the Columbia River and Canada, we refer you to the table of contents of this book.

Asking a lifelong wilderness peripatetic which of the half a thousand miles of the Pacific Crest Trail are his personal Classics is like asking Noah which animals he'd most like to take for a boat ride. As a little kid, a country kid, going to the Big City for dinner and a show was only just rare enough a treat to save my sanity. So few hours in an evening, so many movie palaces, so many funnymen. Harold Lloyd? Laurel and Hardy? The Marx Brothers? Before that, dinner, at the Merry-Go-Round, of course. As we sat on stools at the great circle of the counter, eating soup and salad and main course, before our eyes, in easy child's reach, ceaselessly passed the merry-go-round of desserts. My hand would go out for devil's food cake—but wait, coconut cream pie is looming! Rounding the bend , is that veritably a torte? Yes, and close

Mount Rainier and Pacific Crest National Scenic Trail on side of Kendall Peak

Lower Snowy Lake

Not to knock the other guy's sport, but we've never been end-to-enders on the Pacific Crest Trail in the sense of doing it all in one go, and therefore don't know the speed record. We're better informed about the slow record, that being more our style, going one step at a time from end to end, beginning with early stumblings and continuing to late totterings. Our personal Classics of the Crest Trail are scattered through the other 99 Classics presented here.

Starting in the south, much of the Indian Heaven Loop (Hike 84) is on the Crest Trail, as is much of the Mount Adams Highline (Hike 77); Adams Creek Meadows (Hike 76) is a short sidetrip.

Moving north, the Crest Trail shares a meadow with the Snowgrass Flat trail (Hike 75), looks down on Packwood Lake (Hike 73), and circles Shoe Lake (Hike 72).

In Mount Rainier National Park, the Wonderland Trail (Hike 63) and the Naches Peak Loop (Hike 60) are partly on the Crest Trail. While in William O. Douglas Wilderness, Blankenship Lakes (Hike 69) and Twin Sisters Lakes (Hike 68) are just a hop and skip away.

In Alpine Lakes Wilderness, Kendall Katwalk—Spectacle Point (Hike 55) and Cathedral Rocks—Deception Pass (Hike 52) are on the Crest Trail; close-by sidetrips are Snow Lake (Hike 56), Tuck and Robin Lakes (Hike 53), and Lake Mary (Hike 49).

In Glacier Peak Wilderness, the Crest Trail includes White Chuck Glacier (Hike 32), A Peach, A Pear, and a Topping (Hike 39), Meander Meadow—Kodak Peak—White Pass (Hike 41), and Agnes Creek—Lyman Lake Loop (Hike 46). Connections can be made to Lake Byrne (Hike 33) and Spider Gap—Buck Creek Pass (Hike 43).

Near its north end, the Crest Trail traverses Golden Horn (Hike 17), Windy Pass (Hike 19), and Cascade Loop—Monument 83 (Hike 28); close by is Maple Pass (Hike 16).

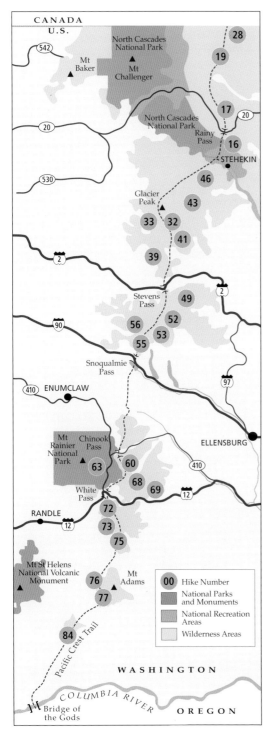

behind, angel food cake pursued by cherry tarts and cream puffs, and I do suspect in the distance a banana split!

The high line along the flanks of Mount Adams is in my memory a seamless succession of meadows and parkland, lava flows and moraines, and rock-milky torrents from one glacier after another. Wilderness all the way, night and day, the wildness accentuated when the sun went down and the anti-wilderness electrically revealed itself, the skyglows (visible, say the astronauts, from the moon) of Columbia River City to the south, and Puget Sound City to the north.

My first visit to the Goat Rocks was on the west side, the Crest Trail side, and I must confess the population density was greater than met the needs of my mood that day. Seeking a place to pick my nose in private, I left the trail and climbed a steep meadow above the headwaters of the Cispus River to a small cirque unsuspected from below, and sat alone beside a snow-melt creek rippling through the flowers and picked my nose.

The trail population was zero-plus-two an autumn midweek north from White Pass. The low sun backlit the cones of subalpine firs, never quite melting the frosts in their long shadows, crisply white stripes in the mellowing-yellow of meadows. This was surely the Crest. The Crest of what? No mountains could be seen beyond the parkland trees. Not until we climbed from the plateau to the summit of Tumac Mountain. I'd always heard it referred to as a cinder cone. But ascending the alternating layers of cinders and hard lava, I recognized it as a composite volcano. An infant. Fated to become—what? Looking to Rainier, Adams, St. Helens, realizing that this was how they began, well. . . . Several years later, on that day in May of 1980, I remembered idly speculating at Sand Lake, where all the sand had come from. . . .

The merry-go-round goes on and on, up and down the half a thousand miles from the Columbia River to Canada. Mount Adams, the Goat Rocks, Tumac Mountain, these are a few of my favorite things.

But hang on! Strawberry shortcake with whipped cream has been sighted, headed this way!

65 | YAKIMA RIM SKYLINE TRAIL

Loop trip: 19 miles
Hiking time: 12 hours (day hike or backpack)
High point: 3550 feet
Elevation gain: 2100 feet
Hikable: late March to early June
Maps: USGS Badger Pocket, Ellensburg, Yakima, Selah
Information: L. T. Murray Wildlife Recreation Area, State Wildlife Department,
Region 3 (509) 575-2740

What does a flower child do for excitement when high-country gardens are a monotonous white? My springtime favorite is the Yakima Rim Skyline Trail. I recall rounding the corner of a ridge and being blinded by a dazzling snowfield. In June, here? No, it was a phlox field. I'd heard rumors of cactus in our state and suspended belief—until I met both our native species, exotic, gorgeous. The drab, sulking plants I walked by on a cloudy-dark morning, their mouths shut tight, opened in afternoon sun to thousands of hysterical bitterroot blossoms. Let us sit upon blocks of basalt and discuss the many hues of buckwheat, and the yellows of desert parsley and stonecrop and wallflower and sunflower, and blues-violets of larkspur and lupine and penstemon and brodiea and mertensia and onion.

When word got around in 1977 that the Wildlife (then, Game) Department had built its very first recreation trail, pedestrians went as berserk as America's wastrels and drifters when gold was found at Sutter's Mill. Why, then, these two decades later, is the treasure trove virtually deserted? Because the trail fell into the obscurity of neglect caused by lack of funds. In *55 Hikes in Central Washington* I've detailed the classic end-to-end route from the South, Middle, and North Trailheads. Following is a recommended introductory looper sampling.

Leave Interstate 90 on Exit 109, turn north 0.6 mile on Canyon Road, and turn left (west) on Dammon Road. At Dammon School, 1.7 miles from Canyon Road, is a four-way intersection. The straight-through road changes

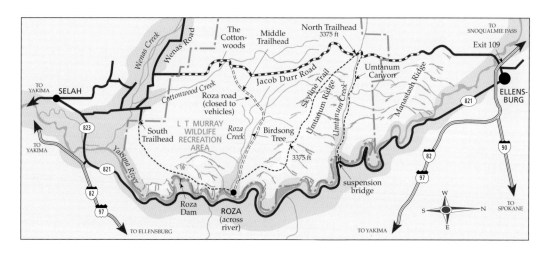

Left, *yellow bell;* right, *Western bluebird*

name to Umtanum. At the far side of the Kittitas Valley floor it abruptly ascends little Shushuskin Canyon. At 5 miles from Canyon Road go left off the paved road onto unpaved, probably unsigned, but very historic Jacob Durr Road. Proceed across the high plateau and commence the steep, narrow, rough descent to the floor of Umtanum Canyon. At 4.1 miles from Umtanum Road is the ford of Umtanum Creek. A 3-mile climb, for a total 12.1 miles from Canyon Road, culminates at the North Trailhead, elevation 3375 feet.

Here begins the most-walked section of the Skyline Trail. The crest of Umtanum Ridge rolls along high in the sky. Views extend from the glaciers of Mount Rainier and Mount Adams in the south to the crags of the Stuart Range in the north.

A day hike out along Umtanum Ridge from Jacob Durr Road is an easy picnic for children. The backpacking is popular—load water and root beer on the back, sup on sandwiches and nibbles, and throw down the sleeping bag where you will. Watch the sun go down, the stars and the lights of farms and cities sparkle out, the sun come up.

The ridge top undulates to the highest point of the Skyline Trail, 3550 feet. The trail, here an old wagon track that unfortunately is still open at the start to wheels, descends to lower sum-

mits and then as true foot trail to the floor of Roza Creek valley and the site of the vanished Roza School, 1300 feet, 8 miles from the North Trailhead.

The end-to-end climbs from the valley to a high point of 3550 feet, and the views, plumb bob-straight-down to the Yakima Canyon, are worth a sidetrip from the loop. (The South Trailhead is about 10 miles from the school.)

The loop ascends the grown-over ruts of the closed-to-vehicles Roza road 2 miles to the only potable water of the route (except in your pack) at Birdsong Spring, 1700 feet. Here is the sweetest camp this side of Heaven, under the spreading Birdsong Tree, a giant, gnarled old locust planted by long-ago homesteaders. At night the bats and nighthawks eclipse the stars and the loudest sounds are crickets and coyotes. At dawn's first light the wings arrive from miles around to strike up the band.

In another 1¼ miles up the foot-only road is the Middle Trailhead, 2100 feet. The loop proceeds on meager roadway, open (just barely) to occasional wheels (very slow) to the height of land, 2260 feet, between Roza and Cottonwood Creeks. Gully-size ruts descend to the 1850-foot junction, 2½ miles from the Middle Trailhead, with the Jacob Durr Road, which in 5¼ miles ascends Cottonwood Creek to the North Trailhead.

00 | CLEAR WEST PEAK

Round trip: 3 miles
Hiking time: 2 hours (day hike or backpack)
High point: 5644 feet
Elevation gain: 900 feet
Hikable: July to October
Map: Green Trails No. 238 Greenwater
Information: White River Ranger District (360) 825-6585

Canada jay

A grand view of Mount Rainier from a small flower-covered meadow, site of a lookout until 1968. The hike is short enough to be good for beginners and families. No virgin forest (logging did it all in) and no wildlife to be seen (hunters took care of that). But The Mountain remains.

Drive east from Enumclaw on US 410 for 21.8 miles and turn right (south) on West Fork road No. 74. At 6.8 miles cross the West Fork of the White River and Wrong Creek (that's right, it's Wrong). At 8.2 miles go left on road No. 7430 for another 7.3 miles to the end, elevation 4726 feet.

Trail No. 1181 begins in a clearcut, a giant flame of brilliant red fireweed in July, and steeply ascends a narrow ridge, at ½ mile entering the Clearwater Wilderness. At 1 mile the trail levels briefly. Switchbacks then begin and soon appears the first overwhelming view south (over your shoulder) to Rainier. A steep hillside

No virgin forest and no wildlife to be seen. But The Mountain remains.

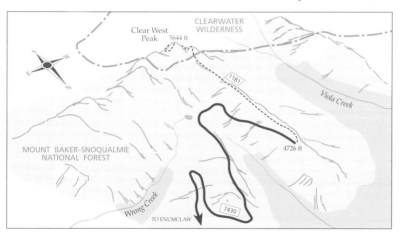

Mount Rainier from Clear West Peak

displays (in season) arnica, lupine, penstemon, blueberries, and beargrass. At 1½ miles is the top of Clear West Peak, 5644 feet.

Sit in the pea-patch-size flower garden and soak up the view: In one direction, a crazy quilt of clearcuts and, in the far distance, a microwave tower; forget that. In the other, Rainier's mile-high ice-and-rock precipice of Willis Wall, the Emmons and Winthrop Glaciers, and the spire of Little Tahoma. If lucky, watch an avalanche of ice blocks crashing down Willis Wall. Silently! Too distant for the crashing to be heard.

By carrying water, camp could be made here to watch the magic of the early dawn light turn the Emmons Glacier to pink-gold.

In 1984 Ira devoted much time and energy lobbying our Congressional delegates for the Washington Wilderness Act. Others spoke to the preservation of the ecosystems; he focused on preserving trails, including that to Clear West. Several years later he was shocked to find the "saved" trail unmarked and, in violation of the Wilderness Act, open to wheels. He contacted the district ranger, who checked with the surveyor, agreed Ira was right, and threw out the wheelers.

67 | NOBLE KNOB

Round trip: 7 miles
Hiking time: 5 hours (day hike or backpack)
High point: 6011 feet
Elevation gain: 500 feet in, 300 feet out
Hikable: July through October
Map: Green Trails No. 239 Lester
Information: White River Ranger District (360) 825-6585

If you want great views, climb to a once-upon-a-time fire lookout. If you want flowers, burn the trees. Because of a fire set by lightning (or somebody) in the 1920s, where eighty years ago was forest there now is a great big splash of color. In brilliant contrast to the little yellows and blues and reds underfoot is the enormous whiteness across the valley, the north side of Mount Rainier, close enough to see crevasses in the Emmons Glacier and cinders of the crater rim. Ira discovered all this while researching his fire lookout book.

Note the extensive rehabilitation work done by the Forest Service in meadows ravaged by jeepers and motorcyclists—destroyers that should not have been allowed on this trail in the first place. In 1984 the boundaries of the Norse Peak Wilderness were drawn to put at least part of the trail out of reach of machines. Then, recently, to accommodate bicycles, the Forest Service rerouted the trail outside the wilderness boundary! So the machines are back, not noisy (the "silent menace") but still mood-destructive.

Drive US 410 east of Enumclaw some 31 miles to an obscure sign on the right side pointing to Corral Pass on the left. At 55 miles an hour, one could easily miss the small sign. Check the odometer reading at the well-signed Buck Creek forest road. In 1.3 miles from Buck Creek, pass Alta Lodge; in 0.5 mile more, turn left on Corral Pass road No. 7174. Drive 6 steep miles to Corral Pass and a junction. To the left is the Noble Knob trail; to the right signed "Campground" is a large parking area with two trailheads, elevation 5650 feet. The Mount Rainier View Trail trailhead is on the uphill side.

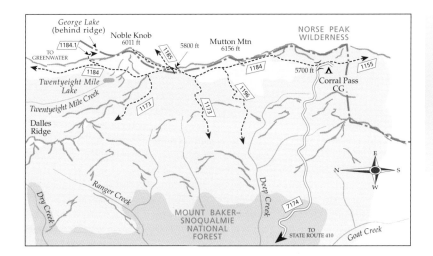

In brilliant contrast to the little yellows and blues and reds underfoot is the enormous whiteness across the valley, the north side of Mount Rainier.

Mount Rainier from Noble Knob trail

The trail contours a hillside, for ¾ mile alternating between flowers and groves of subalpine trees, and then follows the now-abandoned jeep road another ¾ mile. A short, abrupt bit of a climb ends in a resumption of trail. At 2 miles pass Deep Creek trail No. 1196 and at 2½ miles reach a 5900-foot saddle. From here the trail now drops steadily. At 3 miles, directly above Twentyeight Mile Lake, pass Dalles Ridge trail No. 1178.

Shortly beyond, at 5800 feet, is a triple split. The left fork, trail No. 1184, descends to George Lake, 5500 feet, and campsites (the lake can also be reached from road No. 72). The right fork goes down past Lost Lake to the Greenwater trail. Take the middle trail, cross a large meadow, and, with one switchback in a path overgrown in blossoms, traverse completely around the mountain to the old lookout site atop 6011-foot Noble Knob.

When built in the early 1960s, the lookout watched over miles of forest. By the late 1960s both the unbroken forest and the lookout were gone.

TWIN SISTERS LAKES

Round trip to Twin Sisters Lakes: 4 miles
Hiking time: 2½ hours (day hike or backpack)
High point: 5100 feet
Elevation gain: 800 feet
Hikable: July through October
Maps: USFS William O. Douglas Wilderness; Green Trails No. 271 Bumping Lake, No. 303 White Pass
Information: Naches Ranger District (509) 653-2205

The summer of 1980 I chanced to run across Chuck Hessey on a trail. "The Sage of Naches," we called him, because he lived beside that river and over the years had set boots on every trail and scramble path and game trace downwind of the Big Blow of Mount St. Helens. Indeed, he'd been out hiking that momentous morning of May 18, seen a horrid black thunderhead roll over the ridge from a clear blue sky, got out his poncho for the rain—but it wasn't rain that came down. After a musing pause, he reflected, "You know, I'd always wondered why the high country lakes around here have such sandy shores."

Drive Highway 410 east from Chinook Pass 19 miles (or 30 miles from Naches), turn right on Bumping River Road, and follow it 11 miles to the end of pavement, at which point it becomes road No. 1800. Continue 2.5 miles to a junction. Go straight ahead on road No. 1808 (shown on some maps as No. 395) another 7 miles, passing the horse camp at 6.5 miles, to the road-end at Deep Creek Campground, elevation 4300 feet.

Find Twin Sisters trail No. 980 on the north side of the campground. The way gains 800 feet in 2 miles (all in woods) to the smaller of the Twin Sisters Lakes, 5100 feet. The "little" lake (only a comparison, both are quite large) has numerous bays and rocky points. To reach the "larger" Twin Sisters Lake, follow trail No. 980 westward a

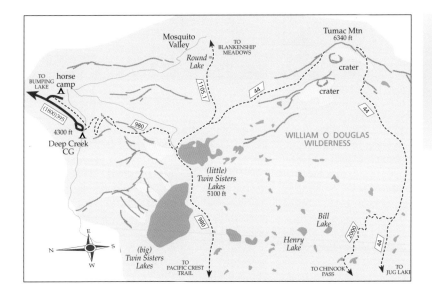

The many delightful sand beaches of the two lakes are all it takes to make the little kids in the party frantic with joy.

(First) Twin Sisters Lakes

scant ½ mile. Both lakes are outstandingly scenic and have beautiful campsites. They have many delightful sand beaches, the more so since the replenishment of May 18, 1980.

That's all it takes to make the little kids in the party frantic with joy, and you'll be hard-pressed to get them any farther. However, we recommend that a kid-watcher be left in charge of the beach and the rest of the group proceed onward and upward. From "Little" Twin Sisters Lake, turn left on trail No. 1104 and cross the outlet stream. In ½ mile the trail turns left toward Blankenship Meadows. Keep straight ahead on Tumac Mountain trail No. 44, which aims at the peak. The way climbs steadily in open meadows 1 mile to the summit, 6340 feet. (See Hike 69, Blankenship Lakes—Tumac Mountain).

Note how small trees are taking over the meadowland, a phenomenon that only recently has received attention. Are the trees just now growing after the Little Ice Age, or are they returning after catastrophic forest fires, insect invasion, or uncontrolled stock-grazing of years ago? Whatever the reason, subalpine meadows all over this portion of the Cascades are rapidly changing to forest, especially here and at Mount Rainier.

69 | BLANKENSHIP LAKES–TUMAC MOUNTAIN

Round trip to Blankenship Lakes: 12 miles
Hiking time: 6 hours (day hike or backpack)
High point: 5200 feet
Elevation gain: 2000 feet in, 200 feet out

Round trip to Tumac Mountain: 20 miles
Hiking time: Allow 3 days
High point: 6340 feet
Elevation gain: 3100 feet in, 200 feet out

Hikable: mid-July through October
Maps: USFS William O. Douglas Wilderness; Green Trails No. 303 White Pass
Information: Naches Ranger District (509) 653-2205

Photos of petite meadows, prairie-vast grasslands, and myriad subalpine lakes capture the eye, entice the feet. Beautiful pictures. Beautiful country. Yet note the name on the map: "Mosquito Valley." We classify the area as "hikable" from mid-July. But you'd never catch *me* there then. After a spell of September frosts, during the poignant colors of October, that's the season to be jolly, chortling at the billions of summer bugs now dead and gone. However, keep another menace in mind. I laughed to hear a comical sound behind a screen of trees, remarking to my companion that it must be a Boy Scout making a bad job of learning the bugle. My companion told me to shut up and run because that was no Scout, that was a bull elk and this was rutting season and he suspected us of flirting with his cows.

Drive US 12 east from White Pass 8.3 miles. A few hundred feet before Indian Creek Campground, turn left on road No. 1308 past summer homes. At a junction in 0.8 mile keep left, still on road No. 1308; at 2.8 miles from the highway is the parking lot by the trailhead signed "Indian Creek trail, No. 1105," elevation 3400 feet.

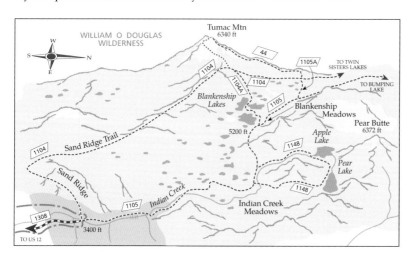

After a spell of September frosts, during the poignant colors of October, that's the season to be jolly.

Mount Aix from Tumac Mountain

The first 2 miles of trail are an old mining road, now closed to wheels because in ¼ mile it enters the William O. Douglas Wilderness. Just before the road-end find the start of true trail, which drops steeply 200 feet into a canyon, crosses Indian Creek, and climbs very steeply out of the canyon. At about 2½ miles listen for a waterfall to the right; step to the canyon rim for a close look. Lovely.

The trail crosses Indian Creek again at about 3 miles, recrosses at 4 miles, and at 4½ miles enters ½-mile-long Indian Creek Meadows. Stay on trail No. 1105, passing trail No. 1148 to Pear and Apple Lakes, a stone's throw from each other. The tread is faint as it traverses the meadow and heads west but becomes distinct again beyond the grass. At 5 miles pass trail No. 1148 to Apple Lake. (No. 1148 is a splendid 3-mile sidetrail loop of Pear and Apple.) At just under 6 miles take a short sidetrail to the first of the three Blankenship Lakes, 5200 feet, a fair spot for a basecamp (as are Indian Creek Meadow and Pear Lake). Another ½ mile along trail No. 1105 are Blankenship Meadows, many little clearings and one huge expanse.

For the trip's topper you must take in Tumac Mountain. (The summit can also be attained from Twin Sisters Lakes, Hike 68.) From Blankenship Lakes follow trail 1105 ½ mile to trail No. 1104, go right ¼ mile toward Twin Sisters Lakes. In meadows leave the trail and contour almost level to intersect trail No. 44 then climb almost 1000 feet in another 1½ miles to the summit, 6340 feet. Though the overlook of tree-ringed lakes and meadows is picturesque, the big feature is the most varied view of vulcanism in the Washington Cascades. Tumac itself—postglacial, and probably younger than 10,000 years—is no simple cone but, rather, built of both cinders and lava and having two craters (both lake-filled), an infant stratovolcano standing on a broad lava plateau. This is how Rainier began. The summit presents a panorama of stratovolcanoes of other ages: Spiral Butte, another infant, at the south end of the lava plateau; youthful St. Helens, expected by geologists to grow and violently blow again and again; bulky, mature, deeply dissected Rainier and Adams; and the old, old Goat Rocks, remnant of a once-mighty Adams-size volcano now reduced to mere roots. Do the climb in mid-July when upper slopes are covered with red and white heather plus a peppering of bright red paintbrush. Or do it in September—no color then, but no mosquitoes, either, and the Boy Scouts are bugling.

Incidentally, don't try to puzzle out an Indian source for "Tumac." Two "Macs," probably McAllister and McCall, grazed sheep in the area.

0 | BEAR CREEK MOUNTAIN

Round trip: 7 miles
Hiking time: 4 hours (day hike or backpack)
High point: 7336 feet
Elevation gain: 1400 feet
Hikable: mid-July through mid-October
Maps: USFS Goat Rocks Wilderness; Green Trails No. 303 White Pass
Information: Naches Ranger District (509) 653-2205

The Goat Rocks Wilderness is a long way from my home and when I undertake that much of an ordeal by highways I aim for familiar favorites, places I know are sure to be worth the trouble. Thus it was that many a year, poking about headwaters of the South Fork Tieton River, I'd look east to the outrigger ridges of the old Goat Rocks volcano and idly wonder what they were like but never did anything about it. A month after the St. Helens cannon went off, pointed right at the Goat Rocks, curiosity led me to go see. The "Ghost Rocks" they were called that summer. I climbed from Conrad Meadows in gray ash that was inches thick atop the snow. I then had to wonder what Bear Creek Mountain was like when the snow had melted and the ash had been washed and blown away. And "so my wealth increases, infinite riches in little room."

Of the two trailheads, the lower one from Conrad Meadows (see Hike 71, South Fork Tieton Headwaters Basin) is recommended in early summer, the flowers then at their best and the higher one usually snowbound until early July. However, the higher provides one of the very greatest backpacks there is for families where some of the young legs are very short and some of the old backs are aching.

Drive US 12 some 9 miles east of White Pass and before reaching Rimrock Reservoir turn right on the paved road signed "Tieton Road" and "Clear Lake." At 3.2 miles cross North Fork Tieton River and at 6.8 miles turn right on gravel road No. 1204; be careful to stick with this road. At about 11 miles is an unmarked junction; go right (uphill) on nongravel and maybe rough and rude road. At 13 miles heave a sigh at the road-end and trailhead a few feet from the murky pond humorously called Section 3 "Lake," elevation 6000 feet.

Trail No. 1130 is a dream, traversing wild-flowers and Christmas trees and creeklets and many a lovely (and little-used) camp. At ½ mile

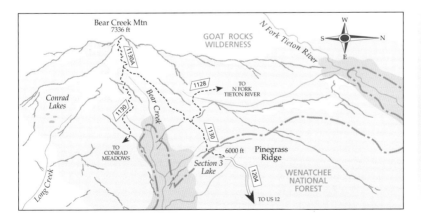

The higher trailhead provides one of the greatest backpacks there is for families where some of the young legs are very short and some of the old backs are aching.

Mount Rainier from Bear Creek Mountain

is a junction with trail No. 1128 from the North Fork. At 2½ miles is a junction with the trail from Conrad Meadows. From here the way winds up through lava rocks and cold-snowy nooks with a variety of different arrays of flowers and still more possible camps and at 3½ miles attains the summit and onetime site of a fire lookout, elevation 7336 feet. Look out to the great volcanoes of Rainier and Adams. Look around you, back down Pinegrass Ridge, and across the valley to Darling Mountain, and to Devils Horns, Tieton, Old Snowy, and Gilbert, and realize you are smack in the middle of a volcano that was worn out and broken down millennia before St. Helens was so much as a puff of steam in a lowland swamp.

71 | SOUTH FORK TIETON HEADWATERS BASIN

Round trip: 15 miles
Hiking time: Allow 3 days
High point: 5500 feet
Elevation gain: 1500 feet
Hikable: July through September
Maps: USFS Goat Rocks Wilderness; Green Trails No. 303 White Pass, No. 335 Walupt Lake
Information: Naches Ranger District (509) 653-2205

The glaciers on 8201-foot Gilbert Peak, highest of the Goat Rocks, gleam as white as the mountain goats often seen traversing the snows. Cliffs are brilliant: the black and gray and brown of Gilbert and Moon Mountain, the yellow and red of Tieton Peak, and the brick-red of Devils Horns. Warm Lake usually is frozen until late summer. Cold Lake floats icebergs from the Conrad Glacier. (Both are pristinely fish-free.) All this and much more invite the off-trail explorer. Yet a hiker never need leave a broad and easy path to rejoice in grand views and sublime flowers, following the South Fork Tieton River from Conrad Meadows to its source and making a long, looping swing around the headwaters basin.

Drive US 12 east from White Pass or west from Yakima to just east of Hause Creek Campground and turn south on South Fork Tieton Road, heading westward along Rimrock Reservoir. At 4.5 miles turn left on road No. 1000, signed "Conrad Meadows," and drive 14 miles to a gate at the edge of private property. Park near here, elevation 3900 feet.

South Fork Tieton trail No. 1120 passes the gate and fords Short Creek and Long Creek into Conrad Meadows, largest midmontane meadow in the Cascades and for that reason alone demanding to be added to the Goat Rocks Wilderness. (The Forest Service has a bushel of reasons why that can't be done; it's up to our letters to tell the rangers why it *must* be done.)

Beware of misleading cow paths in the cropped and flopped meadows and bulldozer roads in the wreckage of a lodgepole pine forest. (Multiple abuse!) At 1½ miles the path crosses the gated private logging road and proceeds to a crossing of Conrad Creek close

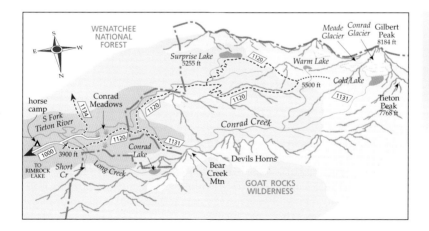

A hiker never need leave a broad and easy path to rejoice in grand views and sublime flowers.

Conrad Meadows and South Fork Tieton trail

above its confluence with the South Fork. The way sidehills the ridge between the two streams and drops to the South Fork valley floor.

At about 4 miles, 4300 feet, is a pair of junctions. The second, the fishermen's thoroughfare leading in 6 miles to the hole in the forest filled with Surprise Lake, 5255 feet, is the return leg of the loop. At the first junction, go right to begin interminable switchbacks nearly to the South Fork–Conrad divide. At the 5300-foot top of a pretty little meadow the trail commences a sublime contour around the South Fork basin, through gardens, by snowmelt waterfalls, to an unmarked junction, 5500 feet, 7½ miles.

The loop, as splendid a ride for equestrians as a walk for pedestrians, ignores this junction, descends to Surprise Lake and in about 7½ miles closes the circle on the valley floor. The Forest Service must insist that horses stay strictly to the loop. The heavy cavalry is logging out subalpine forests and stomping out meadows and no longer can be tolerated up high. Even hikers must take great care in the fragile terrain when they depart from No. 1120 at the unmarked junction, ascend ruins of an old track ½ mile to a 5600-foot saddle in the South Fork–Conrad divide, and commence their all-direction off-trail roaming.

72 | SHOE LAKE

Round trip: 14 miles
Hiking time: 7 hours (day hike)
High point: 6600 feet
Elevation gain: 2200 feet in, 400 feet out
Hikable: mid-July through October
Maps: USFS Goat Rocks Wilderness; Green Trails No. 303 White Pass
Information: Naches Ranger District (509) 653-2205

Meadows and parklands along the Cascade Crest, grand views of the Goat Rocks and Mount Adams, and a beautiful lake (absolutely fish-free, which is a mercy) in a green basin. All this an easy day from the road.

Drive US 12 east from White Pass 0.7 mile to the Pacific Crest Trail parking lot and trailhead opposite Leech Lake Campground, elevation 4400 feet. (For a shorter but steeper hike, park at White Pass ski area, 4400 feet, climb the ski hill

Shoe Lake and the Goat Rocks

Ground squirrel

1½ miles, and intersect the Crest Trail at a point 3 miles from the official trailhead.)

From the official trailhead the way traverses and switchbacks open forest, touching a ski run at one point, and at 3 miles, 5900 feet, reaches the ridge crest and the path from the ski area. The trail ascends into gardens and scattered alpine trees on the slopes of 6789-foot Hogback Mountain and swings to the west side of the crest and a great view of Mount Rainier. Attaining a 6400-foot saddle, the route contours steep, broad shale slopes on the east side of Hogback (an easy scramble from the trail to the summit) above the basin holding little Miriam Lake and climbs to a 6600-foot saddle, 6½ miles, in a spur ridge commanding views of the Goat Rocks and Mount Adams, and, below, the bright waters of Shoe Lake. This is a great place to take pictures and ponder whether the shape of the lake in fact resembles a shoe.

Drop 400 feet in ⅓ mile to the lake, 6200 feet, and fields of flowers. Camping, banned in the entire basin to give meadows a chance to recover from damage by past overuse, is permitted below the lake level and ½ mile beyond, at Hidden Springs. A scar of an old trail climbs the flower-covered hillside and would appear to offer a delightful loop around the lake. However, to keep horses from a former camp, the old tread has been decisively "put to bed."

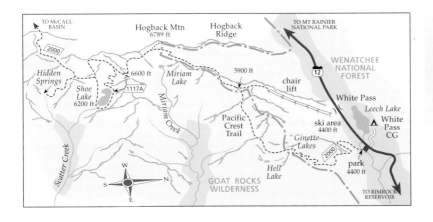

Take pictures and ponder whether the shape of the lake in fact resembles a shoe.

73 | PACKWOOD LAKE

Round trip: 9 miles
Hiking time: 5 hours (day hike or backpack)
High point: 3200 feet
Elevation gain: 500 feet in, 300 feet out
Hikable: June through November
Maps: USFS Goat Rocks Wilderness; Green Trails No. 302 Packwood
Information: Packwood Ranger District (360) 494-0600

A tree-ringed lake on the edge of the Goat Rocks Wilderness. From the outlet, look up to 7487-foot Johnson Peak. From the inlet, look back to Mount Rainier. A wooded island punctuates the picturesque waters. The lake meets three of the six criteria for a Classic—spectacular view of the peak and lake, water (a large lake), and forest (virgin forest lining the trail, 4 miles of it).

In 1959 Ira was asked to do a story on a primitive resort to which guests were flown in by seaplane. He received directions from the Packwood Ranger Station and hiked from the nearest road 6 miles to the resort, housed in attractive shake cabins. The owners, Mr. and Mrs. Martin Nowotny, were in a state of high distress, Washington Public Power having applied for a permit to build a 70-foot-high dam across the outlet, transforming the beautiful lake into an ugly reservoir.

It was deja vu all over again—the David vs. Goliath scenario. However David, backed by public opinion and the Forest Service, hollered loud and long and though Goliath was too big to kill, Nowotny, by good happenstance, had obtained a permit for a tiny paddle-wheel generator just where the dam was to be built; this prior right forced Goliath to compromise and the Forest Service was able to require a steady, non-fluctuating lake level. That's the good news. The bad is that the Federal Power Commission, faithful friend of power companies, mysteriously gave permission for the dam to be built 3 feet higher than specified in the agreement with the Forest Service. Permission so far has not been granted to raise the lake above the natural level. If ever it should be, the shore will be ruined.

More of the bad—the foot trail was built so wide and flat that every weekend hundreds of

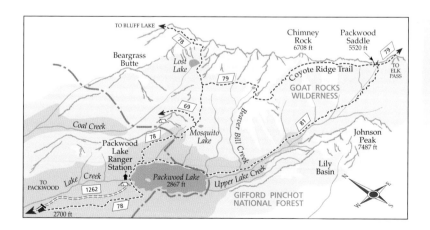

The lake meets three of the six criteria for a Classic— spectacular view, water, and forest.

Packwood Lake and Johnson Peak

children, old folks, and beginning hikers toddle, limp and trot to the lake, and we cheer that because it is good for green-bonding, but too many who cannot bear even briefly to un-bond with the city come carrying radios, beer, and gas lanterns. Further, though forbidden on the foot trail, motorcycles razz up and down the adjoining pipeline road. Best visit the lake on a weekday in bad weather.

From Packwood, next to the Packwood Ranger Station, drive east on road No. 1260, in 6 miles coming to a steel tower and, nearby, a large parking lot and the trailhead, elevation 2700 feet.

Trail No. 78 goes gently through big trees with occasional views over the Cowlitz valley toward Rainier. As the lake is neared, the snowy,

craggy Goat Rocks, dominated by Johnson Peak, appear at the valley head. With ups and downs grossing 400 feet but netting only 167 feet, at 4½ miles the trail reaches Packwood Lake, 2867 feet. The resort and campground are across the outlet. For quiet camping continue around the lakeshore to the inlet.

Actually, one can do a lot better than that with a 12½-mile loop from Packwood Lake. Hike toward Lost Lake and contour airy miles along 6700-foot Coyote Ridge on trail No. 79 to Packwood Saddle, 5520 feet. Return to Packwood Lake on Upper Lake Creek trail No. 81. About half the route is in steep meadows high above timberline, little traveled, very odd considering the population density at the lake and the superb scenery of the loop.

74 | LILY BASIN

Round trip to viewpoint: 8 miles
Hiking time: 5 hours (day hike)
High point: 5700 feet
Elevation gain: 1400 feet
Hikable: late July through mid-October
Maps: USFS Goat Rocks Wilderness; Green Trails No. 302 Packwood
Information: Packwood Ranger District (360) 494-0600

The old Gifford Pinchot National Forest recreation map featured a great picture of a hiker on a point 2000 feet above Packwood Lake, Mount Rainier in the distance. Ira's camera demanded that viewpoint. Rangers directed him to the trail. It was a winner. Spectacular views, lots of flowers, forest, and (at least when Ira was there), solitude, four of the six Classic criteria.

The trail traverses a forested ridge to the viewpoint, then contours Lily Basin, a high cirque under Johnson Peak. This used to be a remote corner of the Goat Rocks, reserved for hikers willing to sweat. Logging roads have ripped up the wildland to an elevation of 4500 feet, making an easy day for the most tender feet. Some would say that's the good news. We beg to differ.

Drive US 12 from Packwood Ranger Station west toward Randle 1.6 miles, passing the Packwood Lumber Company, and approximately opposite a motel turn left on road No. 48. At 8.8 miles from US 12 keep right at an

unmarked junction. At 9.8 miles go left on a seldom-maintained section of road No. 48 another 1.2 miles to the trailhead, on the right side of the road. Park on a wide shoulder just beyond, elevation about 4300 feet.

The trail, signed "Lily Basin Trail No. 86," ascends timber to an old burn, at ¼ mile enters Goat Rocks Wilderness, and at 1½ miles reaches the crest of a wooded ridge, 4900 feet. The path goes up and down along the crest, more ups than downs, occasionally contouring around a bump. At 4 miles, 5700 feet, begin heather and flower meadows and the boggling view of Packwood Lake and Rainier that drew Ira here. A good place for a peanut butter sandwich and the turnaround for a day hike.

At 4½ miles the trail dips under cliffs and regains the ridge top, proceeding to its very end at the base of Johnson Peak. It's only another 3 miles to Heart Lake, 5700 feet, and campsites. For still more, trail No. 86 continues to Jordan Basin, Goat Lake, and Snowgrass Flat.

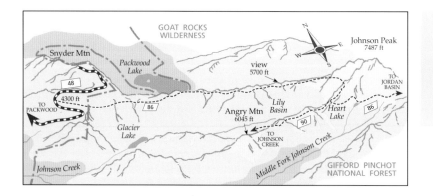

Heather and flower meadows and a boggling view of Packwood Lake and Rainier.

Packwood Lake and Mount Rainier from Lily Basin trail

75 | SNOWGRASS FLAT–GOAT RIDGE LOOP

Round trip to Snowgrass Flat: 8 miles
Hiking time: 5 hours (day hike or backpack)
High point: 5830 feet
Elevation gain: 1200 feet
Hikable: July through November

Loop trip: 13 miles
Hiking time: 8 hours (backpack)
High point: 6500 feet
Elevation gain: 1900 feet
Hikable: August through September

Map: USFS Goat Rocks Wilderness
Information: Packwood Ranger District (360) 494-0600

Until 1980 the sunsets at Snowgrass Flat were famously poignant, the snow cone close to the west shimmering in orange and pink above valleys already deep in night. By day, the meadows of Snowgrass Flat were as rainbow-brilliant as any in the Cascades. Then came the eruption, dumping on the west slope of the Goat Rocks the heaviest fall of ash except on St. Helens itself. Few flowers bloomed that summer. Subsequently, however, paintbrush, lupine and company staged a stunning show. It has been fascinating to watch the meadows recover from the blast, as they have from many other blasts over the centuries and millennia. Even were there no flowers, the views would be a sufficient glory—Adams, what's left of St. Helens,

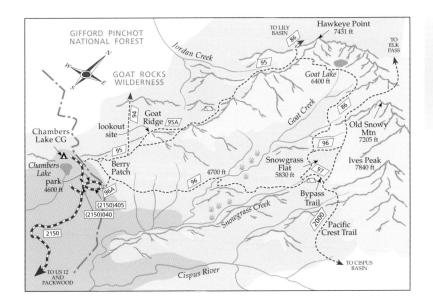

Either of two campsites make a fine base for exploratory walks along the Pacific Crest Trail.

Goat Creek valley from near Goat Lake

and, from the Goat Ridge loop, the Goat Rocks.

Drive US 12 south from Packwood 2.5 miles and turn east on Johnson Creek road No. 21. At 15.7 miles, just past Hugo Lake, turn left on road No. 2150, signed "Chambers Lake," and at 18.5 miles turn right on road No. (2150)040, then right again on No. (2150)405 to the hikers' trailhead at Berry Patch, 21.5 miles from Packwood, elevation 4600 feet.

Set out in the woods on Snowgrass Flat trail No. 96A and soon join trail No. 96. At 1¾ miles cross Goat Creek, 4700 feet. Especially in early summer, stop at the bridge to apply insect repellent, lots of it, because here the trail enters ¼ mile of swampy forest alive with a sound that ain't music. At 2 miles the trail begins climbing from the valley bottom, leaving behind the swarms of bloodsuckers. At 3½ miles reach Bypass Trail; keep left and continue up, emerging occasionally from trees into meadow patches, and at 4 miles finally enter the open expanse of Snowgrass Flat, 5830 feet.

To give nature a chance to repair the damage of chomping jaws and pounding hooves (and boots, too) camping is no longer permitted in the Flat. However, campsites can be found along Bypass Trail only minutes below and along the first mile of trail No. 86 to Goat Lake. Either makes a fine base for exploratory walks south 2 miles along the Pacific Crest Trail to Cispus Basin and north to its 7600-foot high point on the side of Old Snowy.

For the loop (often snow-covered until sometime in August), follow trail No. 86 northward from Snowgrass Flat, contouring a steep hillside 3 miles to Goat Lake, 6400 feet, generally frozen until sometime in August. At 3½ miles are the 6500-foot high point of the loop and a junction with Heart Lake trail No. 86. From here the trail contours the west side of Goat Ridge 2½ miles to a junction with Jordan Creek trail No. 94 and a few feet more to a choice of trails. The left fork climbs 300 feet and traverses the 6240-foot former site of Goat Ridge Lookout, the views panoramic. The right fork contours below the lookout, rejoins the lookout trail in ½ mile, and descends sharply to the starting point at Berry Patch.

76 | ADAMS CREEK MEADOWS

Round trip: 8 miles
Hiking time: 6 hours (day hike or backpack)
High point: 6840 feet
Elevation gain: 2300 feet
Hikable: mid-July through mid-October
Maps: USFS Mt. Adams Wilderness; Green Trails No. 366 Mount Adams West, No. 334 Blue Lake
Information: Mount Adams Ranger District (509) 395-3400

A grand place it is to sit, gazing to Goat Rocks, Rainier, and the truncated cone of St. Helens. A superb place it is to roam, among raw moraines and blocky lava flows, by ponds and waterfalls, in fields of flowers under the "Forgotten Giant," the Adams Glacier tumbling a vertical mile from the summit to the edge of the gardens. A great place, too, to watch sunsets and sunrises, seas of valley clouds, swirls of storm clouds arriving from the ocean, and, at night, the monstrous skyglow of Puget Sound City, visible from outer space.

From the center of Randle drive the road signed "Mt. Adams" a scant 1 mile south to a split. Veer left on road No. 23, signed "Cispus Center, Mt. Adams, Trout Lake, Cispus Road." Stay on road No. 23, paved at first, then gravel, to 32 miles from Randle. Turn left on road No. 2329. In 2 miles pass the sideroad to Takhlakh Lake and at 6 miles (37.7 miles from Randle) find the parking area and trailhead, elevation 4584 feet.

Killen Creek trail No. 113 (which never goes near Killen Creek) enters the Mount Adams Wilderness, ascends open pine forest brightly flowered by beargrass in early summer, and at 2½ miles, 5840 feet, opens out in a broad meadow brilliant early on with shooting star, avalanche lily, and marsh marigold, later with paintbrush and heather, cinquefoil and phlox. Here is the first water, East Fork Adams Creek, and nice camps.

The trail ascends lava-flow steps to cross the Pacific Crest Trail, 3 miles, 6084 feet. Above the Crest Trail intersection is the uprise of a spur ridge that ultimately joins the North Cleaver, a customary route to the summit of Adams. Continue upward 1 long mile from the Crest Trail to a broad meadow swale, 6840 feet, called High Camp, Mountaineers Camp, Adams Glacier Camp, take your pick.

Adams Creek Meadow

The one flaw of High Camp (other than the punishment it takes in storms, evidenced by the streamlined clumps of trees) is that on any fine summer weekend it's a mob scene. On my first camp there, in late June of 1948, the mob was entirely students and faculty of The Mountaineers Climbing Course. I thoughtfully rigged my 7-by-11-foot liferaft sail in the lee of one of those streamlined clumps. At midnight the leader tried to holler the mob out of the bags for the ascent of Mount Adams, but most, wind-smitten and bedraggled, were already fleeing to the cars, and a sizable fraction had somehow squeezed under my sail and in the roaring of wind were deaf to the hollering of leader. My next visit was quiet in the night, our small party sleeping soundly almost to dawn in preparation for the Adams Glacier, which we succeeded in climbing only because one of our bunch was basketball-player tall and just able to leap the ultimate icefall crevasse and reel in the rest of us from the pit in which our short jumps ended.

Since then it's the old story. Never follow the crowd. Go hide. Throughout the vast meadowlands of Adams Creek Meadows on one side of the spur and Killen Meadows on the other are innumerable private nooks. Visit High Camp—and go someplace else to camp. In the woods, please, to permit the meadows to recover from long abuse.

77 | MOUNT ADAMS HIGHLINE

One-way trip from Cold Springs to Devils Gardens: 24½ miles
Hiking time: Allow 3–4 days
High point: 7760 feet
Elevation gain: approximately 4000 feet
Hikable: mid-July through September
Maps: USFS Mount Adams Wilderness; Green Trails No. 366 Mount Adams West, No. 334 Blue Lake
Information: Mount Adams Ranger District (509) 395-3400

The 34-mile timberline circuit of Mount Adams is one of the greatest highland walks in the Cascades. Foregrounds of parkland and flowers and waterfalls rise to lava jumbles that look like yesterday's eruptions, and to a succession of glaciers tumbling from the 12,276-foot summit. By day the hikers look out to miles of forested ridges and three other massive volcanoes. By night they gaze to megalopolitan skyglows of Puget Sound City, Yakima, and Portland.

However, you can't hardly do it. The Great Gap, the 4½ miles between Avalanche Valley

Mount Rainier from Foggy Flat

Mount Adams from northern junction of Round-the-Mountain and Crest Trails

and Bird Creek Meadows, has a half-dozen major glacial torrents to cross; one, the main branch of the Big Muddy, often requires a bypass high on the Klickitat Glacier. There never has been and never can be a trail—not without megabuck outlays and a miles-long detour down the valley to where bridges could be built (and annually rebuilt).

Moreover, 8 miles of the circuit—including The Gap—require a permit from the Yakama Indian Tribal Council in Toppenish, a process as complicated as the Big Muddy. For reasons of

safety and politics, we advise starting the journey at Cold Springs Campground.

From Trout Lake drive north on road No. 80, at the start signed only "Mt. Adams Recreation Area." At about 5 miles go right on road No. 8040 to Morrison Creek Horse Camp at 12 miles, and then right on No. (8040)500 to the road-end at Cold Springs Campground, elevation 5600 feet.

Hike an abandoned road, now called trail No. 183, 1 mile to the Mount Adams Wilderness and a bit more to the Mount Adams Highline

Avalanche lily pushing through winter snow

(or Round-the-Mountain) trail No. 9, elevation 6200 feet.

To the right the trail contours 2 miles into legendary Bird Creek Meadows; the Yakamas allow day-use here for a fee. A sidehilling meadow mile leads to an overlook, 6512 feet, of Hellroaring Valley, this end of the Great Gap.

To the left the trail goes upsy-downsy, mainly in subalpine forest but with many meadow interludes and many vistas and many tempting sidetrips up to moraines and glaciers. Creeks and camps are frequent. At 7¼ miles from Cold Springs Campground, the Pacific Crest Trail is joined at Horseshoe Meadow, 5900 feet; a promontory just beyond gives a four-volcano vista, including the trip's last look at Hood.

Sidetrips continue to beckon as the Crest Trail proceeds north below little Crystal Lake and above little Sheep Lake, beyond the awesome Mutton Creek lava flow. At 14½ miles, 6100 feet,

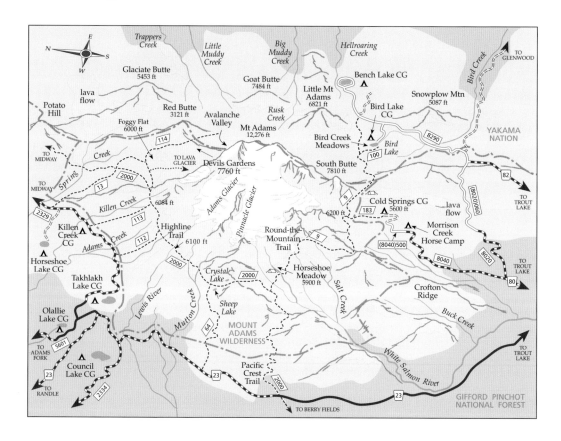

is the headwater creek of Lewis River; for a supreme basecamp, amble up the slope to meadowlands and settle down for days of exploring country below Pinnacle and Adams Glaciers. At 16 miles, 6084 feet, is a junction with Killen Creek trail No. 113 (Hike 76, Adams Creek Meadows), 3 miles from the road; for hikers wishing to focus on Avalanche Valley this is the proper approach.

At 17 miles Killen Creek is crossed. In ¼ mile more Round-the-Mountain Trail, here called Highline Trail No. 114, departs to the right from the Crest Trail, at 19½ miles entering Foggy Flat, 6000 feet. Now a stern uphill commences, from forest to the lava chaos below Lava Glacier, and at 24½ miles tops out in the tundra barrens of Devils Gardens, 7760 feet.

With necessary permits from the Yakama one can proceed 2 miles to Avalanche Valley. What's to say about this vale where cold springs gush from lava tubes and meander through the flowers beneath icefalls of Wilson and Rusk Glaciers, beetling crags of Battlement Ridge, Victory Ridge, The Spearhead, The Castle, and the hanging glaciers on Roosevelt Cliff? Well, when good little hikers finally check in their boots, this is where they go.

Bad little hikers spend eternity in the 4½ miles of The Gap, staggering from moraine boulder to boulder, leaping Big Muddy and Hellroaring, trying to find the one and only semi-easy way over the Ridge of Wonders, never quite attaining Bird Creek Meadows at 34 miles to complete the circuit.

Mount Adams from southern junction of Round-the-Mountain and Crest Trails

78 | BIRD CREEK MEADOWS LOOP

Loop trip: 5 miles
Hiking time: 3 hours (day hike)
High point: 6550 feet
Elevation gain: 1000 feet
Hikable: late July to September
Map: USFS Mount Adams Wilderness
Information: Mount Adams Ranger District (509) 395-3400

The Springs have been pilgrimaging to Bird Creek Meadows since the shorter feet of the family could toddle. While Pat and Ira gawked at the mountain and photographed meadows of wildflowers, the kids chased tadpoles in the three little lakes. For short trips for short legs this is the jewel of Mount Adam's flanks. Meadows, flowers, lakes, tumbling streams, and dotted with tall Christmas-perfect trees.

From Trout Lake (about 60 miles south of Randle on road No.23 or 22 miles from the Columbia River town of White Salmon on Highway 14), follow road No. 23 about 1 mile and turn right (straight ahead) on road No. 80. In another 0.5 mile go right again on road No. 82.

Enter the Yakama Indian Nation, which charges a modest day-use fee to help on the expenses. (Be warned, access roads can be rough and some years may be closed. Check at the Mount Adams Ranger Station in Trout Lake.) Drive to Mirror Lake, turn left on road No. 184 to Bird Lake and the Bird Creek Meadows trailhead, elevation 5585 feet.

A loop via Crooked Creek and Bluff Lake is a good introductory sampling. From Bird Lake cross the outlet to the lake and climb from woods to meadows, crossing Crooked Creek. At about 1 mile pass below Crooked Creek Falls and at 1¼ miles intersect the Round-the-Mountain Trail. For a nice sidetrip go left (west) about

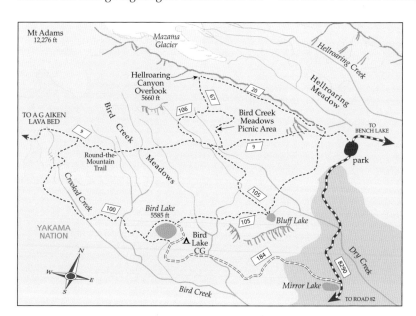

For short trips for short legs this is the jewel of Mount Adam's flanks.

Crooked Creek Falls

1 mile to the top of the 2-mile-long A. G. Aiken Lava Bed, which, except for a few straggly trees, looks like it just happened last week.

To continue the loop, go back to the intersection and follow the Round-the-Mountain Trail a short ½ mile to a mandatory ½-mile sidetrip to the Hellroaring Canyon Overlook, 6550 feet. Look up to the 300-foot headwall below the Mazama Glacier and down to the green meadow below.

Two alternatives for the return to Bird Lake are both nice. Either follow the windswept ridge back down to the Round-the-Mountain Trail and continue down past Bluff Lake to the start at Bird Lake or backtrack a bit and take the Bird Creek Picnic Area path.

79 | MOUNT BELJICA

Round trip: 4 miles
Hiking time: 5 hours (day hike)
High point: 5478 feet
Elevation gain: 1100 feet
Hikable: mid-July through October
Map: Green Trails No. 269 Mount Rainier West
Information: Packwood Ranger District (360) 494-0600

While scanning maps in the course of researching a book on fire lookouts, Ira came upon a strange name. What was a "Beljica"? Who? Why? The mystery demanded investigation. An ascent of the peak failed to solve the puzzle but did add a hike to his personal list of favorites.

On a summer day when the hikers on trails of Mount Rainier National Park outnumber the flowers, dodge away to Glacier View Wilderness. If the meadows and lakes don't quite equal those in the park, the relative solitude and the unsurpassed view of The Mountain more than compensate. The summit of Beljica is close enough to the mighty Tahoma Glacier to see ev-

Mount Rainier under a lenticular cloud

ery crevasse but far enough away to be humbled by the thousands upon thousands of vertical feet it tumbles from the summit icecap virtually to the forests.

Drive Highway 706 (the way to the Nisqually entrance of Mount Rainier National Park) 3.8 miles past Ashford and turn left on Copper Creek road No. 59. At 3.4 miles from the highway keep left at a junction, at 5 miles turn right on road No. 5920, and in 6.5 miles reach Lake Christine trail No. 249, elevation 4400 feet.

Ira remembers the trail was steep when he scouted it for his lookout book but on a recent trip was amazed at how much steeper this trail had become in seventeen years—the explanation being that Beljica must be a lot higher. The trail sternly ascends a short, rough ridge, then on better tread traverses a very airy sidehill to Lake Christine, 1 mile, 4802 feet. Continue past the small, meadow-ringed lake and climb a scant ½ mile to an unmarked and easy-to-miss junction. Turn left on the unmaintained trail ½ mile to the 5478-foot summit. What and why and who is Beljica? The peak was anonymous until climbed in 1897 by members of the Mesler and LaWall families, namely Burgon, Elizabeth, Lucy, Jessie, Isabel, Clara, and Alex—B-E-L-J-I-C-A.

Fill your eyes, exhaust your camera film. Trail No. 249 continues, and so can the trip. From the junction, descend 600 feet to the edge of Beljica

Close up of crevasses on the Tahoma Glacier

Meadows at 3½ miles. Continue to campsites at Goat Lake and, entering Mount Rainier National Park, to Gobblers Knob. If Goat Lake is the destination one can avoid the overwhelming view by shortcutting the trail from road No. 59. But Ira is darned if he will tell how.

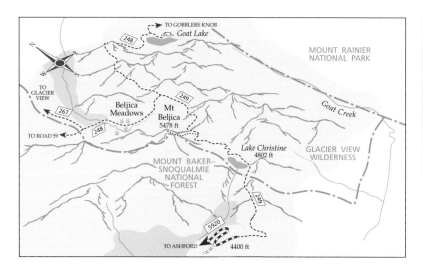

If the meadows and lakes don't quite equal those in the park, the relative solitude and the unsurpassed view of The Mountain more than compensate.

80 | HIGH ROCK

Round trip: 3 miles
Hiking time: 2 hours (day hike)
High point: 5658 feet
Elevation gain: 1400 feet
Hikable: June through October
Map: Green Trails No. 301 Randle
Information: Packwood Ranger District (360) 494-0600

A short, steady climb to a lookout with a breathtaking view of Mount Rainier. The cabin, built in the 1930s, sits on a point of rock that juts out in the sky like the prow of a ship. Once this was a challenging hike, but now, in common with most Forest Service trails south of Rainier, it is barely an afternoon walk—or better, a morning walk, when the lighting is more striking. A good trip for small children, but hold their hands tight on the last bit to the summit. For a number of years the building was abandoned and left to the mercies of vandals. To photograph The Mountain at sunrise, Ira carried his sleeping bag and spent the night; just his luck, clouds blew in. Before he had another chance the Forest Service reactivated the lookout.

Drive Highway 706 east from Ashford 3.8 miles and turn right on Kernahan Road, signed "Big Creek Campground–Packwood," about 1 mile to a steel bridge crossing the Nisqually River. At 1.5 miles is another junction. The easiest way to the trailhead is to go right on road No. 85 about 6 miles, then 5 miles more on No. 8400 to Towhead Gap, elevation 4301 feet. However, if sidetrips to Cora, Bertha May, or Granite Lakes are contemplated, go left on road No. 52, signed "Packwood." At 4.3 miles turn right on road No. 84, cross Big Creek, and start climbing. At 11.3 miles keep right on road No. 8400 and at 14 miles reach Towhead Gap.

Trail No. 266 starts on the north side of the gap, ascends a clearcut a few hundred feet, and enters forest. The first mile is mostly through trees, gradually thinning. The final ½ mile to the

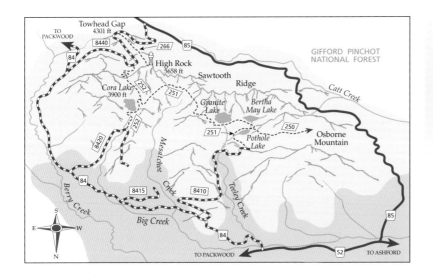

No vantage in the national park gives this magnificent sweep from Columbia Crest down to the Nisqually entrance.

lookout is fairly open, with views to Adams and St. Helens.

Climaxing all is the eye-popping panorama of Mount Rainier. No vantage in the national park gives this magnificent sweep from Columbia Crest down to the Nisqually entrance. Observe the outwash from the catastrophic 1947 flood of Kautz Creek. Note hanging ice on the Kautz Glacier ready to do it again. Pick out Mount Wow and peaks of the Tatoosh Range. See the green gardens of Indian Henry's Hunting Ground. When your eye shifts from The Mountain to your feet, hang on! Cora Lake is 1750 feet below, almost in spitting range.

At midday Rainier is a big, flat curtain of white. The best views are when the sun slants over the face of the mountain, the contrast of bright light and dark shadows delineating every ridge and valley, even the trees in the parklands and crevasses on glaciers. Therefore plan to be at the lookout before 10 in the morning or after 4 in the afternoon.

To while away the heat and flat light of midday, before or after the summit climb, visit lovely Cora Lake, reached by a ½-mile trail from road No. 8420, a spur from Big Creek road No. 84, or visit Bertha May and Granite Lakes on a 1-mile trail from Teeley Creek road No. 8410. A very nice 3-mile trail runs along under Sawtooth Ridge, connecting the lakes, but logging roads are so close and motorcycles so numerous that the lakes are mobbed by noisemakers. A dirty shame.

High Rock Lookout and Mount Rainier

81 | JUNIPER RIDGE

Round trip to Juniper Peak: 8 miles
Hiking time: 5 hours (day hike)
High point: 5593 feet
Elevation gain: 2000 feet
Hikable: mid-June through November
Maps: USGS McCoy Peak; Green Trails No. 333 McCoy Peak
Information: Randle Ranger District (360) 497-1100

Juniper Ridge bountifully satisfies two of the six criteria for a Classic—a museum display of volcano giants and a vastness of flowery meadows. The hiker with a bit of luck may also meet wildlife—elk and mountain goats. Paradoxically, he may also find, thanks (no thanks) to motorcycles, solitude.

Ira has made this area, together with the Mad River country and the Golden Lakes, virtually a career, ceaselessly nagging the Forest Service, flying to Washington at his own expense to lobby Congress. Progress has been made, but victory lies with letters by hikers to the Forest Service and Congresspeople.

Ira asks, how in the name of decency could the Forest Service serve up on a platter for the cavorting of a handful of ORVers a trail that in pristine peace safeguarded from racketing wheels would be delighting throngs of happy feet? Nearby wilderness areas (Indian Heaven, Goat Rocks, and Mount Adams) are so popular that the Forest Service advises hikers to go elsewhere. Where indeed? Juniper Ridge is a superb alternative—or would be were it not for motorcycles. Something there is in the spirit of a hiker that cannot abide machinery on the trail. When the wheels are let in, the feet fly out. Bureaucrats have been deafened by the archaic dogma of multiple-abuse. However, the Washington Trails Association, utilizing the legal skills of Karl Forsgaard, is seeking justice in the federal courts. The ORV use on Juniper Ridge has been slowed and ultimately may be stopped.

Views are dramatic up the Cispus River to Adams, out to Rainier and St. Helens and a seeming infinity of forested hills and valleys.

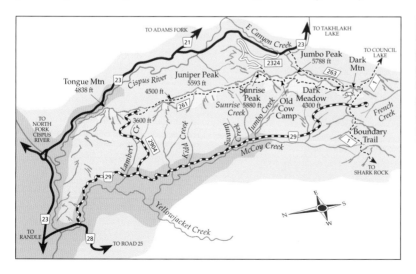

The route lends itself to a variety of trips: an easy afternoon stroll, a day hike, or an overnight backpack.

Mount Adams from the side of Sunrise Peak

The long ridge alternates between open slopes of huckleberries, beargrass, and flowers and young forest dating from the horrendous Cispus firestorms of 1902 and 1918. The route lends itself to a variety of trips: an easy afternoon stroll to a 4500-foot saddle (the trail this far generally is free of snow in early or mid-June); a day hike to Juniper Peak; an overnight backpack on a long approach to the Boundary Trail. After the snow melts (sometime in July), the ridge is too dry for camping unless water is carried. Day hikes thus are recommended to Tongue Mountain, Sunrise Peak–Jumbo's Shoulder, and Juniper Peak.

Turn south in Randle, cross the Cowlitz River, and drive 1 mile. Turn left on road No. 23 and in 9 miles (from Randle) turn right on road No. 28. At 10 miles leave pavement and go straight ahead on road No. 29. In 14 miles turn left on road No. 2904 and at 18 miles from Randle find trail No. 261 on the south side of the road, elevation about 3600 feet.

The trail goes a few hundred feet through a clearcut, enters second-growth forest, and traverses beneath two prominent knolls, ascending steadily, in frequent views, 2¼ miles to a 4500-foot saddle. The trail continues climbing, gaining 1100 feet, to within a few feet of the top of 5593-foot Juniper Peak, 4 miles, views far and near, and a good turnaround for day hikers.

To hike the full length, continue southward, dropping about 400 feet to pass beneath cliffs. At 5½ miles is a super-great huckleberry patch—outstanding even in an area legendary for berries. At 5¾ miles pass campsites at a tiny lake, dry in summer. At 7 miles is the Sunrise Peak trail, a ¼-mile sidetrip to the 5880-foot site of a former lookout. At 7¾ miles, after losing almost 1000 feet to a broad saddle, is Old Cow Camp (no water). The trail again climbs, passing beneath cliffs of 5788-foot Jumbo Peak, 9 miles, with a late July snowpatch (possible camping), and descends to the Boundary Trail at Dark Meadow, 12 miles, 4300 feet; campsites here with water. From Dark Meadow the Boundary Trail leads in 2 miles to road No. 29 at McCoy Pass. For a shorter trip try Sunrise Peak from Road 2324.

82 | COUNCIL BLUFF

Round trip: 3 miles
Hiking time: 3 hours (day hike)
High point: 5180 feet
Elevation gain: 960 feet
Hikable: mid-June through October
Map: Green Trails No. 334 Blue Lake
Information: Randle Ranger District (360) 497-1100

A name like Council Bluff implies that before Europeans arrived, the Original Inhabitants gathered there to contemplate the majesty of Mount Adams. Ira didn't find Originals, but in 1996 did come upon two women who had spent the night on top watching a total eclipse of the moon.

The ascent is easy in forest, then rock gardens, to the great circle of Hood, Adams, Rainier, Goat Rocks, St. Helens, and Potato Hill. With all that country in view, the summit was an obvious spot for the fire lookout which stood here from 1932 to 1960.

Drive south from Randle on road No. 23 to a junction 1 mile beyond Babyshoe Pass. Go straight ahead on road No. 2334 another 1.9 miles to Council Lake Campground, elevation 4221 feet. A badly eroded road that once served the lookout atop the bluff is still driveable, sort of, but we recommend that you park at the campground and walk the extra mile. If you walk to the road-end and find cars, you'll wish you had driven. On the other hand, if you drive you'll probably wish you had walked.

Find the road/trail at the upper edge of the

Council Bluff and Mount Rainier

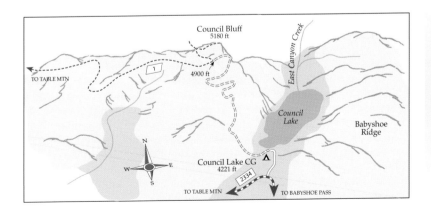

The ascent is easy in forest, then rock gardens, to the great circle of Hood, Adams, Rainier, Goat Rocks, St. Helens, and Potato Hill.

Mount Adams and fall color on Council Bluff

campground. Near the first switchback is a great view of Council Lake and Mount Adams. The road/trail ends in about 1 mile where a storage shed-garage once stood, elevation 4900 feet. From here a real trail climbs to the 5180-foot top. The almost level ¼-mile-long summit invites exploring.

Other than volcanic giants, the scenery includes Council Lake, Steamboat Mountain, Sleeping Beauty, and Indian Heaven. Potato Hill? That's the partly wooded, cone-shaped hill to the north. It, too, is a volcano, a little one, now extinct. Lots of those around here, and a number are "potatoes." Is it because they look like the tuber or is it because the Originals used to dig on their slopes for eatable roots?

83 | LEWIS RIVER

Round trip to Quartz Creek Camp: 9 miles
Hiking time: 7 hours (day hike or backpack)
High point: 2500 feet
Elevation gain: 500 feet, plus innumerable ups and downs
Hikable: June through November
Maps: USGS Quartz Creek Butte; Green Trails No. 365 Lone Butte
Information: Mount St. Helens National Volcanic Monument Headquarters (360) 247-3900

In the 1960s much of the Lewis River trail was bulldozed to make room for road No. 90. However, three surviving segments offer raging streams and tumbling waterfalls and cathedral groves of ancient trees. When Ira first walked here in the 1970s, red "cut here" signs marked many of the big trees. Thanks to some nameless forest ranger, not all the signs were obeyed and trees up to 8 feet in diameter still line the trail, rising 100 feet limb-free and straight—from one

Middle Falls on Lewis River

standpoint some of the best sawlogs left in Gifford Pinchot National Forest; from another, a superb example of ancient lowland forest, an ecosystem becoming rare almost to the vanishing point.

Drive either road No. 25 south from Randle or road No. 90 east from Cougar. At the north end of Swift Reservoir, just north of the Pine Creek Information Center, turn onto road No. 90. To find the first of the three "survivals" drive 5.2 miles and turn left on road No. 9039 for 1 mile to the Lewis River bridge. Park here and cross the bridge to find the lower trailhead, elevation about 1100 feet. For the second segment, featuring three splendid waterfalls, continue on road No. 90 another 9 miles to Lower Falls Campground. For the third go 2 more miles on road No. 90 to the Quartz Creek bridge and trail No. 5, elevation 1800 feet. If you have time for just one of the survivals do this third segment, described here.

The trail is seldom level, repeatedly climbing steeply over obstacles and dropping just as steeply. The first ⅔ mile is along Quartz Creek on an old miners' road, the trees here as yet unmolested. Above the trail, just before dropping to Platinum Creek, is the miners' rusted machinery. Platinum Creek is the first "interesting" stream crossing, which is to say, difficult in high water.

The way climbs steeply, then traverses the edge of a twenty-year-old clearcut with a healthy stand of young trees. At 2 miles cross Straight Creek on a large log with ax-flattened top; a nervous person might feel better scooting across on what climbers know as the fifth point of suspension. On the far side is a good camp

Forest along the Lewis River trail

and just downstream are Quartz Creek Falls; other falls are upstream on Straight Creek.

At 4 miles are a log bridge over Snagtooth Creek and more camps. At 4½ miles is an unsigned junction. The main trail, marked by two blazes, goes left, uphill. Take the right, marked by four slash-line blazes, and drop ¼ mile to the magnificent trees of delightful Quartz Creek Camp, 2300 feet.

Quartz Creek trail continues, albeit lacking the preceding loving care, to a junction at 6 miles with the Snagtooth Mountain trail leading to road No. 9341. At 10½ miles the way intersects Boundary Trail No. 1 near road No. 2325.

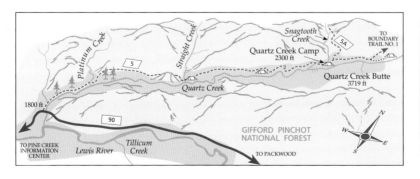

Three surviving segments of trail offer raging streams and tumbling waterfalls and cathedral groves of ancient trees.

84 | INDIAN HEAVEN LOOP

Loop trip: 9½ miles
Hiking time: 6 hours (day hike or backpack)
High point: 5237 feet
Elevation gain: 1700 feet
Hikable: July through October
Maps: USFS Indian Heaven Wilderness; Green Trails No. 365 Lone Butte, No. 397
    Wind River
Information: Wind River Ranger District (509) 427-3200

A fascinating portion of the Pacific Crest Trail, 23 lakes big enough to have names and almost 100 smaller lakes, ponds, and tadpole pools, all in an area at about 5000 feet elevation, a medley of forest, groves of subalpine trees, and flat, grassy meadows, the foregrounds complemented by glimpses of glaciered volcanoes.

Indian Heaven has been fondly known to hikers and horsemen for many years, but remoteness used to keep their visits to a minimum. In recent years logging roads have given quick access to the innermost lakes and meadows, and in 1984 Congress designated the Indian Heaven Wilderness, spreading the fame across the nation. Trails in the soft pumice meant for occasional use could not withstand the heavier traffic, especially the heavy pounding by horses. So the Forest Service abandoned the

old trails and built new and tougher ones.

In Ira's file of Forest Service maps from the 1950s he found the abandoned trails and when seeking a bit of solitude has no trouble following them. Unfortunately, solitude-loving horsepeople also use these unstable trails and the resource damage the Forest Service tried to eliminate continues. (The recent 7.5-minute USGS maps do not show the old trails but did help Ira find his way down into the flower-covered bottom of East Crater.)

The new trails can be sampled on a day-long 9½-mile loop, an overnight 18-mile loop, or by half a week or more checking off all 23 lakes plus as many tadpole pools as the heart desires. Usually the snow melts out early in July, when Indian Heaven is appropriately called "Mosquito Heaven"; late August or September are

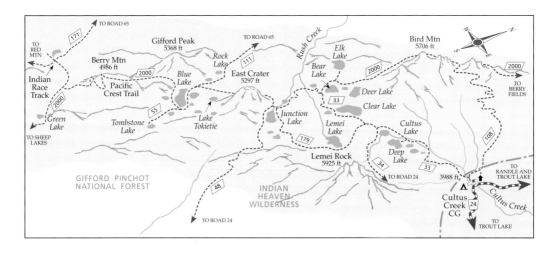

Indian Race Track

recommended, the bugs gone and, incidentally, the blueberries ripe. Don't be fooled by the seemingly flat terrain—the paths have many little ups and downs. Campsites are numerous, some near lakes and others by streams.

Maps show many roads and many trailheads. Because much of it is paved, Ira recommends road No. 88. From Trout Lake drive past the ranger station on Highway 141. Opposite the gravel pit, turn right on road No. 88. Pass by Big Tire Junction and Mosquito Lakes and continue to the end of the pavement at the junction with road No. 30. Go left on road No. 24 to Cultus Creek Campground, elevation 3988 feet. Do not park in campsites.

Trail No. 33 begins in forest, climbing to Cultus Lake at 2 miles, 5050 feet, a body of water typical of many of the lakes, trees around half the shore, meadows around the rest. To the southeast is 5925-foot Lemei Rock and to the northwest 5706-foot Bird Mountain; these peaks are useful landmarks, visible from a number of the lakes. Dig out the map and plan your long loop, or short loop, or maybe this lake is far enough.

Recommended as one long sidetrip from the loop (or an in-out from road No. 65 on trail No. 171), is the Indian Race Track. From far around the Original Inhabitants gathered annually for the blueberry harvest and autumn frolic. The 2000-foot-long rut worn in the meadow by racing horses can still be seen in part.

85 | NORWAY PASS–MOUNT MARGARET

Round trip to Norway Pass: 5 miles
Hiking time: 3 hours (day hike)
High point: 4508 feet
Elevation gain: 900 feet
Hikable: July through September

Round trip to Mount Margaret: 11 miles
Hiking time: 6 hours (day hike)
High point: 5858 feet
Elevation gain: 2300 feet
Hikable: August through September

Map: Green Trails No. 332 Spirit Lake
Information: Mount St. Helens National Volcanic Monument Headquarters (360) 247-3400

The cataclysm of 1980 flattened the forest along the trail to Norway Pass. Two years passed before Mount St. Helens was deemed quiet enough for visitors anywhere near the ridges above Spirit Lake. Wishing to duplicate a pre-eruption picture, as soon as restrictions were relaxed Ira and wife Pat set out for the pass. Mile after mile they waded in deep pumice, crawled over, under, and around logs. The sky cloudless, the sun merciless, the hills steep and barren, no shade, no water. But there was a reward: a view about as awesome as Ira expects ever to see this side of Hades.

Well, that was 1982. A good trail now makes their 10-hour ordeal an easy 2 hours (still no shade, though). Also, the wildflowers are coming back. Of course, the awesome view is what draws the throngs.

The Boundary Trail (as it is now called) to Norway Pass, Mount Margaret, and to Johnston Ridge is the best vantage from which to *feel* the devastation of May 1980, to gaze open-jawed at the new (and ghostly) Spirit Lake and the crater that destroyed the perfect symmetry of the "Fujiyama of the West." Carry water and perhaps a parasol. *Note:* Steep snow slopes below Mount

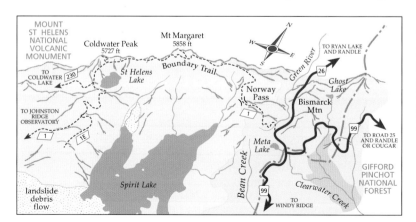

Gaze open-jawed at the new Spirit Lake and the crater that destroyed the perfect symmetry of the "Fujiyama of the West."

Beargrass on side of Mount Margaret, Spirit Lake and Mount St. Helens

Margaret may not be safe until late summer.

Drive road No. 25 south from Randle 22 miles and turn uphill on road No. 99, signed "Mount St. Helens–Windy Ridge Viewpoint." At 8.9 miles from road No. 25 turn right on Ryan Lake road No. 26 and in 1 mile reach Norway Pass trailhead, elevation 3600 feet.

The trail switchbacks up through blown-down forest. On slopes where the blast of hot gas and ash blew straight out from the mountain the trees lie flat in tidy parallel lines; where the blast eddied in the lee of a hill, they are piled one atop the other in a haphazard jackstraw.

At Norway Pass, the old mining machinery that used to be of interest disappeared in the blast, but a badly dented boiler thrown up from the Campfire Girls camp on Spirit Lake can be seen—if one can take eyes off the view down to Spirit Lake, half-filled with logs. Note how a giant "tidal" wave (the technically accurate term is *seiche*) washed away the forests 500 feet above the shore.

From the pass continue climbing westward, with several substantial ups and downs, into the flower gardens of Mount Margaret and views down to the Mount Margaret backcountry lakes—first Grizzly, then Boot and Obscurity. At about 5½ miles a short spur from the Boundary Trail climbs to within 20 feet of the 5858-foot summit of Mount Margaret and aerial views of Spirit Lake and Mount St. Helens. To the north is Rainier, east Adams, and south Hood. The Boundary Trail continues to Johnston Ridge Observatory at 10 miles.

215

Chapter 5

OLYMPICS

Ocean beaches, rainforest valleys, meadow ridges, cirque lakes, rock peaks standing tall above broad glaciers—is there in the old 48 states, or for that matter in the 50, such another wilderness cornucopia?

How is it fixed for day hikes and short backpacks, edge wilderness for introductory greenbonding? An abundance of that, on the ocean at Toleak Point and Hole-in-the-Wall. In valleys of the Hoh and Quinault. Along Grand Ridge from Deer Park to Obstruction Point. Lower Lena Lake to Upper. Mount Olympus and the Blue Glacier, as viewed from the High Divide having the look of a chunk of Alaska broken loose from its moorings.

Wilderness for semi-expeditions? It doesn't get much deeper in the old 48 than O'Neil Pass, two or more days from the road by any trail, or the mythic off-trail traverse of the Bailey Range from the High Divide to Cream Lake to Queets Basin. In my time at Camp Parsons and Ira's at Camp Cleland, Scout parties looped far and wide, on and off trails, and if in four or five days did no better than 50–60 miles, no bragging. Equally memorable for me in my post-Scouting was crossing the range from the Hoh River to the Blue Glacier, over Glacier Pass to the Hoh Glacier, over Blizzard Pass to the Humes Glacier, to Queets Basin and down to Elwah Basin, up to Low Divide and out the Quinault; peaks bagged on the rainy way, Olympus, Barnes, Christie, and a then-nameless summit while searching in the clouds for Blizzard Pass.

One visit (of his many) to a certain Classic that Ira doesn't talk about a lot is the time he took the lazy way home from the Wilderness Beach. Subsequently he suggested to the Park Service that to "BEWARE OF GIARDIA" signs it add "BEWARE OF SLIPPERY ROCKS." He was just minding his own business, studying a tide pool, and WHAM, there's the Coast Guard air taxi.

As Scouts in the 1930s we didn't fall down on beaches, though occasionally we might get a scalp creased by a falling rock or legs and arms abraded during a head-over-heels glissade. Neither did we suffer giardiasis, which hadn't yet been invented; now and then a weak-willed companion would be driven witless by thirst and drink from a tadpole pond and come down with the "Boy Scout trots." Good for laughs. I kept myself physically strong, mentally awake, and morally straight by sucking a prune pit.

The Classics chosen for this book tell how our romances with the Olympics began, years ago, at Mount Ellinor and Lake of the Angels, the Poop-Out Drag and Flypaper Pass. No matter how far we philander in other wildlands, we're both still sweet on our first love.

Hart Lake and Mount Duckabush

86 | MOUNT ELLINOR

Round trip to summit: 4½ miles
Hiking time: 5 hours (day hike)
High point: 5944 feet
Elevation gain: 2100 feet
Hikable: mid-July through October
Maps: Custom Correct Mt. Skokomish–Lake Cushman; Green Trails No. 167 Mount Steel, No. 168 The Brothers
Information: Hood Canal Ranger District (360) 877-5254

From the top of Mount Ellinor, Puget Sound and Hood Canal are laid out like a map, Rainier, Adams, and St. Helens on the horizon. In the other direction are Mount Olympus, the twin ears of Mount Stone, the double top of The Brothers, and the cliffs of Mount Washington. Below in the Jefferson Creek valley, 2000 feet down, is inviting Ellinor Pond. This—the spectacular view—is the trip's only solid claim left to status as Classic. Not on the criteria list is another—Memories.

Ira spent his boyhood in Shelton, where Mount Ellinor lay outside the Springs' living room window. In 1932 their father led Ira and twin brother Bob to the top of their first real mountain. During school years they repeated the climb many times, and the day of high school graduation returned from Mount Ellinor with faces sunburned brilliant. In 1932 the trail began on the shores of Lake Cushman, elevation 750 feet. The ascent gained 5200 feet, a vertical mile. Logging roads have cut the elevation gain to 2100 feet, cut the virgin forest altogether, and pretty much destroyed the solitude. But there are still, as ever, the spectacular views.

From 1853 to 1857 George Davidson surveyed Puget Sound, working from the brig *R. H. Fauntleroy,* named for his superior, the head of the U.S. Coast and Geodetic Survey. Needing names for the maps he was making, he drew upon the Fauntleroy family, calling the southernmost peak on the Olympic skyline Ellinor for the youngest daughter, the double-

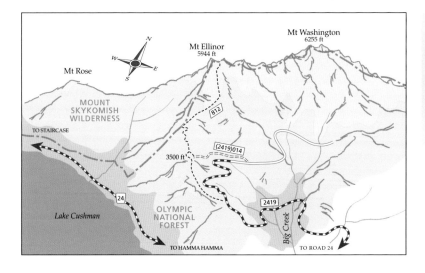

The new Summit Trail climbs forest, heather meadows, rockslides, scree slopes, and flower gardens.

Mountain goat near the summit of Mount Ellinor

summited peak for her Brothers, and the highest point for her older sister Constance. Later, Davidson and Ellinor were married. Because of her mountain's striking resemblance to the profile of the Father of Our Country, subsequent mappers shifted Ellinor to a lower peak, and her original namesake became Mount Washington.

In 1932 the official trail ended at the first meadow. From there to the top was a wild and dangerous rock scramble. A snap for hikers with more energy than skill. However, the logging road brought the danger within reach of folks with no experience and less sense. Slippery slabs, steep snowfields, and boulders let loose by careless feet made many pay a high price. In 1990 volunteers Frank Maranville (age 71), Frank Heuston (76), and Tom Weilepp (61), helped by the Olympia branch of The Mountaineers and Olympic National Forest, built a new, safe (relatively) trail to the top, steep all the way, but much less dangerous. In 1998 the three are still diligently maintaining their trail.

Drive US 101 along Hood Canal to the center of Hoodsport. Turn west and go 9 miles on Lake Cushman road to a junction. Turn right for 1.6 miles on road No. 24, then left on Big Creek road No. 2419, past the lower trailhead at 4.8 miles from road No. 24. At 6.4 miles go left on road No. (2419)014 to the road-end and trailhead, elevation about 3500 feet. Carry a full canteen; the slopes are dry.

Find the path ascending very steeply up the nose of the ridge. At ¼ mile go left at a junction and continue up. At a long 1 mile, about the time the first heather appears, is the start of the new Summit Trail, climbing forest, heather meadows, rockslides, scree slopes, and flower gardens. The only consistency is steepness, gaining another 1100 feet in a scant mile, the tread faint in rocky stretches. The final 50 feet are still a scramble. When the trail emerges on the summit rocks, watch carefully to note where the tread ends, lest on the way down you stray into cliffs.

87 | FLAPJACK LAKES

Round trip to lakes: 16 miles
Hiking time: 10 hours (day hike or backpack)
High point: 3850 feet
Elevation gain: 3200 feet
Hikable: mid-June through October
Maps: Custom Correct Mount Skokomish–Lake Cushman; Green Trails No. 167
    Mount Steel
Information: Olympic National Park Wilderness Information Center (360) 452-0300
Backcountry reservation and use permit required for overnight stay

Two subalpine lakes set side by side like flap-jacks in a frying pan. Above the waters and the forests rise sharp summits of the Sawtooth Range, a group of peaks noted among climbers for the oddness of the rock, which largely consists of "pillow lava" erupted under the surface of an ancient sea.

In 1940 Ira was part of a crew from the Shelton Ridge Runners, a ski club, and the Bremerton Ski Cruisers who built a two-story cabin on the shore of Upper Flapjack Lake. While the work was in progress they stayed in one of the two three-sided shelters that stood between the lakes.

They had anticipated great skiing on the wide-open slopes of Mount Gladys. However, it so happened that whenever a storm came through it washed out the Staircase road. Further, snow deep enough for good skiing made the trail a misery. To cap their woes, Pearl Harbor was bombed and between the army and gas rationing there wasn't much skiing for a while. While they were away at the war their cabin was damaged beyond repair by a falling tree.

The road beyond Staircase proved so difficult to keep open that the desires of Mother Nature at length were heeded and the road abandoned, deepening the wilderness. Not deep enough to dampen ardor for the lakes. Don't expect solitude, just tall trees 5 and 6 feet thick, views from the top of Mount Gladys, flowers and heather on its slopes, two beautiful lakes and wildlife, if

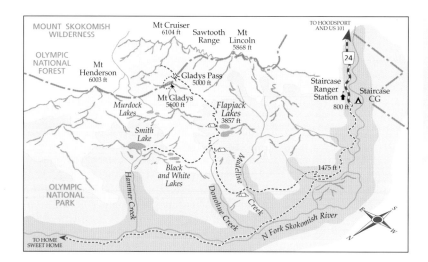

Roam flower gardens to the summit of Mount Gladys and stare at the frightening walls of Mount Cruiser ("Bruiser").

that's the proper term for the deer that wander past the tent and the bear who will be glad to share a meal—yours.

Drive US 101 along Hood Canal to Hoodsport. Turn west, pass Lake Cushman, go left on road No. 24, and follow the North Fork Skokomish River Road to Staircase Ranger Station and trailhead, elevation 800 feet, some 16 miles from Hoodsport.

The North Fork Skokomish River trail follows the abandoned road the first 3¾ miles to a junction, elevation 1475 feet. Turn right on the Flapjack Lakes trail—genuine trail—ascending steadily in cool forest to Madeline Creek at 5¼ miles and a campsite across the bridge. The way steepens. At 7½ miles are more campsites beside Donahue Creek, where a way trail goes left to Black and White Lakes. At 8 miles reach the Flapjacks, 3857 feet.

The Sawtooth Ridge is a ragged skyline. To the left is Mount Cruiser, to the right Mount Lincoln.

In the middle is a prominent tooth that Ira's gang, in the 1930s, called "The Chipmunk." On an autumn night of 1946 with the full moon (made of green cheese, then) touching its yearning snout, I called it "The Mouse." Ira has come to agree that in moonlight it is indubitably a mouse but insists that in daylight it's a chipmunk.

The trip only just begins for real at the lakes. For high and wide meadows and broad views, walk the Mount Gladys way trail 1½ miles up a lovely valley of rocks and flowers to Gladys Pass, 5000 feet, between a rounded garden peak and a vicious finger of lava. Roam the gardens to the 5600-foot summit of Mount Gladys. Stare at the frightening walls of 6104-foot Mount Cruiser ("Bruiser"), whose tower is visible from Seattle, standing like a boundary monument on the southeast corner of Olympic National Park.

Popularity has forced stringent restrictions on camping at the lakes. However, day hikes from Donahue Creek are practical.

Lower Flapjack Lake and Sawtooth Ridge

88 | HOME SWEET HOME

Round trip to Home Sweet Home: 27 miles
Hiking time: Allow 2 days
High point: 4688 feet
Elevation gain: 4000 feet in, 500 feet out
Hikable: July through October
Maps: Custom Correct Mount Skokomish–Lake Cushman; Green Trails No.167
　Mount Steel
Information: Olympic National Park Wilderness Information Center (360) 452-0300
Backcountry use permit required for overnight stay

In early May a small elk band is still in the Skokomish valley and trillium and calypso orchids are in bloom. When growing up in Shelton, Ira often in that season walked the gentle trail 7½ miles to Camp Pleasant. Twice, with friends, he carried skis and climbed over First Divide to Home Sweet Home's three-sided shelter, a cozy nest in a cold white world.

Drive US 101 to the center of Hoodsport and turn west, pass Lake Cushman, and go left on road No. 24 to the Staircase Ranger Station, elevation 800 feet.

The first 3¾ miles of the North Fork Skokomish River trail follow an abandoned, revegetated road which in the era of the Works Progress Administration (WPA) was headed over First Divide to Home Sweet Home and would have wound up at Lake Quinault. Had this highway engineers' scheme prevailed—and the companion scheme for a highway up the Dosewallips to Anderson Pass and down the Quinault to the ocean—precious little deep wilderness would have remained in the Olympics.

At 6 miles pass Big Log Camp, a spacious area beside the stream. At 6½ miles the path bridges the river over a deep, quiet pool. Immediately beyond is a junction; go right. The trail climbs slightly to Camp Pleasant, 7½ miles, 1600 feet, on a large maple flat. This appropriately named spot is a good overnight stop for springtime backpackers. At 10 miles, 2091 feet, is Nine Stream and the end of level walking. In the next mile the trail ascends at a comfortable rate through a big meadow, then forest. After that the way is continuously steep and often rough. Flower gardens become more frequent. Mount Hopper and Mount Stone appear to the southeast. At 12½ miles the trail enters a meadow below Mount Steel, turns sharply right, and climbs to the crest of 4688-foot First Divide, 13 miles,

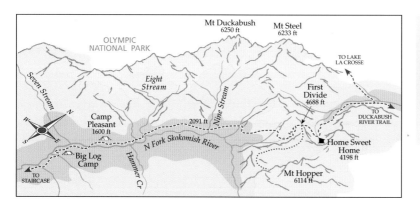

Depending on the season, that sweetness in the air is from the blossoms of avalanche lilies or the beautiful field of lupine.

Flower garden at Home Sweet Home, and Mount Steel

and views across the Duckabush valley to Mount La Crosse, White Mountain, and the greenery of La Crosse Pass. The path descends ½ mile to Home Sweet Home, 4198 feet. Depending on the season, that sweetness in the air is from the blossoms of avalanche lilies or the beautiful field of lupine. The view of 6233-foot Mount Steel is superb.

Many hikers continue 2 miles to the Duckabush River trail, losing 2000 feet. They then either proceed onward, climbing 2500 feet to Lake La Crosse and over O'Neil Pass to the Enchanted Valley (Hike 96), or hike 1½ miles downstream and climb a grueling 3000 feet to 5566-foot La Crosse Pass, the route to Honeymoon Meadows on the Dosewallips.

89 | UPPER LENA LAKE

Round trip to upper lake: 14 miles
Hiking time: 12 hours (backpack)
High point: 4600 feet
Elevation gain: 3900 feet
Hikable: to lower lake April through November, to upper lake July through October
Maps: Custom Correct The Brothers–Mount Anderson; Green Trails No. 168 The Brothers
Information: Olympic National Park Wilderness Information Center (360) 452-0300
Backcountry use permit required for overnight stay

An easy trail, free of snow most of the year, ascends splendid forest to popular and often crowded Lena Lake—which should be in The Brothers Wilderness but was omitted because of a proposed hydroelectric project—a project so preposterously destructive that not only environmental groups but the Forest Service are protesting. To add immediate insult to possible injury, the Forest Service has opened the trail to bicycles, thus effectively closing it to happy walking the first 3 miles.

This was Ira's summer country of Boy Scout years, starting in 1931. Camp Cleland, on Lena Lake, had eight patrol cabins, several staff buildings, a large cookhouse, a water system, six wooden rowboats, and an eight-hole outhouse. Many, many are the golden memories of that basecamp, its traces obliterated by time. But the proof of a basecamp lies in what is beyond: The Brothers, Upper Lena Lake, and roaming to Mount Stone, Lake of the Angels, and wherever. The Scouts did all that and more. But life doesn't end with Boy Scouts. Pat and Ira spent their honeymoon at Upper Lena Lake, returned for their twenty-fifth wedding anniversary, and who knows, with help from grandchildren may get back for their fiftieth.

Ira admits to being prejudiced. He concedes

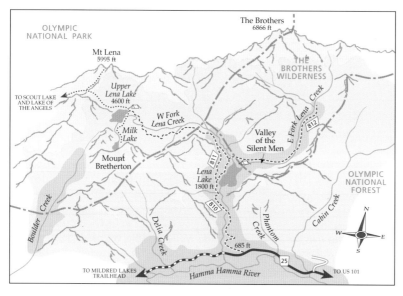

Upper Lena Lake meets five of the six criteria for a Classic: views, lakes, flowers, heather-covered alpine meadows, and, if lucky, herds of elk.

Tarn below Mount Stone

there are more spectacular mountains in the North Cascades and more flowers around Mount Rainier. However, he defies anyone to deny that Upper Lena Lake meets five of the six criteria for a Classic: views, lakes, flowers, heather-covered alpine meadows, and, if lucky, herds of elk.

Drive US 101 along Hood Canal some 14 miles north of Hoodsport, cross the Hamma Hamma River bridge, and 0.5 mile beyond Waketickeh Creek turn left on Hamma Hamma River road No. 25 and drive 8 miles to the trailhead, elevation 685 feet.

The wide trail switchbacks gently and endlessly in forest shadows. The trees look respectable now but in 1931, Ira's first year at camp, the initial ½ mile was being clearcut and the Scouts had to go straight up a fire line. At 1½ miles today's plush path crosses the dry streambed of Lena Creek, which runs underground most of the year. At 3 miles is Lena Lake, 1800 feet. Here the trail splits. The right fork drops to campsites by the lake and rounds the west shore ½ mile to more.

For Upper Lena Lake, stay left, following West Fork Lena Creek, entering Olympic National Park at 4 miles. At approximately 5 miles, 2700 feet, the trail crosses a small creek which can be hazardous during spring runoff. Beyond, the trail deteriorates to a boot-beaten path. As the way climbs, the vegetation changes to subalpine forest, heather and huckleberry and Alaska cedar. Occasional views open down the valley toward The Brothers. The steepness ends abruptly at Upper Lena Lake, 4600 feet, 7 miles. A rough up-and-down way trail rounds the north side.

Camping, which over the years has trampled large areas to bare dirt, is now restricted to designated sites; many former sites are being revegetated by the Park Service. The shore demands roaming, as do the meadows and screes ringing the cirque. For more ambitious explorations scramble to the summit of 5995-foot Mount Lena, or follow a boot-beaten track over a 5000-foot ridge near Mount Lena to Scout Lake, or follow the ridge by its numerous tarns toward Mount Stone and Lake of the Angels.

90 | ANDERSON GLACIER

Round trip: 22 miles
Hiking time: Allow 3 days
High point: 5000 feet
Elevation gain: 3500 feet
Hikable: mid-July through October
Maps: Custom Correct The Brothers–Mount Anderson; Green Trails No.167 Mount Steel, No. 168 The Brothers
Information: Olympic National Park Wilderness Information Center (360) 452-0300
Backcountry use permit required for overnight stay

A long trail leads to a luscious meadow and climbs onward to the edge of one of the largest glaciers in the eastern Olympics. Enjoy glorious views down the Dosewallips River to Mount Constance, over Anderson Pass to Mount La Crosse and White Mountain, down into the Enchanted Valley at the head of the Quinault River, and, of course, across the Anderson Glacier to the summits of Mount Anderson. In early August a wild array of flowers blooms, including fields of lupine and paintbrush that stand out dramatically against the rugged background.

Quartz crystals were discovered on Mount Anderson by a prospector in 1890, and Ira recalls anticipating treasures and finding none when

their Dad took him and Bob to the East Peak of Anderson in 1934. I came along five years later, my first time on a glacier. Our party of Boy Scouts from Camp Parsons got from the glacier floor almost to the top of Flypaper Pass, on the way to the summit of the peak, before falling rock split open a Scout's scalp, not mortally, but bloodying an incredible amount of snow. The leader sounded the retreat, which was via the longest, fastest, wildest sitting glissade I know of that didn't kill anybody.

Drive US 101 along Hood Canal to just north of Brinnon and turn west on the Dosewallips River road; continue to the end of pavement in 4.7 miles, Elkhorn Campground junction at 10.7 miles, Constance Creek at 13.5 miles, and at 16

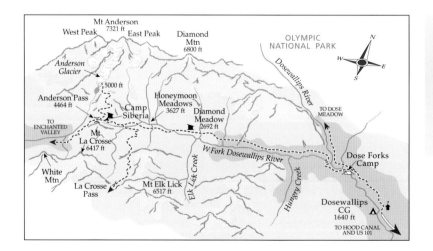

The trail crosses the West Fork Dosewallips River on a bridge perched spectacularly some 100 feet above the water.

Mount Anderson and Anderson Glacier above a sea of clouds

miles the road-end campground, guard station, and trailhead, elevation 1640 feet.

The trail starts in deep forest (a showing of rhododendrons in late June) and, after going up and down a bit, reaches a junction at 1½ miles. Turn left to Dose Forks Camp and cross the river. At about 2½ miles the way again crosses the river, now the West Fork Dosewallips, this time on a bridge perched spectacularly some 100 feet above the water. The trail climbs steeply to dry forests far from the stream, which flows in so deep a gorge that often it cannot be heard.

The trail descends a bit to campsites at 6 miles, then climbs again, and with minor ups and downs reaches the pleasant campsites of Diamond Meadow at 6¾ miles, 2692 feet. At 7¼ miles the trail once more crosses the river and begins a steady ascent, at about 8 miles climb-ing steeply beside the raging torrent as it tumbles through a narrow gorge. At 8¾ miles, 3627 feet, the valley opens into the broad, flat expanse and good camps of Honeymoon Meadows, named years ago by a Seattle couple who long since have celebrated their golden wedding anniversary. The valley is a happy hunting ground for a number of bears, so watch your groceries. One final time the trail crosses the river, here a jump wide (a big jump), and as-cends to Camp Siberia at 10 miles and Ander-son Pass at 10½ miles, 4464 feet.

The Anderson Glacier Overlook way trail climbs steeply from the north side of the wooded pass, emerging from trees and in ¾ mile ending at a small tarn amid boulders and mead-ows. A few feet farther are the edge of moraine and the views, 5000 feet.

91 | MARMOT PASS

Round trip to Marmot Pass: 10½ miles
Hiking time: 9 hours (day hike or backpack)
High point: 6000 feet
Elevation gain: 3500 feet
Hikable: July through mid-November
Maps: Custom Correct Buckhorn Wilderness; Green Trails No. 136 Tyler Peak
Information: Quilcene Ranger District (360) 765-3368

At each slow step up the Poop-Out Drag the Ten Can tied to my Trapper Nelson clanked, and the nickels and dimes in my pocket clinked, the one for boiling the supper rice at Camp Mystery, the other for the ice cream cone and bottle of pop at Marmot Pass. But the suspicion grew that the big guys were fooling us new guys. No rangers were around to mow the lawns and weed the gardens of the meadows above Mystery, as I figured they did at Mount Rainier on weekdays, when no tourists were watching. And in my experience, a "pass" was a place where a highway crosses the mountains, like Snoqualmie Pass, but the forest road sure was no highway and anyway it had ended at Bark Shanty Shelter, 9 clanking-clinking miles down the valley.

Fawn hiding in the woods

After supper I took a walk, by myself, the final mile above camp. I came to a creek tumbling from under a boulder. Books told of explorers spending lifetimes searching for the Source of the Nile. On this, my very first mountain hike, I'd found the Source of the Big Quilcene! I came to where the meadows ran out into a sky of sunset colors and I gazed down to shadows of a great unknown valley, and out to a ragged line of peaks that might not even have names, so far as I knew. I didn't miss the ice cream cone and bottle of pop. This was *wilderness*. I'd thought all the wilderness was in Darkest Africa, the Polar Wastes, the Roof of the World. But here it was, and here I was, and though not for years would I ever hear the word, that evening at Marmot Pass must have been about as good an epiphany as any twelve-year-old Boy Scout ever had.

I was unaware, in that epiphany year of 1938, that Olympic National Park had just been established. Neither did I know that President Franklin D. Roosevelt had wanted Marmot Pass in "his" park but been forced by machinations of the forest industry and the U.S. Forest Service and the Republican Party to accept its omission as a trade-off to preserve the coastal rain forests. The years passed, the machinations proceeded, and the Quilcene road was extended beyond Bark Shanty to haul virgin forests to the sawmills, and then motorcycles snarled up the Poop-Out Drag and their fumes overpowered the flowers, and so it came about that multiple-

Lewis monkeyflower

use sacrilege drove me into the ranks of what a newspaper editorial of the times sneeringly called "bird watchers and mountain climbers." And then, in 1984, Congress passed the Washington Wilderness Act establishing the Buckhorn Wilderness, and so in 1985 I returned, proving that if you keep the faith maybe you *can* "go home again."

Drive US 101 along Hood Canal to 0.9 mile south of the Quilcene Ranger Station and turn

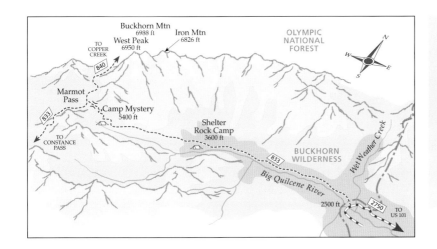

The trail follows the Big Quilcene River through intensely green forest, crossing numerous step-across creeks, passing many close-up looks at the lovely river.

west on Penny Creek Road. At 1.4 miles go left on Big Quilcene River Road, which becomes road No. 27. Stick with that number 9 miles, then go left for 4.5 miles on road No. 2750 to the start of Big Quilcene trail No. 833, elevation 2500 feet, 14.8 miles from US 101.

The trail immediately enters the Buckhorn Wilderness and follows the river through intensely green forest, all moss and ferns and lichen, crossing numerous step-across creeks, passing many close-up looks at the lovely river. At 2½ miles is Shelter Rock Camp, 3600 feet, and the last water for 2 miles.

Now the way turns steeply upward from big trees to little, to the hot, dry scree of the infamous Poop-Out Drag. At 4½ miles the suffering ends as the trail abruptly flattens out at Camp Mystery, 5400 feet, with two delightful springs and campsites in alpine trees. Except for snow-

melt there is no water above, so hikers preferring to bed down privately in secluded nooks higher up should pause here to fill jugs.

The trail continues upward, passing under a cliff and opening into a wide flat meadow, marmots whistling up a storm. At 5¼ miles, 6000 feet, the way attains the Buckhorn Botanical Area and, a bit farther, Marmot Pass and panoramas westward to Mount Mystery, Mount Deception, second-highest in the Olympics, and the jagged line of The Needles.

The Three Rivers Hike of Camp Parsons saga and myth descended the trail 1½ miles to Boulder Shelter, followed Dungeness trail No. 833 to Home Lake and Constance Pass in Olympic National Park, climbed Del Monte Ridge, and plunged down the interminable short switchbacks of the Sunnybrook trail to the Dosewallips River trail, and thence to the road. The trip is

Piper's bellflower, indigenous to the Olympic Mountains

Flower field at Marmot Pass

still extremely popular, using a two-car shuttle.

Fine as the views are from Marmot Pass, nearby are even better ones. For a quick sample, scramble up the 6300-foot knoll directly south of the pass. For the full display, at the pass turn north on trail No. 840, follow it 1½ miles to just short of Buckhorn Pass, and find a path climbing to the 6950-foot west summit of Buckhorn Mountain. Especially striking are the dramatic crags of 7300-foot Warrior Peak and 7743-foot Mount Constance and the views north to the Strait of Juan de Fuca and Vancouver Island.

92 | GRAND RIDGE

One-way trip: 7¾ miles
Hiking time: 5 hours (day hike)
High point: 6600 feet
Elevation gain (from Deer Park trailhead): 2250 feet, loss 1300 feet
Hikable: mid-July through September
Maps: Green Trails No. 135 Mt. Angeles; Custom Correct Hurricane Ridge
Information: Olympic National Park Wilderness Information Center (360) 452-0300

I knew Grand Ridge before ever I saw it. We (the Rangers from Camp Parsons) had pounded up the Dose valley, run Lost Ridge, and slid down the Lillian Glacier. Next morning we would run Lillian Ridge to Obstruction Point and, the day after, run Grand Ridge to Deer Park. Ridge-runners we were, a snooty step up from valley-pounders, barely half a leap from peak-baggers, and Everest probably had not been climbed (though we hoped to be

Grand Ridge trail

the ones to find evidence that Mallory and Irvine had). But next morning there wasn't any morning. A Three-Day Blow blew us back along Lost Ridge. I would return.... And I did, to walk the crest "between heaven and earth," between Olympic wilderness on the one hand, the Strait of Juan de Fuca on the other.

The only water after the snowfields drip dry is what you carry on your back (a gallon a day per back, a burden which may well be thought worth it for a camp's light show of mankind and starkind). A day hike of 15½ miles round trip (only one gallon per back) is grueling in the hot sun—but then, doing the whole thing isn't mandatory. For the whole thing, a one-way trip is perfect, ideally with a friendly driver dropping you off at one end and picking you up at the other.

To start at Obstruction Point, from Port Angeles drive 17 miles to Hurricane Ridge on the Olympic National Park Highway; just before the lodge turn left and go 7.9 miles on the steep, narrow Obstruction Point road (which many of us feel should be abandoned to deepen the wilderness) to its end, elevation 6200 feet.

In my opinion, the classier way to go is from Deer Park, preserving the feeling of steadily deepening wilderness as the ridge is run. Drive US 101 to milepost 253, about 3 miles east of Port Angeles and about 11 miles west of Sequim, and turn off on the Deer Park road. The first 5 miles are paved, then the way gets progressively steeper and narrower and vertiginous. At 16 miles go right to the ranger

station and trailhead, elevation 5250 feet.

The trail descends ¾ mile to a 4900-foot saddle on an abandoned 1930s road—which in that age of exuberant car-touring was planned to go all the way to Obstruction Point! The trail served as a fire line during the 1988 Deer Park blaze. From the low point the trail is mostly up and often very steep, traversing forests of Green Mountain. It levels off along a 5500-foot ridge top and little pockets of lush flowers begin. Forest is left behind in ascending a large meadow to a 6000-foot shoulder of Maiden Peak, 3 miles, in views of Port Angeles, Vancouver, and Mount Baker. A good turnaround for day-trippers. Continuing, the way traverses tundra close below the twin summits of 6434-foot Maiden Peak, 4 miles.

The crags of Warrior and Constance and the glaciers of Anderson dominate to the south. To the east are Deer Park and the saltwater and, to the north, Mount Angeles. Ahead are the naked slopes of Elk Mountain, daunting indeed on a day of blistering sun or roaring winds. The trail drops to Roaring Winds Camp (snowmelt only) and begins the 600-foot ascent of Elk Mountain. At 5¼ miles Mount Olympus comes in view. At 5½ miles, near the 6600-foot high point of the trail, pass the Badger Mountain trail. In the final 2 miles along the broad, naked slopes of Elk Mountain, Olympus' glaciers give a striking imitation of Alaska. Across Badger Valley can be seen Grand Lake and Moose Lake and a tiny unnamed lake set in green meadows. Steep scree slopes lead down to the road-end at Obstruction Point.

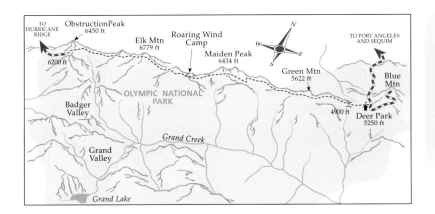

In the final miles along the slopes of Elk Mountain, Olympus' glaciers give a striking imitation of Alaska.

93 | GRAND VALLEY

Round trip to Moose Lake: 9 miles
Hiking time: 6 hours (day hike or backpack)
High point: 6450 feet
Elevation gain: 300 feet in, 1800 feet out
Hikable: July through October
Maps: Custom Correct Gray Wolf–Dosewallips; Green Trails No. 135
    Mount Angeles
Information: Olympic National Park Wilderness Information Center (360) 452-0300
Backcountry use permit required for overnight stay

A Grand Valley it surely is, the three lakes and a half-dozen ponds in glacier-scooped bowls, meadows to roam and rushing streams and views to admire. However, when Ira and Pat camped there they were most impressed by the crowds of deer and grouse and the whistlers beyond counting, all seeming as interested in Springs as the Springs were in them. Yes, Grand is the Valley, but Ira calls it "The Kingdom of Marmots."

This is an upside-down trip—the trail starts high and descends to the valley; the hard hauling is on the return. Usually open in July, after a winter of heavy snow the road may not open until August; ask the rangers before setting out.

Drive US 101 to Port Angeles and turn south for 17 miles on the Olympic National Park Highway to Hurricane Ridge. Just before the lodge

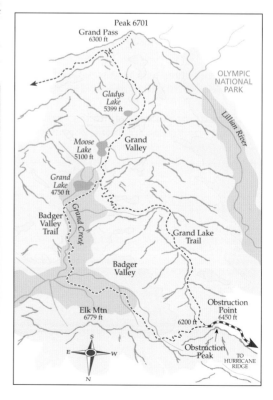

Marsh marigold

Camp near Moose Lake

turn left on a narrow and scenic dirt road through parklands along the ridge crest. In 7.9 miles, on the side of Obstruction Point, is the road-end, elevation 6200 feet.

The drive is beautiful and so is the first mile of trail south along the meadow crest of Lillian Ridge, in views over Elwha River forests to Mount Olympus, then swinging around rocky slopes of a small peak to a notch in the ridge, 6450 feet. The way drops steeply down slate scree and lush flowers to open forest on the floor of Grand Valley, and a junction at 3½ miles, 5000 feet.

The left fork leads in ½ mile to Grand Lake, 4750 feet, then descends Grand Creek to 4000 feet and climbs through Badger Valley back to Obstruction Point, reached in 5 miles from the junction. (The "badgers" actually are marmots; listen for their whistles.) This route makes an excellent loop return to the road.

The right fork ascends ½ mile to Moose Lake, 5100 feet, and another ½ mile to little Gladys Lake. There are nice camps near Moose and Grand Lakes.

For more alpine wanderings, continue on the trail to 6300-foot Grand Pass, 6½ miles from Obstruction Point, then scramble up Peak 6701 to the west, with views to the Bailey Range and Mount Olympus and Mount Anderson and more.

To append a footnote to Ira's trip, my most vivid memory of the valley is when my companion demonstrated for me and his son how a mosquito operates. He gave one complete freedom to sink test holes in his arm, locate a gusher, and fill its abdomen with red blood. The crime over, execution followed instantly. He—my companion, that is—was a professor of philosophy, subsequently fired by the University of Washington. Not for the mosquito. Politics.

94 | HIGH DIVIDE

Loop trip: 19 miles
Hiking time: Allow 3 days
High point: 5474 feet
Elevation gain: 4000 feet
Hikable: August through October
Maps: Custom Correct Seven Lakes Basin–Hoh; Green Trails No. 133 Mount Tom,
    No. 134 Mount Olympus
Information: Olympic National Park Wilderness Information Center (360) 452-0300
Backcountry use permit required for overnight stay

Ira's first visit to High Divide was in 1929, he and twin brother Bob led by their father. From that introduction at the age of eleven all he remembers is the marmots and that in the morning the water pail at their Deer Lake camp was frozen over. In the summer! From repeat trips he remembers the Sol Duc forests, tarns and gardens of Seven Lakes Basin, meadows of the High Divide, and views across the green gulf of the Hoh River to glaciers of Mount Olympus and far west to the Pacific Ocean.

They saw no other hiker then. Now the fame of the area draws thousands of feet annually. The trail is so busy and the lakes so crowded that the biowelfare of the area has required camping to be limited. If no permits are available at the lakes, do not be dismayed; day visits from the numerous camps in valley forests (which have a better chance of solitude) are practical. The loop trip described here is a fine sampler, but the country offers a variety of wanderings short and long.

Drive US 101 west from Lake Crescent (Fairholm) 2 miles to the Sol Duc River road, signed "Soleduc Hot Springs," and turn left. At 14.2 miles are the road-end and trailhead, elevation 1900 feet.

The trail gently ascends splendid old forest 1 mile to the misty and mossy gorge of Sol Duck Falls. Close by is a junction with the Deer Lake

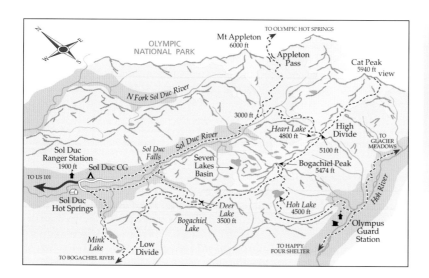

Forests, tarns and gardens , meadows, and views across the green gulf of the Hoh River to glaciers of Mount Olympus and far west to the Pacific Ocean.

Avalanche lilies on side of Bogachiel Peak, and Mount Olympus

trail—the concluding segment of the clockwise loop described here.

The Sol Duc River trail continues up the valley of gorgeous trees, passes the Appleton Pass trail at 5 miles, 3000 feet, and soon thereafter crosses the river and climbs steeply to grasslands and silver forest of Sol Duc Park and Heart Lake, 7½ miles, 4800 feet.

Shortly above, at 8½ miles, the way attains the 5100-foot crest of the High Divide and a junction. The left fork runs the ridge 3 miles to a dead-end on the side of Cat Peak, offering close looks at the Bailey and Olympus Ranges.

Turn west on the right fork into a ridge-top succession of views far down to trees of the Hoh valley and across to ice of Mount Olympus. At 10½ miles a sidetrail descends 1½ miles left to 4500-foot Hoh Lake, and from there to the Hoh River. Here, too, a path

climbs a bit to the 5474-foot summit of Bogachiel Peak, a former lookout site, and the climax panoramas. Plan to spend a lot of time gazing the full round of the compass.

The route swings along the side of the peak, at 11¾ miles passing the sidetrail to Seven Lakes Basin (often snowbound on the north side until mid-August), and traverses Bogachiel Ridge above the greenery (and often, a band of elk) in Bogachiel Basin. Snowfields linger late on this stretch and may be troublesome or dangerous for inexperienced hikers who try the trip too early in the summer.

The trail contours the ridge above the Bogachiel River for almost 2 miles, then in subalpine trees drops to Deer Lake at 3500 feet and a junction with the Bogachiel River trail at 15 miles. Past the lake the trail descends in lush forest to Sol Duc Falls at 18 miles and another mile to the road.

95 | HOH RIVER–GLACIER MEADOWS

Round trip to Glacier Meadows: 37 miles
Hiking time: Allow 3 days
High point: 4200 feet
Elevation gain: 3700 feet
Hikable: mid-July through October
Maps: Custom Correct Seven Lakes Basin–Hoh; Green Trails No. 133 Mount Tom,
   No. 134 Mount Olympus
Information: Olympic National Park Wilderness Information Center (360) 452-0300
Backcountry use permit required for overnight stay

From around the world travelers are drawn to the Hoh River by the fame of the Olympic rainforest. Most of the 100,000 annual visitors are richly satisfied by the self-guiding nature walks at the road-end, but the more ambitious can continue for miles on the nearly flat trail through huge trees draped with moss and then climb to alpine meadows and the edge of the Blue Glacier.

Ira had climbed Olympus twice before he was married in 1949, and was in no hurry to do it again, but as part of the marriage proposal had promised his bride, Pat, to lead her up the peak. They had only three days for the trip. Going in the 18 miles with heavy packs the first day blistered their feet a bit. The climb the next day was great fun, but crampons on already sore feet

were no treat. The final day's 18-mile return to the car was agony. Rubber-lug soles had not yet come to America, and the hobnails and tricounis studding their boots gave good grip on the trail but further tenderized the feet. A dozen hours under heavy packs brought the newlyweds limping into the Hoh Ranger Station. The ranger's wife earned a niche in the Spring gallery of saints by allowing the use of her shower and setting out a hot dinner.

Drive US 101 to the Hoh River Road, turn east and go 19 miles to the Hoh Ranger Station, elevation 578 feet. The hike begins on a nature trail starting at the visitor center.

The way lies amid superb, large specimens of Douglas-fir, western hemlock, Sitka spruce, and western red cedar, groves of bigleaf maple

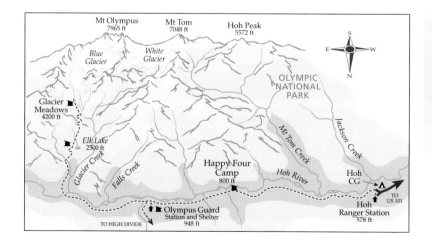

The way lies amid superb, large specimens of Douglas-fir, western hemlock, Sitka spruce, and western red cedar.

Blue Glacier on side of Mount Olympus

swollen with moss, and shrubs and ferns. Gravel bars and cold rapids of the river are never far away, inviting sidetrips. Here and there are glimpses upward to snows of Mount Tom and Mount Carrie. In winter one often may see herds of Roosevelt elk; were it not for their constant grazing the relatively open forest floor would be a dense jungle.

Any distance can make a full day, what with long, lingering pauses. Happy Four Camp, at 5¾ miles, 800 feet, is a logical turnaround for a day hike. The trail remains level to Olympus Guard Station, 9 miles, 948 feet. At 9¾ miles is a junction with the trail to High Divide. The valley trail then climbs a bit to the bridge over the spectacular canyon of the Hoh at 13¼ miles, 1400 feet, leaves the Hoh valley and climbs more to forest-surrounded Elk Lake at 15 miles, 2500 feet.

Now the grade becomes steep, ascending through steadily smaller trees, in views across Glacier Creek to Mount Tom. At 17¼ miles are Glacier Meadows, 4200 feet. Wander a short way in flowers and parkland ¼ mile to the end of the bouldery crest of a lateral moraine. Admire crevasses and icefalls of the glacier and the summit tower of 7965-foot Mount Olympus.

96 | LAKE LA CROSSE–O'NEIL PASS

Round trip to Lake La Crosse: 55 miles
Hiking time: Allow 7 days minimum
High point: 4900 feet
Elevation gain: 4000 feet
Hikable: mid-July through September
Maps: Custom Correct Enchanted Valley–Skokomish; Green Trails No. 167 Mount
    Steel, No. 166 Mount Christie
Information: Olympic National Park Wilderness Information Center (360) 452-0300
Backcountry use permit required for overnight stay

Of all the wondrous places Ira and twin brother Bob were led to by their father in the 1930s, this is the one remembered well. A group of beautiful alpine lakes. Water sparkling amid the heather and huckleberries. Far far away from humdrum reality. A golden dream. Indeed, it's so far away, so deep in the heart of the Olympic wilderness, that Ira seldom finds time to get back. Except, of course, in dreams. Other routes to the lakes are good, but the one described here is the 24-carat Classic on one of the most spectacular trails in the National Park, traversing ridges high above the Enchanted Valley of the Quinault, in magnificent views and flower fields.

Drive US 101 to the South Shore Lake Quinault Road. Turn easterly, skirting the lake and winding up the valley. Pavement ends at 12 miles. In 13 miles pass the bridge to the North Fork and at 18 miles Graves Creek Campground. Continue on the final narrow road to the trailhead 18.5 miles from US 101, elevation 646 feet.

Hike the Quinault Valley Trail 13 miles to the Enchanted Valley Chalet and continue up the trail another 3½ miles to a junction, 16½ miles from the road, elevation 3300 feet. Go right on the O'Neil Pass trail beside a small torrent, westward and up, alternating between forest and wide-view meadows. One mile farther are

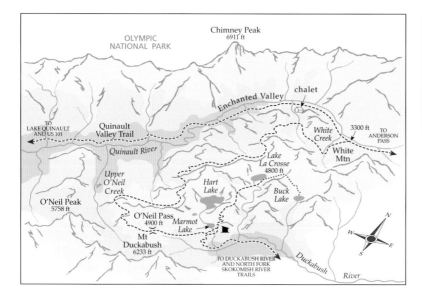

The route described here is the 24-carat Classic on one of the most spectacular trails in the National Park.

Lake La Crosse

camps and a crossing of White Creek; a hillside beyond gives the best look at Mount Anderson.

The trail climbs to 4500 feet and then contours for miles, mainly in grass and blossoms. Directly across the valley is Chimney Peak, an impressive 6911 feet. Views are breathtaking down the Quinault River to Lake Quinault and, in clear air, the ocean. The trail drops a bit, rounds a shoulder of the ridge, and ascends to 4900-foot O'Neil Pass, 25 miles from the road; a close-up here of Mount Duckabush. Still in meadows, the way descends to Marmot Lake, 26 miles, 4400 feet. The O'Neil Pass trail ends here in a junction with the Duckabush River trail.

Scattered through higher gardens are Hart Lake and Lake La Crosse. Find the trail at Marmot Lake and switchback upward ¾ mile to a junction. The left fork contours ½ mile to Hart Lake, enclosed on three sides by vertical cliffs. The right fork continues ¾ mile uphill to Lake La Crosse, 4800 feet, Ira's nomination for the most splendid alpine lake in the Olympics, views across the water to graceful 6300-foot Mount Steel and more massive 6233-foot Mount Duckabush. An experienced cross-country hiker can find tiny Buck Lake under an 5986-foot unnamed peak that the Spring family trekkers of the 1930s called Buck Mountain.

97 | POINT OF THE ARCHES

Round trip to Point of the Arches: 7 miles
Hiking time: 4 hours (day hike or backpack)
High point: 150 feet
Hikable: all year
Maps: Custom Correct North Olympic Coast; Green Trails No. 98S Cape Flattery
Information: Olympic National Park Wilderness Information Center (360) 452-0300
Backcountry use permit required for overnight stay

Pushed into a corner and forced to choose, Ira votes for this as the single most scenic stretch of the Washington ocean coast—needle-like sea stacks, caves, arches, tidal pools, and a long

Sanderlings

sandy beach. Once threatened by road-building and subdivision, in 1976 Shi-Shi Beach and the Point were added to the wilderness-ocean section of Olympic National Park.

Of the two accesses to the Point of the Arches, the Park Service—of course—has to recommend the one entirely on public land, a difficult and hazardous route from Cape Alava. The only one reasonable for the average hiker is from the north by permission of the landowner, the Makah Indian Nation, obtained, for now, by paying a modest parking fee.

Drive Highway 112 past Sekiu to Neah Bay in the Makah Indian Nation. At the west side of town go left on a paved road, following signs to "fish hatchery" and "Hoback Beach." At 2.5 miles go left on a dirt road, cross the Waatch River, stay right at the following intersection, still following fish hatchery signs. At 4.3 miles the road turns left; go straight ahead to a gate signed "Car Vandalism–No Parking." Unload

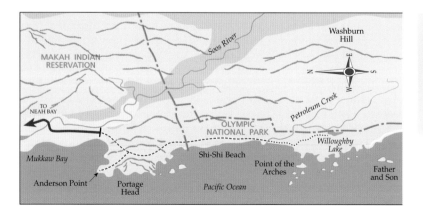

The trail leads to spectacular sea stacks, tidal pools, and whatever is left of a 1950s shipwreck.

Point of Arches

packs here and drive the car back to the last house and pay the parking fee.

Beyond the gate over Portage Head, the road no longer drivable, is pleasant walking under a canopy of trees. During wet weather be prepared for much mud. In about 1 mile push through the brush for dramatic looks down to the surf. At 2 miles, where the way comes to the edge of the bluff for the first unobstructed views of the ocean, is the park boundary and permit box. A trail drops to the north end of Shi-Shi Beach. (If the tide is high, follow the "road," which in a mile nearly touches the beach.)

A short sidetrip north from the foot of the trail is Portage Head, with spectacular sea stacks, tidal pools, and whatever is left of a 1950s shipwreck. For Point of the Arches, hike about 2 miles south on the beach, passing a number of good camps (the most reliable source of water in summer is Petroleum Creek). The long string of stacks and islands can be explored at extreme low tide; the going is rough over sharp and slippery rocks and involves some wading.

Although Shi-Shi Beach is in Olympic National Park, the mineral rights obtained years and years ago by legal chicanery and since passed from one speculator to another now are held by a private corporation that says it intends to placer mine the sand for gold. (Does it really want to mine the sand? Or the public pocketbook by blackmail typical of the modern "miner"?)

Environmentalists, hikers, and the Park Service are working together to stop this legal nonsense. Sooner or later Congress is going to have to face up to the fact that the nineteenth century is dead and with it must be buried the frontier permissiveness of mining law. Have you written your letter today?

98 | CAPE ALAVA–SAND POINT LOOP

Loop trip: 9½ miles
Hiking time: 6 hours (day hike or backpack)
High point: 170 feet
Elevation gain: about 500 feet
Hikable: all year
Maps: Custom Correct Ozette Beach Loop; Green Trails No. 130S Ozette
Information: Olympic National Park Wilderness Information Center (360) 452-0300
Backcountry use permit required for overnight stay

Two trails from Ozette Lake to the ocean, plus the connecting stretch of Olympic National Park wilderness beach, make a memorable loop hike for one day or several, for winter as well as summer.

Drive from Port Angeles on Highway 112 past Sekiu and turn left on Ozette Lake Road to the road-end ranger station, campground, and parking lot where the Ozette River flows from the lake, elevation 36 feet. Both trails depart from the open-air information booth. The loop

is equally good in either direction. The trail begins by crossing a bridge over the Ozette and in a few feet splits.

Though camping has a strict quota, good sites are sufficient to make room (usually) for everyone. The location of the campsite one is assigned will determine which direction one goes. If the counterclockwise loop is given, take the Cape Alava trail which starts on abandoned road and soon plunges into dense greenery of salal, hemlock, and other shrubs and trees. The

Pictographs at Wedding Rock, obviously carved after the first Europeans came sailing by

Black turnstones

onetime lake filled in by natural processes, partly a pasture cleared early in the century by a homesteader, Lars Ahlstrom. Again the trail enters greenery, a far-off roar can be heard, the way tops a forested crest—and below are the breakers and beyond is the Pacific horizon. The trail drops abruptly to the beach of Cape Alava, 3½ miles.

Scores of people (very chummy) can be complexly accommodated in camps on a grassy wave-cut bench, site of an Indian village occupied for centuries. Ghosts are many, many here; archaeologists have excavated houses buried in a mudslide 500 years ago; other buried houses, dating back at least 2500 years, are awaiting excavation. Artifacts are on display at the Makah Museum in Neah Bay. For a sidetrip, hike 1½ miles north to the Ozette River and a far look toward Point of the Arches.

path is sometimes flat, sometimes undulating a little, much of the way on planks—which may puzzle and irritate summertime hikers but not those who do the trip in fall or spring when all the bare ground is black muck, or in winter when every depression is feet deep in water. Walk with caution—the planks can be slippery and memories of the average hiker include a pratfall or two. Ripple or smooth rubber soles give better traction than lugs.

At 2 miles the route opens out magically into a broad bog—Ahlstroms Prairie, partly a

The beach south 3 miles to Sand Point is easy walking at anything less than high tide and offers an assortment of sands and rocks and tidal pools; camps and dependable water at several places. A third of the way south, 1 mile, is Wedding Rock, inscribed with easy-to-miss petroglyphs. A dozen or more are scattered over rocks near the line of high tide.

In trees along the beach south of Sand Point are countless good (and in summer, crowded) camping areas. To complete the loop, find the trail in the woods at Sand Point and hike 3 miles to Ozette Lake, again on planks in lush brush and forest.

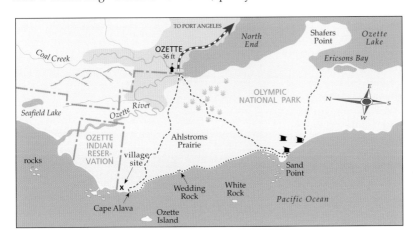

The way tops a forested crest— and below are the breakers and beyond is the Pacific horizon.

99 | RIALTO BEACH

Round trip: 3 miles
Hiking time: 3 hours (day hike or backpack)
High point: 10 feet
Hikable: all year
Maps: Custom Correct North Olympic Coast; Green Trails No. 130S Ozette
Information: Olympic National Park Wilderness Information Center (360) 452-0300
Backcountry use permit required for overnight stay

Olympic National Park first became famous for rainforests and glaciers set within a magnificently large area of mountain wilderness. Now, though, it is known far and wide for still another glory—the last long stretch of wilderness ocean beach remaining in the coterminous United States. North and south from the Quillayute River extend miles and miles of coastline that are now almost exactly as they were before Columbus—except that in 1492 (and until fairly recent times) Indians had permanent homes and temporary camps at many places along the coast now deserted.

We found it impossible to choose any of the beach walks as "the best." All four in this book are Classics. But we can say of Hole in the Wall that it has best tidal pools, so plan your hike for very low tide.

Drive US 101 to 2 miles north of Forks. Turn west on the La Push road, go 8 miles, then turn right on the Mora Campground–Rialto Beach road and continue 5 miles to the parking lot at the beach and head north.

The way starts on steep rounded rock "shingles." In ½ mile is Ellen Creek, the first permissible campsite. Here and elsewhere the "ocean tea," the creek's water colored by bark tannin dissolved in headwater swamps, is perfectly drinkable when treated as you would any other water in the wilds. At 1 mile are three sea stacks that at low tide can be walked between. At 1½ miles, the camera has a frenzy inside and outside the Hole-in-the-Wall, a large tunnel through a headland. (Ira has a photo of it taken in 1929.) On the far side are some of the richest tide pools on the coast, a gaudy display of seaweed, anemones, and starfish.

The Hole-in-the-Wall is everybody's favorite day hike. It is also the start of the 23-mile backpack to Cape Alava; whole guidebooks have been devoted to that very big Classic.

The first headland beyond the Hole requires

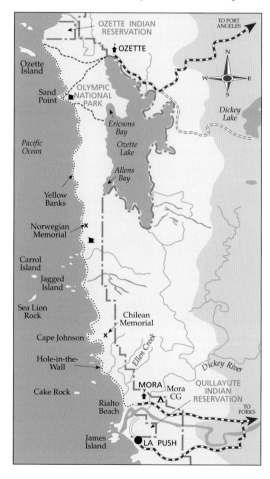

Hole-in-the-Wall

a low tide to get around. At 2½ miles are camps near the Chilean Memorial, which commemorates one of the countless ships wrecked on this cruel coast—said to have, except for Cape Horn, the most violent seas in the world. At 3 miles begins the long, rough rounding of Cape Johnson; no trail over the top and the beach passable at low tide only. A point at 6 miles must be climbed over on a short trail and the next one can be rounded at low tide. At 6½ miles are campsites at Cedar Creek.

At 7½ miles is Norwegian Memorial (another shipwreck and more camps) and at 10 miles a low-tide-only point. At 13½ miles are Yellow Banks; the point at the north end must be rounded at low tide.

At Sand Point, 15½ miles, are innumerable campsites in the woods and a trail leading 3 miles to the Ozette Lake road. But the wilderness beach continues 3 miles to Cape Alava, 18½ miles. Finish the trip by following the trail 3½ miles back to Ozette Lake for a total of 23 miles.

100 | TOLEAK POINT TO HOH RIVER

One-way trip: 17 miles
Hiking time: Allow 3 days
High point: 250 feet
Hikable: all year
Maps: Custom Correct South Olympic Coast; Green Trails No. 163S LaPush
Information: Olympic National Park Wilderness Information Center (360) 452-0300
Backcountry use permit required for overnight stay

Wild forest and wild ocean, woods animals and sea birds, tidal pools and a series of wave-carved stacks called the Graveyard of the Giants, the constant thunder of surf, and always the vast Pacific, where mariners of old heard the dragons that lurk in ambush at the edge of the world. This south section of the Olympic National Park wilderness ocean strip is shorter but more complicated than the northern one, requiring detours inland to cross headlands and creeks and demanding even closer attention to the tide chart. A one-way hike as described here is the most desirable—though arranging transportation back to the starting point is complicated. Also recommended is a 13-mile round trip to Ira's favorite spot, Toleak Point, where sandy beaches are wide and sea stacks picturesque.

Warning: Goodman Creek, Falls Creek, and Mosquito Creeks are high all winter and after periods of heavy rain are virtually unfordable.

Drive US 101 to 2 miles north of Forks. Turn west on the La Push road and continue for 12 miles to the parking lot at the Third Beach Trail, elevation 240 feet.

Warning: Cars at the Third Beach parking area are occasionally broken into. Do not leave any valuables.

Hike the forest trail, descending abruptly to the beach and campsites at 1½ miles. Head south along the sand and in ½ mile look for a prominent marker on a tree above the beach, indicating the route over Taylor Point—which cannot be rounded at the base. The "trail" up a cliff composed not of rock but mud, is a rope ladder! In about ½ mile the trail drops from forest back to the beach beside a small head that can be rounded at a medium tide or climbed over on a steep path.

At 3½ miles, after another mud climb and forest descent, is Scott Creek, campsites in the woods. At 5 miles is Strawberry Point, low and forested and simple. At 6½ miles is Ira's joy, Toleak Point.

At 7 miles is Jackson Creek (camps). A trail ascends a steep bluff and proceeds inland

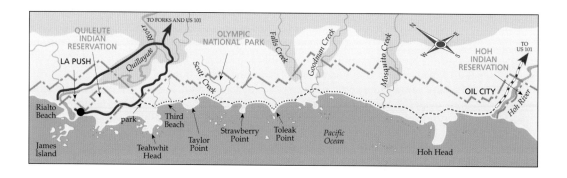

Toleak Point

through beautiful forest to crossings of Falls and Goodman Creeks (cliffs rule out a shore passage), returning to the surf at 8¾ miles. The beach is then easy to camps at Mosquito Creek, 11 miles; ford the stream at low tide. There now is a choice of routes. On a *minus tide in calm weather* follow the beach, crossing four or five small points; less exciting but more certain, take the overland trail.

At 13½ miles a trail climbs the large promontory of Hoh Head, which cannot be rounded in any tide, and regains the beach at 14½ miles. Going by a campsite or two, at 15 miles the way comes to the last point, a heap of big rocks that must be rounded at low tide. From here a narrow, low-tide-only strip of beach leads to the mouth of the Hoh River, 16 miles. A trail follows the river inland to the Oil City road-end, 17 miles. To find the Oil City Road drive US 101 about 0.5 mile north of the Hoh River bridge; go west at the sign "Cottonwood Recreation Area" then 12 miles to the road-end.

INDEX

ABOUT THE AUTHORS

A well-known outdoor photographer, Ira Spring devoted much of his time to organizations advocating trail and wildlife preservation. He was a co-founder of the Washington Trails Association and was one of twenty-four Americans to receive the Theodore Roosevelt Conservation Award in 1992. Harvey Manning is one of the Pacific Northwest's most influential and outspoken advocates of wilderness preservation. The founder of the Issaquah Alps Trail Club, Manning was instrumental in the fight to preserve the Alpine Lakes area and to establish North Cascades National Park. Both Spring and Manning played key roles in the passage of the 1984 Washington Wilderness Act.

Over the past thirty years, their guidebooks have introduced legions of hikers, and future environmentalists, to the Northwest wilderness. Spring and Manning have collaborated on over twenty books, including the award-winning *Cool, Clear Water; Wildlife Encounters; the four-volume Footsore series; Hiking the Great Northwest; Hiking the Mountains to Sound Greenway; 50 Hikes in Mount Rainier National Park; 55 Hikes in Central Washington;* and four titles in the *100 Hikes in*™ series.

THE MOUNTAINEERS, founded in 1906, is a nonprofit outdoor activity and conservation club, whose mission is "to explore, study, preserve, and enjoy the natural beauty of the outdoors. . . . " Based in Seattle, Washington, the club is now the third-largest such organization in the United States, with 15,000 members and five branches throughout Washington State.

The Mountaineers sponsors both classes and year-round outdoor activities in the Pacific Northwest, which include hiking, mountain climbing, ski-touring, snowshoeing, bicycling, camping, kayaking and canoeing, nature study, sailing, and adventure travel. The club's conservation division supports environmental causes through educational activities, sponsoring legislation, and presenting informational programs. All club activities are led by skilled, experienced volunteers, who are dedicated to promoting safe and responsible enjoyment and preservation of the outdoors.

If you would like to participate in these organized outdoor activities or the club's programs, consider a membership in The Mountaineers. For information and an application, write or call The Mountaineers, Club Headquarters, 300 Third Avenue West, Seattle, Washington 98119; (206) 284-6310.

The Mountaineers Books, an active, nonprofit publishing program of the club, produces guidebooks, instructional texts, historical works, natural history guides, and works on environmental conservation. All books produced by The Mountaineers are aimed at fulfilling the club's mission.

Send or call for our catalog of more than 300 outdoor titles:

The Mountaineers Books
1001 SW Klickitat Way, Suite 201
Seattle, WA 98134
1-800-553-4453
e-mail: mbooks@mountaineers.org
website: www.mountaineers.org

Other titles you may enjoy from The Mountaineers:

100 HIKES IN™ WASHINGTON'S SOUTH CASCADES AND OLYMPICS: Chinook Pass, White Pass, Goat Rocks, Mount St. Helens, Mount Adams, Third Edition,
Ira Spring & Harvey Manning
The best-selling hiking guide to this region, newly revised and featuring the new series design and new color photos, with thoroughly researched, succinct hike descriptions by the area's most respected hiking gurus.

HIKING THE GREAT NORTHWEST: The 55 Greatest Trails in Washington, Oregon, Idaho, Montana, Wyoming, Northern California, British Columbia, and the Canadian Rockies, Second Edition,
Ira Spring, Harvey Manning, & Vicky Spring
The latest edition of this classic hiking guide to the most spectacular trails in the region, featuring new color photos and the personal picks of a trail-tested team of Northwest hiking gurus.

A WATERFALL LOVER'S GUIDE TO THE PACIFIC NORTHWEST:
Where to Find Hundreds of Spectacular Waterfalls in Washington, Oregon, and Idaho, Third Edition, *Greg Plumb*
The complete, newly revised guide to Pacific Northwest waterfalls accessible by foot, car, and boat, with fifty new waterfalls described and rated for aesthetic value.

BEST HIKES WITH CHILDREN, IN WESTERN WASHINGTON AND THE CASCADES, VOL. 1, Second Edition, *Joan Burton*
A thoroughly revised edition of the best-selling book in the *Best Hikes with Children*, series, with approximately twenty new hikes appropriate for families, seniors, and anyone who enjoys an easy dayhike.

AN OUTDOOR FAMILY GUIDE TO WASHINGTON'S NATIONAL PARKS AND MONUMENT: Olympic, Mount Rainier, North Cascades, Mount St. Helens,
Vicky Spring & Tom Kirkendall
A three-season guide to the best selection of outdoor activities in Washington's spectacular national parks, with information on flora and fauna, history, safety, and tips on successful outdoor outings with children.

SEATTLE'S LAKES, BAYS & WATERWAYS: AFOOT & AFLOAT Including the Eastside, *Marge & Ted Mueller*
The newest in the popular *Afoot & Afloat* series, featuring city escapes for boaters and shoreside explorers.

WASHINGTON'S BACKCOUNTRY ACCESS GUIDE: National Parks, National Forests, Wilderness Areas, *Ken Lans, Editor*
Completely updated compilation of Washington backcountry information from a variety of sources, highlighting recent regulation changes and featuring the latest access, trail conditions, and permit information.